Mothers
Beyond Maternalism

Mothers
Beyond Maternalism

Edited by
Samita Manna
Sujit Roy
Soumyajit Patra

KALPAZ

First Published, 2021

Published by

Kalpaz Publications
C-30, Satyawati Nagar,
Delhi - 110052
Ph.: 011-47034999, 9811692060
www.kalpazpublications.com
E-mail: kalpaz@hotmail.com

Printed at: Gyan Press, Delhi.

Cataloging in Publication Data—DK
Courtesy: D.K. Agencies (P) Ltd. <docinfo@dkagencies.com>

All India Sociological Conference (43rd : 2017 : Lucknow, India)
Mothers : beyond maternalism / edited by Samita Manna, Sujit Roy, Soumyajit Patra.
pages cm
"... papers presented in the Mother and Motherhood Adhoc Group in the 43rd All India Sociological Conference organised by the Indian Sociological Society (ISS) at the University of Lucknow, U.P. in November, 2017"—Preface.
ISBN 9789353246198

1. Motherhood—India—Congresses. 2. Motherhood—Social aspects—India—Congresses. 3. Mothers—India—Social conditions—Congresses. 4. Mother and child—India—Congresses. I. Manna, Samita, 1954- editor. II. Roy, Sujit, editor. III. Patra, Soumyajit, editor. IV. Indian Sociological Society, organizer. V. Lucknow University, host institution. VI. Indian Sociological Society. Mother and Motherhood Adhoc Group. VII. Title.

LCC HQ759.A45 2017 | DDC 306.87430954 23

Contents

To

All

Mothers

Preface

Whatever be the name, a mother is always adored as a mother. Her presence is so natural that no one can deny her eternal essence and entity, begetting new lives entailing every creation of the nature. That is why the term 'mothers' points not only to human mothers but also to the mothers among non-humans, and for that matter, to the Mother Nature as a whole. As reality and language create each other through a meaningful interaction, mother as a term and as a social entity also interacts with other social entities in infinite ways creating new connotations. Then, mother is ubiquitous in nature and is alike from the East to the West and from the North to the South.

But, mothers are so 'culture-specific' that mothers as 'social' entities are different from 'biological' realities. As a result, the issues of motherhood automatically come to the fore. We can use the Sanskrit term *matritva* to refer to the term motherhood in English. But *matritva* cannot be equated mechanically with motherhood as every term is contextual with its multi-dimensionality within a cultural framework that the connotation of the term 'motherhood' cannot be a 'cultural universal'.

That is why in the present volume our endeavour to study mothers and motherhood goes beyond universalistic narratives, not only of western maternalism but also of European construct of motherhood. And, therein lays the basic paradigmatic difference between mothers of the two worlds of the East and the West.

Matritva in Indic culture is more than a concept unlike that of motherhood in the West. It has been a reality with multi-ramifications in Indian *dharmic* society from time immemorial. Then the study of motherhood in Indian context should consider the hermeneutics of motherhood focusing on 'existential understanding' of mothers with their 'feelings'. Despite the patriarchal nature of human society all over the world including the Indian society, *matritva* or motherhood has bestowed a special status to Indian women. As a mother, a woman in Indic culture has controlling power over children with 'motherly' independence making motherhood positive and satisfying for Indian mothers.

Then the 'mother-child unit' has assumed a particular contextual significance in Indian *dharmic* society considering the agency of Indian mothers where the whole of *matritva* or motherhood gets transformed into a divinity. And, this divine paradigm of motherhood has been so unique in Indian society that it requires 'particularistic' study of mothers with the emphasis on the feelings of the Indian mothers.

This volume is primarily based on the papers presented in the *Mother and Motherhood* Adhoc Group in the 43rd All India Sociological Conference organised by the Indian Sociological Society (ISS) at the University of Lucknow, U.P. in November, 2017. Like the prior two volumes on motherhood, we have touched and traversed new horizons on motherhood in the present volume.

We pay our gratitude to Prof. Sujata Patel, the President, Prof. Abha Chauhan, the Secretary of ISS, and Prof. D. R. Sahu, the Organising Secretary of the Conference for their cooperation in organising paper presentations in the Group. We also convey our heartfelt thanks to Prof. Biswajit Ghosh for his unstinted support to this Group.

We are ever thankful to our energetic members of this Group and the contributors of this volume. Lastly, we are thankful to the authority of Kalpaz Publications, New Delhi who has taken much efforts to publish the volume during this Covid-19 pandemic situation. We really hope that this volume would again provide valuable insights on motherhood from different perspectives, particularly the East and the West way of perceiving motherhood, not only to the special readers of sociology but also to the general readers at large.

August, 2021

Samita Manna
Sujit Roy
Soumyajit Patra

List of Contributors

Dr. Aritra Ghosh is an Assistant Professor of Sociology in Serampore Girls' College, Hooghly, West Bengal.

Dr. Sujit Roy is a Research Analyst and Management Consultant, Kolkata, West Bengal.

Dr. Anushua Roy is an Assistant Professor of Sociology in Government General Degree College, Manbazar II, Purulia, West Bengal.

Dr. Samita Manna is a retired Professor of Sociology, Department of Sociology, University of Kalyani, West Bengal and former Vice Chancellor of Sidho-Kanho-Birsha University, Purulia, West Bengal.

Dr. Soumyajit Patra is Professor in the Department of Sociology, Sidho-Kanho-Birsha University, Purulia, West Bengal.

Dr. C.K. Manna is a retired Professor of Zoology, University of Kalyani, Kalyani, Nadia, West Bengal.

Biswajit Ghosh is a State Aided College Teacher (SACT) of Sociology in Kalyani Mahavidyalaya, Nadia, West Bengal.

Dr. Kaushik Chattopadhyay is an Assistant Professor of Sociology at Prof. Syed Nurul Hassan College, Farakka, Murshidabad, West Bengal.

Soumya Narayan Datta is a State Aided College Teacher (SACT) of Sociology in Bijoy Krishna Girls' College, Howrah, West Bengal.

Dr. Pankaj Kumar is an Assistant Professor in Sociology in Asansol Girls' College, Asansol, Burdwan, West Bengal.

Dr. Sadhna Gupta is an Assistant Professor in Law at Hooghly Mohsin College, Hooghly, West Bengal.

Dr. Reshmi Chakraborty is a State Aided College Teacher (SACT) of Sociology in Kalyani Mahavidyalaya, Nadia, West Bengal.

Dibakar Bera is a Research Scholar in the Department of Sociology, Vidyasagar University, Paschim Medinipur, West Bengal.

Kaynat Kenukhan is an M.Phil. Scholar in the Department of Folklore, University of Kalyani, Nadia, West Bengal.

Soumik Bhattacharjee is a State Aided College Teacher (SACT) in Muzaffar Ahmed Mahavidyalaya, Murshidabad, West Bengal.

Abhra Chanda is a State Aided College Teacher (SACT) in Ranaghat College, Nadia, West Bengal.

Tania Upadhaya is an M.Phil student in the University of Kalyani, Nadia, West Bengal.

Rimi Sarkar is an Assistant Professor of Sociology in Hijli College, Kharagpur, West Bengal.

Dr. Suchismita Majumder is an Assistant Professor of Sociology in Raiganj University, Raiganj, Uttar Dinajpur, West Bengal.

Atulita Banerjee is M.A. in Sociology, University of Kalyani, Nadia, West Bengal.

Sajal Sammadder is a Visual Anthropologist, West Bengal.

Introduction

Mother is the most enduring phenomenon encompassing every aspect of life with her eternal essence. Her status is unparallel and uncompetitive in nature. She gives shelter to her children in her lap. She gives security, protection, love and feeds her child when no one can take part in it. Rich (1976) says, 'All human life on the planet is born of women'. She is the mother. Sometimes she is also called as mummy, mom, *maa*, *amma* etc. From these perspectives can we say that gender fails to construct its space among the wider arena of mother? Since the inception of the living world she was and she is with us. Her presence makes the society vibrant and dynamic. Will it be unjustified if we say that mother is ubiquitous in nature and is alike from the East to the West and from the South to the North? Mother's love and emotion, sacrifice and tolerance for bearing her baby are unique. It brings unity in diversity. Leick (2003) has pointed out that 'the worship of the mother entity can be traced back to early Vedic culture, and perhaps, even before that time'. The *Rig Veda* calls the divine female power as *Maimata*, a term which literally means 'Mother Earth'. Nine months and nine days she keeps her baby in her womb keeping well till birth. Even the most powerful and powerless men and women take birth in their mothers' womb. Miller (2005) has rightly pointed out that 'becoming a mother changes lives in all sorts of ways. It has major significance for individual biographies, yet expectations and experiences will be shaped by the social and cultural contexts in which women live their lives'.

Mother is sometimes considered as living goddess. This is true in one hand; but on the other hand, if this mother becomes the wife of another or becomes the daughter-in-law or sister-in-law or the mother-in-law then the total situation varies discursively. Sometimes the mother becomes the role model of her daughter. Throughout the world when a woman becomes a mother her sacrifice, love and caring are considered as unparallel. With these characteristics she is honoured and respected. Especially in Indian society mothers are worshipped for her *seva* (service) and *tyaga* (sacrifice). All Indian languages have referred to the Divine Mother as *Devi* or *Mahadevi* representing *shakti* that is divine power (Rao, 2013). In our country there was a heinous practice, *Satidaha*. India is such a country where sometimes mothers are tortured and killed or are forced to commit suicide when they give birth to daughters. So, the study of mother and motherhood is very complicated. Situation comes when motherhood becomes critical and context-specific. Time-space dimension creates various domains for interpretative understanding of mother and motherhood. Leskosek (2011) has rightly said that 'throughout the history motherhood was described as the woman's basic mission, profession, and an inseparable part of her nature. Women are supposedly drawn into motherhood by their instincts which at the same time guarantee their children's healthy growth and development'.

Since the inception of the human society in this earth (approx. six million years ago) the primitive men lived in forest. There was no demarcation of areas. One part of the world was demarcated either by forest, or by hills, mountains, deserts or big oceans. Extreme form of primitivism persisted everywhere. Primitive men were known as paleolithic men. They lived in forests. Gradually, they established themselves as different species other than the primates. That primitive society was known as savage society. Promiscuity prevailed at that time. The children were identified by their mother. Since that time the children are protected, nourished and identified by their mothers. The mothers had primarily protected their babies from the crude, uncomfortable nature. This type of unstable, fluid, unstructured, nomadic society got its identities only through the identity of the mothers.

With this trajectory, society took its various dimensions. Gradually human became the members of different continents. The geographical boundaries made the people to become a member of that particular locality. Shchurko (2012) comments that motherhood is a discursive strategy that makes women's bodies the object of disciplining practices and bio-politics.

In this way the continents like Asia, Africa, Australia, and America were developed. The roots of human civilisation traced back through matriarchal, matrilocal and matrilineal patterns of human social relations. 'Mother right', however, still prevails in the matriarchy, which is founded, of course, on 'natural law'. Bachofen said in his book, *Myth, Religion and Mother Right* (1967), that mother right included not only the reckoning of kinship and descent according to the mother, but also the inheritance of property by the daughter (Bachofen, 1967). On the other hand, Love and Shanklin (1983) wrote that matriarchy is a non-alienated society: a society in which women, those who produce the next generation, define motherhood, determine the conditions of motherhood, and determine the environment in which the next generation is reared. Many studies were done by British and American Anthropologists justifying the facts of mother-line societies.

Today majority of the societies throughout the world are patriarchal in nature. India is no exception. According to Sagade, gender differences are reflected in the sexual division of labour between the 'productive' and 're-productive activities'. This differential status and power create imbalance between the sexes (Sagade, 2005). It is assumed that the tribal societies are our ancestors. Many pristine traits are carried out by them proving the no denying of the fact that they were our original ancestors.

Edward Burnett Taylor and Herbert Spencer deemed ancestor worship to be a first inchoate religion (not as one phase). They assumed that primitive people were unable to comprehend the unseen. Taylor remarked that the worship of the Manes, or ancestors, is one of the great branches of religion. Its principles are not difficult to understand, as they plainly keep up the social relations of the living world (Taylor, 1871). Different tribal groups throughout India worship mother goddess. Bias free motherhood in respect of gendersex was prevalent in our primordial societies. No exception was found. The entire world was created by her hand. So before starting any ritual they worship the goddess mother. Anthropologists Hoebel and Frost (1976) affirm that social conservatism is a feature of ancestor-worshipping religions. These ancestors do not favour change in the social practices, they knew while alive.

Especially from the second half of the nineteenth century onwards the situation has changed throughout the world up to the second half of the twentieth century. Asian countries are no exception. Motherhood takes a different shape when women are accorded subordinate status in patriarchal societies. The role of mothers and the meaning of 'motherhood' are not same in all socio-cultural contexts. In India, there is a religious and historical tradition of equating woman with 'mother'. Motherhood in this country has always been glorified from the ancient times. But this glorification is more a myth than a reality as motherhood has often to be surrendered to different social forces that mould and shape the ethos of motherhood as such (Dutta, 2014).

Feminists' views on mothers always reflect that they are at all times distressed, oppressed, and subjugated. The notion of motherhood has been developed as a social category by the male dominated society. Arcana (1979) opined that within the framework of motherhood, women are most often depicted in saint like fashion, as passive, caring, patient, loving human being.

The modernisation and emergence of new roles and power centres during the late nineteenth century also deprived women from enjoying those rights which prevailed at that time. There were several ways in which they were restricted and their roles and social positions were determined (Leskosek, 2011).

II

Janani is a Sanskrit word meant for mother. In *Bhagavad Gita*, *janani* was referred as a *Devi* who was also divine. *Janani* was referred to as *Trideva-janani* i.e., the mother of the three deities which represented an epithet of goddess *Durga* who was omnipotent, eternal and most powerful (*Sivapurana* 2.2.11-accessed on 29.4.2020 www.archive.org; Shivapurana). So *janani* took a noble position in the history of India. Since then up to modern India we refer to mother as *janani*. The mothers of Indian society are always holding special position though the evil practices like *sati* and child marriage were also in vogue in particular time-space dimensions. The famous Sanskrit *shloka* '*Janani Janmabhoomischa Swargadapi Gariyasi*' means mother and motherland are even superior to heaven. This special emotional attachment of the people with their mother and motherland is not only seen in India but also in South Asian and South East countries showing the equal type of reverence towards their mother and motherland. Similar types of religio-cultural solidarity perhaps develop the same identical sense of belongingness towards their life and works. Temples, sculptures, mythological stories reveal the glorification of mother and motherhood. The notion of subjectivity of mother and motherhood develops through their culture and heritages. Two great epics - the *Ramayana* and *Mahabharata* have deeply influenced their mind and behavioural practices. The enlightening stories of the *Ramayana* and *Mahabharata* along with some brightening women characteristics of the epics have always been echoing in each and every house glorifying the essence of ideal mothers which are often accepted as sacred books of them. Nevertheless as a perfect wife (Leslie, 1989 referred by Tryambakayajvan's treatise) we also mention the names of ideal wives like Sita, Savitri and Dayamanti and like. On the other hand, women's captive condition of womanhood was well quoted down in the following:

> It is woman. ... who gives and gives endlessly, gracefully, smilingly, whatever the demand, however unreasonable and harmful to herself. ... Sita, Savitri, Anusuya and various others mythological heroines are used as the archetypes of such a woman and women themselves are deeply influenced by these cultural ideals. ... This ideology of slavery and contempt for women in the family plays a more important part than even beatings or bullets in keeping women oppressed (*KishwarandVanita*, 1984: 46-7 cited in Leslie, 1989: 2).

They were also ideal mothers as they were perfect ideal wives, *pativrata* who dedicated their lives to their husbands (Leslie, 1989). So marriage is essentially a sacred ritual and the wife must be a perfect partner by following the scriptures of the society. 'A family that is *sunya* is one without children. Since in the orthodox view a woman's primary function is to bear children (e.g. Manu 1x.96); this is a dire threat indeed' (Leslie, 1989:63).

But here one thing should be mentioned which is often overlooked. The analysis or interpretive understanding of mother and motherhood should have to be empathetic keeping in mind the subjectivity of the incumbent and her associates. Indian civilisation and culture could have not been made only by the great men of history keeping the women under lock and key. Women might have been subordinated, but it was not the success story behind the screen; they might have enjoyed the healthy space for living where social conditions and forces of religion often made them ready to accept it. Indian mothers were not always humble and occupant of second grade citizenship.

'Universal subordination of women' should not be accepted which came from the West. Indian women as mothers always enjoyed special privilege unlike their western counterparts. Oppressed status of women often be viewed due to colonial legacy that created a situation of acceptance of cultural hegemony of the West (Channa, 2007). This view is also expressed in Chatterjee's (1989) article 'Colonialism, Nationalism and Colonised Women: The Context of India'. Indian mothers are always attached with the socio-religious values. Since our Vedic period of *Srutis* and *Upanishads* to the time of *Smritis* and *Dharmashastras* the famous religious leaders like the Manu, Yajnavalkya, Triambakayajvan and others wrote many important laws or codes of conduct to maintain *dharma* (religious dictum) where male child is essential to maintain the lineage of a patriarchal society. In Hindu *Shastra,* birth and re-birth are directly associated with *karma* (deed).The term *atma* i.e., the soul or spirit is real essence for each individual. The body is temporary and after death to make the soul free from *bandhan, mukti* or salvation is necessary which is only possible through a male child. After death during the time of *sraddh* ceremony, '*pindadan*' (a special food for ancestors) is necessary and this is done only by a male child.

In Hindu *shastra* becoming a mother of a son is the utmost duty of a married woman. 'Because the son protects his ancestors from the hell called put, he has been called putra' (Man.ix, 138; aha. Adi. 74,27; cf. also ama, ii 107- 12 cited in Prabhu, 1940.)

'... for the salvation and peace of a man's soul a son had to make a spiritual ceremony called *pindadan*' (Chakravarty, 1957: 82). Even the position of the eldest son is very important in the Hindu family. He has the authority to offer the funeral cake (*pinda*) at the *Sradh* ceremony on the death anniversary of the father and the ancestors (Prabhu, 1940).

Indian society is an exceptional one. Here *dharma* plays an important role to maintain the wellbeing of the people and society. The importance of *dharma* stands for ever more perfection and it is as old as the Vedic period. Many changes took place over time but India remains a '*Dharmic Bharat*' forever inspite of many challenges faced, especially by the Indian women. The rigidity and stereotyped religious codes are well maintained by the religious leaders.

In later phases some changes are seen but *dharma* directly or indirectly remains associated with the activities of our everyday life. Although the impact of caste system and the role of Brahmins cannot be ignored in our daily life where different forms of sacred rituals in the name of performing *dharma* are carried out to maintain *pobitrata* (divineness). It helps maintain the religious fraternity of Indian society where the unequal status of women is highlighted. The females are not allowed to take part in the worshipping process as they are not considered as pure. As a result they are not allowed to wear sacred thread. So the priest as a male must have the power of wearing sacred thread. The married women are always welcome to becoming a mother of a son. The common proverb '*putravati bhaba*' is popular like the ancient society. In 2002, one UGC project was conducted where it was observed that most of the working women were eager to get a son (Manna, 2002). In 2014, another UGC major project highlighted that son is preferred so the female fetus is being killed (Ghosh and Manna, 2013). The importance of male child is highly acclaimed in Indian society as the lineage of a family is maintained through the male child. Mortuary rites and rituals have to be performed only by the male child to get *uddhar* or salvation. The woman must be a mother of a son. This *parampara* (tradition) is going on. This is one of the significant reasons of distinctiveness of Indian mothers from the West.

The flavour of motherhood is great and uncompetitive in nature. Glorification of mother and motherhood since time immemorial up to the early Vedic period was very enriched and well revered which attracted the western society too. Even today the new challenging domain of women is once again reverberating the society where women are going to celebrate their new challenges at the juncture of the third wave of feminism (Snyder, 2008).

The symphony of mother is ringing from every corner of society originating from the emotion of mother itself. The subjectivity of motherhood perhaps has had to be understood till the appearance of mother in this earth. Epistemological understanding of mother has its yawning connotation which largely affects the society in time-space dimension.

With the passage of time gradually the mother was and is considered as the object of study especially in the West first and then in India. It is not an exception when mothers have become an object, considered merely as a reproductive organic entity. Gradually the women were treated as others. 'To call the "other" sex, the opposite sex obscures in many ways we are alike' (Kimmel, 2000:14). Consequently they were the victims of men's state power and domination with physical strength.

Unlike hunting-gathering society, agricultural society needed more man-power. As a result more wealth wished more members. In this way women were reduced to mere reproductive organic bodies. Large numbers of children were considered as the property of a family. Gradually the women were treated merely as the organs of reproduction. Not only they were intended to giving birth of the child but proper care of the children, nursing and giving food to other family members were the necessary duties of women. In early Vedic period the women enjoyed equal power like men. A perfect wife was supposed to follow certain codes of conduct where *Sati* was implemented to justify the chastity of women. The root of caste system deeply penetrated the soil of Indian society. The Brahmins controlling the society were just next to god. The lower caste people were treated as beasts or animals. The mothers were important only to giving birth of the male baby. Polygyny was also in vogue. Women were relegated as inferior in consideration to males. In this situation religion played the dogmatic role to justify the inferior position of women. Not only in India but throughout the world the status of women was inferior (Beauvoir, 1954).

It is accepted everywhere that without the contribution of woman the existence of neither great man nor normal man is possible. Especially in India the women are considered as inferior in holding power but they should be respected when they become mother. Women are the mothers of great men. Even the unknown person or strangers often address the senior female as '*maa*' i.e., mother. It is, till today, found that the poor, stranger and even beggar ask for alms by saying '*maa*'.

In earlier period, male folk were well aware that the women would be more powerful if they were given equal access like men and even they might challenge the authority to control the society. With the passage of time throughout the world the religious leaders justified the inferior position of women through the prescribed religious dogmas. But special attention was given to mother as they were the creator of male child.

> In truth women have never set up female values in opposition to male values; it is man who, desirous of maintaining masculine prerogatives, has invented that divergence. Men have presumed to create a feminine domain-the kingdom of life, of immanence only in order to lock up women therein (Beauvoir, 1949).

Regarding the healthy child and 'good mother', Beauvoir nicely pointed out in her book *The Second Sex* (1997: 537): 'They are neither play things, nor tools for the fulfilment of parental needs or ungratified ambitions. Children are obligations; they should be brought up so as to become happy human beings'. Only the woman who is well balanced, healthy, and aware of her responsibilities is capable of being a 'good' mother (*ibid:* 537).

Indian society is enriched with its culture and heritage where women play significant role. But throughout history the role differences between men and women are accepted. Women's biological capacity for child birth and breast feeding and their generally lesser physical strength are seen as determining their social role in home, occupying themselves with domestic chores and bringing up children. But it was also claimed that these biological differences made them unfit to participate in the public sphere (Freedman, 2019).

In Indian society the mother is a power figure which is not accepted in Western society. Since the Vedic period to modern society (early twenty-first century) women had and have the power to share equal role with their husbands. Many creative and extraordinary women throughout the history in different time periods had shown their talents and ability to justify their position amidst the non-favourable social forces.

An Indian male respects his wife as the mother of his children, rather than as a sexual object in the conjugal family life. Right from childhood, in a traditional family, a man grows up to respect his mother and his sisters, and the sentiments are quite absent in western societies. An Indian woman gains the highest status for being a mother. This is something totally unfamiliar to a western culture, especially among the White middle class. Although among the Afro-Americans, this situation may prevail albeit in a different form (Channa, 2007:33). Even Channa (2007) in her article mentioned that she is really astonished when one British scholar in his research work has changed his earlier conception and said:

> In India he found that it was a socially accepted and normal situation that a woman should be in control in the domestic domain, and that included the husband as well. Before

> leaving he told me that he had totally revised his opinion about gender relation in Asia (Channa, 2007:36).

In this connection we would like to quote a few lines of Jawaharlal Nehru mentioned in the foreword of the book *Women of India* written by Tara Ali Baig (1957):

> There are two views, among others, about Indian woman. One is the typical old Indian viewpoint of the Indian woman being a symbol of purity, faithfulness and submission and devotion to her husband. The great symbols are Sita and Savitri. The other view, mostly to be found in some western countries, is that the Indian woman is backward, suppressed and treated almost as a chattel. Both these views are far from the truth, and deal with some imaginary conceptions little related to life.

So motherhood as a particular stage in life and as a social institution has been manifested in the role prescriptions of a particular group, which are conditioned by the group culture. There may be oriental and occidental variations in the notion and realisation of motherhood. Indian society, in many senses, worships 'mothers' and develops a kind of imagery paralleling divine personifications.

III

Human being is embedded in reality of both objective as well as subjective world. From the lap of a mother, a child begins his/her journey of social life and gradually develops a worldview following a way of life of the land, called the 'culture' of land. Then, every human being must be 'culture-specific' having a complex language structure to share feelings, information and ideas with others with an evolutionary advantage. So, language is unique to humans and a defining feature of humanity and a cultural universal. And, language shapes how people understand causality, and is also shaped and governed by social convention, and norms and practices. The world is linguistically constituted and we cannot exist apart from language and every language constitutes a world-view, because the linguistic nature of the world frees each individual from an objective environment (Gadamer, 1989).

Thus, we come to the very words of *mata/matri* and *matritva* as the Sanskrit terms for English mother and motherhood. *Mata* is also *janani* in Sanskrit. *Mataji* is used as a respectful term to address an older woman in Indian culture, particularly if she is unknown to the speaker, because according to Vedic culture, all women who are not one's wife are to be treated as one's mother, where *ji* is an honorific suffix used to indicate respect.

Sanskrit *matritva* can be translated as motherhood in English. But *matritva* is more than motherhood as *dharma* is more than what is known as religion in the West. The term *matritva* is composed of two words: *matri* meaning mother and *tattva* (or *tattwa*) meaning 'reality', 'principle', 'truth' or 'thatness' in English. In Indic way of life, a *tattva* is an element or aspect of reality. Each and every culture provides its own way of understanding and interpretations of reality which connote a unique 'contextual meaning' of the social world to its members. *Matritva* in Indic culture is merely not a concept like that of motherhood in the West. But it has been a reality with multi-ramifications in Indian society from time immemorial.

Now, the question is: what do we mean by the East and the West? Simply put, the East we refer to here is the way of life led by the people following 'ethnic' religious system characterised by plurality of beliefs, cultural systems and worldviews in the Eastern parts of the world of non-Western cultures and epitomised by the *dharmic* way of life in the Land of Bharat. And, the West here is referred by the way of life led by the people following 'Abrahamic' religions in the Western parts of the world, where religion has emerged as a category separate from culture and society, demonstrating the superiority of the 'living' or 'universal'. European worldview compared to the 'dead' or 'ethnic' religions practised in other parts of the world. Thus, the West is defined by a worldwide ideal religiousness (Dubuisson, 2007).

Our studies on mothers rest on these paradigmatic differences of two worlds of the East and the West with respect to the worldviews relating to life experiences, meaningfulness of life and 'essence' of life as practiced by the people (Smith, 1978).

Mothers of the East and its study require us to go through the hermeneutics of motherhood, particularly of *matritva* in *dharmic* culture in the 'Land of Bharat'. Now, what is hermeneutics? In general, hermeneutics refers to analysis, interpretation and understanding of texts, especially religious texts. Again, hermeneutics in modern and contemporary ages focus not only on texts but also both on verbal and nonverbal communication as well as semiotics, presuppositions and preunderstandings. Hermeneutics in English may be what is meant by '*Bhashya*' in Sanskrit. In Indian context *Bhashya* means literally 'spelling, talking, any work in the current vernacular speech' (Monier-Williams, 2002) and any 'explanatory work, exposition, commentary' (*ibid.*) that brings to light something else. The root *Bhash* means 'speak about, describe, declare, tell' (*ibid.*). Then *Bhashya* is a commentary or exposition of any primary or secondary text in ancient or medieval Indian literature.

Thus, from the perspective of hermeneutical circle, the study of *matritva* with the reciprocity between text and context shifts the focus from 'interpretation' to 'existential understanding' by 'way of being' as a mother in the world than merely as 'a way of knowing' motherhood. Then, it is no denying the fact that 'faith' still has been the dominant factor of 'modern' social life. In Indian subcontinent and also in East Asian countries, *dharma* constitutes the basic building block of Eastern society. *Dharmic* religions have been Hinduism/*Sanatana Dharma*, Jainism and Buddhism from the ancient time and Sikhism from the medieval India. The Indian subcontinental culture has been heavily influenced by all these *dharmic* religious systems cumulatively (Mohammada, 2007). Hinduism and Buddhism have also been influencing the Eastern Asian societies from ancient times. Thus, Indic culture has been an amalgamation of several cultures spanning across the Indian subcontinent. The Indic society has been influenced by a history that is several millennia old (Keay, 2011).

Although almost all societies and communities in the world have been patriarchal in nature, *matritva* has bestowed a special status to Indian women who have been traditionally given inferior socio-cultural positions in a patriarchal society of Indian subcontinent, particularly since last thousand years. It is true that there has been no clear-cut role model in *dharmic* scriptures for good motherhood. But it is no denying the fact that there has certainly been a cultural and ideological understanding of motherhood as a pre-eminent status and positional roles in Indic society. Mothers have been depicted as sacrificing, loving women who, unlike the wife, have been in control of themselves and their children. And, as a mother, a woman in Indic culture has controlling power over children. Indic culture has a whole body of oral tradition and literature that glorify *matritva*, which influences, shapes and somehow transfers a natural role into a 'supernatural' one.

Matritva really confers Indian women a purpose and identity amid dismal poverty, disempowerment and drudgery of child rearing. Here we must take note of the point that traditionally Indian brides enter their husbands' families not as wives but as daughters-in-law where intimacy with husbands has been consciously discouraged by the extended family. Here lies the basic difference of the status of daughters-in-law in the East from that of the West. The daughter-in-law or future mother in her husband's family has been accepted and revered as *kulabadhu* (daughter-in-law of the family) who becomes a mother of the family. Thus, Indian mothers have often been related with their children. So, in Indic culture, a mother is expected and encouraged traditionally to find emotional fulfillment primarily in her relationship with her children. Being a mother with shared responsibility of parenthood and caring for the next generation, an Indian wife gradually develops later much intimacy with her husband. Thus, it is only through motherhood or *matritva* that an Indian bride has traditionally come into her as a woman. In the whole process motherhood role alone has given recognition of worth to an Indian woman in the family, in the community and in the life cycle in Indic culture.

Now come to another important point of asexuality of *matritva*. Traditionally, mother of the East has been held to be asexual. The East society, particularly the Indian society is unique in bestowing religio-cultural respect for mothers which has increased safety and security for mothers in their interactions with other males. This reality has been translated into a relaxation of controls, and an exercise of independence and power available to them as women who never before experience that aspect in social relationship. This newly found 'motherly' independence and power of Indian mothers, highlighting dual ideas of feminity as wife and mother, have been playing a significant role in the immense emotional investment in mothers of *dharmic* culture. Thus, all these realities of *matritva* make motherhood positive and satisfying for Indian mothers disapproving negative aspects and thoughts about their so-called confinement in a 'motherly' role.

Here arise the pertinent questions: Hasn't this eulogisation of motherhood actually imposed a socially constructed role on women in Indic culture? Hasn't it in reality gratified the patriarchy of this society that gives little actual power to mothers? Has not it made *matritva* an emotional and ideational compensation for an otherwise exploited gender? Let us examine all these issues critically from a *dharmic* perspective.

It is no denying the hard fact that there are biological differences between men and women as well as between women and mothers. That is why the 'mother-child unit' has been a 'natural' and constituent part of all cultures (Moore, 1988). This 'unit' has assumed a particular significance in Indian socio-religious context. In Indian subcontinent all indigenous *dharmic* religions of *Sanatana Dharma*/Hinduism, Jain *Dharma*/Jainism, Bouddha *Dharma*/Buddhism, Sikh *Dharma*/Sikhism, and other sub-religious faith systems have sanctified *matritva*/motherhood with deep rooted tenets and rituals which have made this continuous Indic culture very distinctive and vibrant since prehistoric time.

Then the most important question arises whether there can be of any East motherhood, particularly Indic motherhood i.e. *Bharatiyamatritva,* that can be observed, measured and analysed from the perspective of social ontology. The answer to this question probably lies in the resolution of 'big three' dichotomies: subjectivity and objectivity, structure and agency, and synchrony and diachrony (Archer *et al,* 2013). The first dichotomy deals with knowledge, the second with action, and the last with time. Again comes the problem of integrating or transcending the divide between micro, meso and macro-scale social phenomena of *matritva* in Indian subcontinental context.

The knowledge of *matritva* in the context of Indic culture has to be gained through the resolution of the dichotomy of subjectivity and objectivity. The subjective here is the individual mother of the East, and her intensions, interpretations and interactions with the objective. The objective here is public or external action or outcome of a mother in discharging her mothering actions. Here comes the paradox of a social researcher from the fact that a social scientist is 'part of the very object they seek to explain' (Bourdieu, 1992). So, mothers and motherhood of the East should be analysed by taking into consideration the continuing cultural heritage writ large in East society influenced and shaped by pre-Vedic traditions through Vedic-Puranic continuum.

Next is the structure-agency dichotomy, which forms an enduring ontological debate in social theory, and it is also relevant in interpreting and understanding Bharatiya *matritva* and mothers of the East. In social theories, agency is the capacity of individuals to act independently and make free choices, and structure refers to the factors that limit or affect or shapes the choices and actions of individuals. These limiting factors in society have been gender, religion, social class, caste, ethnicity etc. The core of sociological epistemology has been the case of which factor(s) takes over other, which opens up the debate over social reproduction: how are structures reproduced through the choices of individual actor(s) or agency?

Here arises a critical dilemma. If we consider *matritva*/ motherhood in Indian society merely as a social construction by patriarchy, then we have to deny any type of autonomy to Indian mothers, which defy the basic logic of existence and essence of human being as a conscious being. We cannot deny the agency of human beings. So we have to study Indic motherhood and mothers of the East from a deeper as well as larger perspective. When a Hindu *Shakta* saint proclaims that *Kali Brahmn, Brahmn Kali,* the whole paradigm of motherhood/ *matritva* gets transformed into the divinity, which has been unparalleled in any other organised religio-cultural society. This divine paradigm of *matritva* remains the basic source of agency of mothers of the East in general and mothers of the Indic culture in particular from time immemorial.

The synchrony-diachrony dichotomy or statics and dynamics (Lizardo, 2010) is related to a distinction of social reality with respect to time. Synchrony refers to an analysis of static social reality slicing moments of time, and diachrony tries to analyse dynamic sequences of social reality within the context of time-space relations inherent in the constitution of all social interaction (Giddens, 2006). Thus, synchrony considers social phenomena as static concepts like a *language* and diachrony would refer to unfolding processes like actual *speech*. These 'speeches' of mothers of the East have to be sensed, understood and interpreted by analysing particularly vast Indic texts as well as ways of life of mothers as *living heritage* in Indic land from the pre-historic time.

Then the study of mothers of the East should be 'particularistic' in nature with the emphasis on the 'feelings' of Indic mothers in particular in different social locations and their worldviews entwined with the quest for identity as mothers.

If we want to study Indic mothers and their feelings, we should go through the *dharmic* texts of the Land of Bharat. *Dharmic* texts comprise both Hindu and other non-Hindu *dharmic* scriptures. Hindu texts are of two major types: *Sruti* ('revealed') and *Smriti* ('remembered'). Major Hindu scriptures include the *Vedas, Upanishads, Puranas, Manusmriti and Agamas* (all *Smriti*). And, there are other *dharmic* texts of Jainism, Buddhism and Sikhism.

Other important Hindu texts include *Devi Mahatmya,* the *Tantras,* the *Yoga Sutras* etc. As Hindu *Dharma* grants absolute and complete freedom of belief and worship, it conceives the *Brahman/Brahmn* as the Ultimate Reality, which is gender-neutral and formless in nature. But the *Brahmn* can take the form of personal *Ishvara* (God) who may be male god or female goddess. Hinduism has no central doctrinal authority. However, Shaktism has been one of the major denominations. The denominations differ primarily in the god/goddess worshipped as the Supreme One and devotees worship that god/goddess following a tradition making that denomination a distinct path for liberation. From that perspective, we get into *Shakta* tradition where devotees worship *Shakti* (power) personified through a female divinity or Mother Goddess *Devi.*

IV

The roots of Indic motherhood have to be traced through Rig Vedic society of Bharat. Rig Vedic society was relatively egalitarian with the absence of strict social hierarchy and the existence of social mobility. Though the Vedic household was patriarchal and patrilineal in nature, people worship both male and female gods. Women could choose their husbands and could remarry if their husbands died or disappeared. This independence of women has been behind the worship of female gods. In later period, there arose a distinct social system and tradition of worshipping female gods and consideration of goddesses as mothers.

However, the worship of mother as deity dated back to the pre-Vedic age with the coincidence of Harappan civilisation in Indian subcontinent. The tradition of worshipping mother has been going through the Vedic age down the line of classical, *Puranic* age and *Dharmic* age up to the present modern age. In Hindu religious life *Smarta* traditions with the *Puranas*' genre of literature have assumed a very distinct character. This tradition is notable for the domestic worship of five shrines with five deities - Vishnu, Shiva, Ganesha, Surya and Devi (*Shakti*) and all deities have been treated as equal. Here comes the importance of Mother Goddess in *dharmic* religious tradition of the East.

As Hindu *dharmic* tradition consists of diverse system of thoughts with various types of belief systems, the concept of god is much complex and depends upon concerned individuals and the tradition and philosophy followed. However, the concept of Brahman/*Brahmn* is unique in this tradition in that the *Nasadiya Sukta* (Creation Hymn) of the Rig Veda speaks of

'The One' and this One is Brahman. As per the *Rig Vedic* pronouncement – Truth is One but appears as Many for different perceivers – *Ekam Satya Bipra Bahudha Badanti.* From Brahman sprang first *Dharma* – universal principle of law, order, harmony, all in all truth. *Dharma* is pure Reality as conceived by the *Brihadaranyaka Upanishad*. Brahman is *Sacchidananda* (Truth-Consciousness-Bliss). And, this Brahman is conceived both as *Saguna* (with attributes) and *Nirguna* (without attributes). *Saguna* Brahman is worshipped as personified *Ishvara* – both as male and female form. In *Shakta* tradition, female *Ishvara* is worshipped as *Devi.*

In the Land of Bharat 'cults of goddess' worship is so ancient and this tradition is Shaktism where *Shakti* is the power that underlies the male principle. *Shakti* has been the concept or personification of divine feminism creative power, and sometimes *Shakti* has been referred to as 'The Great Divine Mother' in Hindu tradition. In Indic tradition, *Shakti* is responsible both for creation and change, and *Shakti* is cosmic existence as well as liberation with its most significant form being the *Kundalini Shakti* in Tantric tradition (Klostermaier, 1989).

In South India the *Shakti* goddess is also known as *Amma,* meaning mother and has been considered as the protector of the village. In this tradition, *Devi* is the Supreme Brahman itself with all other forms of divinity considered to be merely her diverse manifestations, and her main three transformative forms, known as *Tridevi.* This *Tridevi* is connected to *Trideva* separately as the complementary conjugal forms of *Brahma-Sarasvati* with creative *Rajas Guna, Vishnu-Lakshmi* with preservative *Sattva Guna*, and *Kali-Rudra* with destructive *Tamas Guna.*

In *Shakta* philosophy and practices, the Supreme Divine is feminine, called *Adi Parashsakti,* whose material manifestation is *Tripura Sundari,* a Hindu *dharmic* concept of the Ultimate

Shakti or *Mahashakti*, the ultimate power inherent in all Creation. But it is also interesting to note that as mother-father duo has been in a complementary role, so is the conjugal forms of *Tridevi-Trideva*. However, in *Shakti* tradition, *Devi* or *Adi Parashakti* is the Ultimate Reality as conceived in *Devi-Mahatmya* and *Shaktisangama Tantra*, both of which declared:

> Woman is the Creator of the universe, the universe is her form; woman is the foundation of the world, she is the true form of the body (*ibid.*).

It is also to be noted that there has always been a counter-narrative to androcentric denominations of Hindu *dharmic* traditions. While the feminine *Tridevi* goddesses have been relegated as consorts and auxiliary deities to the more eminent masculine *Trideva/Trimurti* gods, the feminine *Shaktidharma* denomination has given the eminent roles of the feminine *Tridevi*. In that tradition, the three *Devis* – Creator (Mahasarasvati), Preserver (Mahalaxmi) and Destroyer (Mahakali) – the *Tridevi/Matadi* have assumed the vital roles with the masculine *Trimurti* gods being relegated as the auxiliary deities as agents of the feminine *Tridevi*.

Of course, in Hindu meta-philosophy there have been no basic differences between Shiva and *Shakti*, Power and Powerful, and Brahman and *Atma*. From this perspective, God is both male and female, and *Shakti*/power of God is essential to create, sustain and destroy. As in modern science, energy can never be created or be destroyed, which changes from one form to another, *Adi Parashakti* took many forms/incarnations to do different tasks.

As *Brahman/Brahmn*, having all attributes/*gunas* in an equilibrium in *nirguna* state, desires to create this universe/*Jagat*, Brahman, being a non-dimensional God, becomes a dimensional God with attributes/*gunas* and creates this world through *Srishti-Shakti* (Mahasarasvati or Sound or knowledge), preserves through *Sthiti-Shakti* (Mahalaxmi or Light or resources), and destroys through *Samhara-Shakti* (Mahakali or Heat or strength).

This *Tridevi* philosophy and practices have gone outside the Indic land through Hinduism and Buddhism to all of the East Asian regions and took a syncretic form in local traditions. The *Tridevi* entered Japanese mythological tradition as the goddesses Benzaitennyo (Sarasvati), Kisshoutennyo (Laxmi) and Daikokutennyo (Mahakali).

So, the Mothers of the East consider themselves as a part of the Divinity of *Tridevi* and feel themselves empowered as the power given by the *Tridevi*. It is no denying that the mothers of the East have been so rooted in their traditions that they define themselves something uniquely in contrast to the mothers of the West.

V

The present volume intends to divulge different dimensions of this deep-rooted social institution that determines the course of life in many ways from birth to death. Altogether nineteen articles have been included to understand its specific ramifications and meanings in different social contexts and different life worlds. The first article is written by Aritra Ghosh, who has examined the institution from a feminist perspective. He points out that 'motherhood is culture specific and each culture has its own specific rules that define the role of motherhood'. In this way motherhood is institutionalised. Sujit Roy has tried to find out the ethos of motherhood in Indic culture from the perspective of hermeneutics. He explained the word *matritva* with the 'reciprocity between text and context, which shifts the focus from "interpretation" to "existential understanding" by "way of being" as a mother in the world than merely as "a way of knowing" motherhood'. He opined that *matritva* has been one of the defining characteristics of the Indic culture. Anushua Roy explains the significance of motherhood from the narratives of the *Ramayana*. She opines that the *Ramayana* enunciates 'quixotic parenting guidelines', while depicting different archetypal characters. The depiction of motherhood in another epic in the *Mahabharata* has been examined by Samita Manna. She has tried to find out the changing meanings of motherhood in the life of Kunti by following the socio-cultural compulsions to become a perfect mother. This article has also focused on the dual roles played by Kunti as a mother of her five sons as well as the mother of her eldest son Karna. Soumyajit Patra analyses the concept of 'motherhood' or 'mother' from the point of view of 'mother-child relationship'. In his words, the notion of 'mother' is relational. This relationship points to a set of responsibilities and obligations of the 'mother' towards her offspring(s). With the help of a particular case of Purulia District of West Bengal he has tried to point out that construction of 'mother' is situation-specific and so it is family-specific.

C.K. Manna tries to find out the existence of proto-motherhood in some animal species, particularly among a group of Ophidian (belong to the Class: Reptilia), the deadly poisonous rattle snake, widely available in India. He observes that the rattle snakes (Pit viper, *Crotalus cerastes*), give birth to the new born snake-lets (baby snakes) after incubation of eggs within the mothers' body for a certain period. For this specific reason they are termed as ovoviviparous. The variant of motherhood found among them needs further explorations and comparisons. Biswajit Ghosh and Kaushik Chattopadhyay have examined the idea of reproduction of motherhood from the perspective of the growing consumerism. They observed that globalisation of mothering is indicative of a new direction where gender role is reconstructing identity in a new array. They termed it as the deconstructed form of identity. Soumya Narayan Datta in his article develops the idea of scientific motherhood which refers to the practice of mothering informed by expert knowledge. This practice has evolved as medicine and science have replaced traditional domains of knowledge related to fertility and birth. From this point of view the movement to scientific motherhood redefined the concept of child and child-raising.

Pankaj Kumar analyses the challenges of single motherhood. He observes that the women who choose to remain single often face multiple disadvantages as a result of social and cultural, often legal and administrative constuctions of singleness. The rights of motherhood as protected by the Hindu Personal Law have been depicted by Sadhna Gupta. She has observed that the issue of gender justice has always been a concern in many nations despite the fact that laws enacted profess and mandate formal removal of institutionalised discrimination. This is because of the fact that the mindset and the attitudes ingrained in the cultural psyche have not been changed. The same can be said of the queering motherhood. Reshmi Chakraborty in her article has opined that motherhood is not a static phenomenon. It has cosmic connotation in all over the civilisation. At the same time it is not limited to gender identities. She used the term 'Queering motherhood' as a disjunction of the context of motherhood from the concept of womanhood and explored the idea of motherhood from the data collected from the eunuchs of various parts of North 24 Parganas, Nadia and Hooghly districts of West Bengal. Dibakar Bera, on the other hand, has examined the notion of motherhood among the eunuchs from the *guru-chela* relationships. He found that in the relationship between the *gurus* and *chelas*, the *gurus* are often equated with mothers among the eunuchs. This type of motherhood adds a different dimension to the study of motherhood itself.

The challenges of the mothers of the children with special needs have been studied by Kaynat Kenukhan. After analysing a number of case studies the author has opined that the parents, particularly the mothers of such children, are the worst sufferers. A child with special needs may impact his parent's quality of life as well and to overcome these special care and attention are required. Soumik Bhattacharjee and Abhra Chanda have divulged the anxieties of the mothers of the students of English Medium schools. They have studied fifty mothers each having one child from Kalyani municipality area of Nadia District of West Bengal. This study points out that these mothers always feel that their children have been underperforming in schools and this results in deteriorating the state of the mental health of the children, as the mothers always put pressure on them. Tania Upadhaya has analysed the role of the working mothers and grandparents in taking care of the children from a few case studies collected from North 24 Parganas, her area of study. She found that in case of the working mothers the role of grandparents cannot be undermined.

The notion of motherhood takes a different connotation among the tribal people of our country. In many senses, gender divisions in their communities take new meanings and principles. Rimi Sarkar and Samita Manna have found that among the Birhors, Souria Paharias and Mal Paharias of Jharkhand, motherhood is considered as a natural phase of life. This study has examined the practices associated with motherhood in these three tribal communities. The challenges of mothering among the imprisoned Rohingya mothers, living in West Bengal, have been analysed by Suchismita Majumder. She found that due to lack of any concrete policy for the Rohingya Muslims the problems of Rohingya mothers have been aggravated significantly.

In order to depict a holistic imagery of the 'mothers' and their challenges in mothering, the present volume has incorporated two articles that have focused on the issues of the sex workers. Atulita Banerjee in her study, conducted in a red-light area of North 24 Parganas District of West Bengal, has observed that the sex workers do not get the scope of fantasising motherhood because of the harsh reality of their life. The ghoulish atmosphere of the brothels disturbs the socialisation process of the children and as a result the ideal mother-child relationship fails to develop in such cases. In a similar study conducted in Kalighat red-light area under Kolkata (South) of West Bengal, Sajal Samadder examined the challenges of the sex workers and focused on the needs of their children along with their problem of social stigmatisation.

The bio-social realities of motherhood, thus, manifest itself in different forms depending on the culture-specific contexts. With some universal feelings and subjective orientations, the institution of motherhood appears as different form of cultural representations. In this sense 'mother' is a metaphor, which creates a wide gap between the 'signifier' and 'signified'. The present volume is an attempt to encapsulate some of its meanings in the present context, particularly in Indian sub-continental way of life.

References

Arcana, J. 1979. *Our Mother's Daughters*. California: Shameless Hussy Press.

Archer, M. S. and Tritter, J. Q. 2013. *Rational Choice Theory: Resisting Colonisation*. London: Routledge.

Bachofen, J.J. 1967. *Myth, Religion and Mother Right*. New Jersey: Princeton University Press.

Baig, T. A. 1957. *Women of India*. Ministry of Information and Broadcasting: Government of India. New Delhi: Sales Emporia Publications Divisions.

Bourdieu, P. and Wacquant, L. J. D. 1992. *An Invitation to Reflexive Sociology*. Chicago: University of Chicago Press.

Chakravarty, R. 1957. 'The Law as It Affects Women' in *Women of India*. Tara Ali Baig (Eds.). Ministry of Information and Broadcasting: Government of India. New Delhi: Sales Emporia Publications Divisions.

Channa, S.M. 2007. *Feminism and Empowerment in an Indian context: A Critical Analysis in Indian Women- Broken Words, Distant Dreams*. Kolkata: Levant Books.

Chatterjee, P. 1989. 'Colonialism, Nationalism and Colonised Women: The Context in India', *American Ethnologist*, 16 (4): 622-633.

Dubuisson, D. 2007. 'Exporting the Local: Recent Perspectives on 'Religion' as a Cultural Category', *Religion Compass,* 1.6, pp. 792.

Dutta, A. 2014. 'Glorified Motherhood: The Power of Identity', *Mainstream Weekly*. LII (11): 207-229.

Freedman, J. 1919. *Feminism*. New Delhi: Rawat Publications.

Gadamer, H. G. 1989. *Truth and Method.* 2nd Ed. New York: Crossroad.

Ghosh, A. and Manna, S. 2013. 'Declining Child Sex Ratio: Trends in West Bengal', *International Journal of Scientific Research.* 2 (8): 493-494.

Giddens, A. 2006. *Sociology* (5th Edition). Cambridge: Polity.

Hoebel, A.E. and Frost, E. L. 1976. *Cultural and Social Anthropology*. New York: McGraw-Hill.

Keay, J. 2011. *India: A History.* 2nd Ed. Revised and updated. New York: Grove Press/Harper Collins.

Kimmel, M.S. 2000. *The Gendered Society*. Oxford: Oxford University Press.

Klostermaier, K. K. 1989. *A Survey of Hinduism.* NY: State University of New York.

Leick, G. 2003. *Sex, Love and Eroticism in Mesopotamian Literature*. London: Routledge.

Leskolek, V. 2011. 'Historical Perspective on the Ideologies of Motherhood and its Impact on Social Work', *Social Work and Society- International Online Journal*. 9 (2): 1-10.

Leslie, I.J. 1989. *The Perfect Wife - The Orthodox Hindu Woman according to the Stridharmapaddhati of Tryambakayajavan*. New Delhi: Oxford University Press.

Lizardo, O. 2010. 'Beyond the antimonies of structure: Levi-Strauss, Giddens, Bourdieu, and Sewell', *Theory and Society.* 39.6: 651-688.

Love, B. and S. E. 1983. 'The answer is matriarchy', in Joyce Trebilcot (ed.). *Mothering: Essays in Feminist Theory*. New Jersy: Rowman & Allenheld.

Miller, T. 2005. *Making Sense of Motherhood: A Narrative Approach*. Cambridge: Cambridge University Press.

Mohammada, M. 2007. *The Foundations of the Composite Culture in India.* New Delhi: Aakar Books.

Monier, M.W. 2002. *A Sanskrit-English Dictionary, Etymologically and Philologically Arranged to cognate Indo-European Languages.* New Delhi: Motilal Banarsidass.

Moore, H. L. 1988. *Feminism and Anthropology: Feminist Perspectives.* Minneapolis: University of Minnesota Press.

Prabhu, P. H. 1940. *Hindu Social Organisation*. Bombay: Popular Prakashan.

Pramanick, S.K. and Manna, S. 2010. *Women in India: Motherhood and Multiple Identities*. New Delhi: Serial Publications.

Rao, D. J. 2013. *Adi Shakti: The Mother Goddess*. New Delhi: Viva Books.

Rich, A. 1976. *Of Women Born: Motherhood as Experience and Institution*. New York: Norton and Company.

Sagade, J. 2005. *Child Marriage in India: Socio-Legal and Human Rights Dimensions*. New Delhi: Oxford University Press.

Shchurko, T. 2012. 'Compulsory Motherhood: The female reproductive body as regulated by the state', *Summary Laboratorium*. Vol.4 (2): 259-263.

Smith, W. C. 1978. *The Meaning and End of Religion*. New York: Harper and Row.

Synder, R.C. 2008. 'What is Third Wave Feminism? A New Directions Essay', *Signs*. 34 (1): 175-196.

Taylor, E.B. 1871. *Primitive Culture*. London: J. Murray Publication.

Chapter - 1

Sociology of Motherhood: A Discussion from Feminist Perspective

Aritra Ghosh

In our society, as in most societies, women not only bear children, but also take the primary responsibility for infant care, spend more time with infants and children than men do, and sustain primary emotional ties with infants.

Sociology of motherhood is a field of sociology that examines gender, family and parenting, with primary emphasis on motherhood. Over time, numerous trends have emerged within the sociology of motherhood. Some of these themes are: motherhood and the sociology of gender; motherhood as an experience and an institution; motherhood ideologies; motherhood and separate spheres; motherhood and paid employment; care giving practices; and changing notion of motherhood.

Psychoanalytic theorists have examined mother's unconscious actions, exploring her deep attachment to her children. Sociologists have attempted to trace mother's actual experience of child rearing, identifying the way society and culture have affected her behaviour and her attitudes. But feminists, especially since the beginning of the liberation movement in the late 1960s, have been concerned with the subordination of women in the mothering role and have offered impassioned and often contradictory ways of thinking about motherhood. The essential contribution of feminism to the understanding of motherhood as a structuring category has been its insistence on the distinction between biological and social motherhood.

Motherhood: From the Perspective of Western Feminists

Simone De Beauvoir was one of the first and, perhaps, the most influential to proclaim that women's ability to give birth was the source of their subordination. In her view, motherhood signalled that women were twice doomed: biologically, during pregnancy when they lacked control over their bodies; and socially, when children restricted them to the home (Beauvoir, 1953:199-236). Fourteen years later, Betty Friedan diagnosed what she called 'the problem that has no name'. She identified the unhappiness of middle-class, educated, suburban housewives who were pressured into their maternal role and, consequently, felt unfulfilled and discontented (Friedan, 1963:272).

The radical feminist Shulamith Firestone argued that women's oppression lies in her child bearing and child rearing role. For Firestone, the denial of the mother's sexual desire within the social organisation of the family was the primary instrument of female control (Firestone, 1970). Clearly, an expectation, that mothers were pure and chaste, limited their expression of sexuality. Furthermore, for some women the prohibition of sexual enjoyment was linked to restrictions on the joy of bonding with their children (Weisskopf, 1980).

Iris Young pointed out that cultural pressures condemned the mother's pleasure even in breast-feeding. At the base of this, she argued, was the husband's requirement that his wife depend solely on him for sexual pleasure (Young, 1990). In Western society, a good mother was seen as pure and 'self-effacing' and the bad mother as 'sexually active and self-interested' (Flax, 1990:125).

Adrienne Rich urged women to become educated about their corporeal processes in order to reclaim their sexuality and form a united female culture. Her book, *Of Woman Born* was pivotal to mothering theories because it investigated women's experience with their children and related it to their subordination in society. Writing from the mother's point-of-view, Rich criticised the ideological base of motherhood. She argued that by commandeering the birth process, male institutions had 'devalued motherhood and kept women in an inferior position' (Rich, 1981: 256-280).

At the same time, Rich extolled the practice of mothering. Unlike Beauvoir and Firestone, she considered that women's ability to give birth could become the main source of their power. Rich's idea to 'think through the body' was, perhaps, impractical for busy mothers. The main benefit of her work came from her compassion and understanding of the experience of mothering. Although her writing has an essentialist, biological base, she explored her own maternal ambivalence in her relationship with her three sons in a candid and enlightening manner.

Sociologist Alice Rossi also highlighted the connection of the mother to her children. In 1964, Rossi had advocated shared parenting in order to reduce the woman's involvement in mothering duties so that she would be able to work outside the home (Rossi, 1964). By 1974, she had changed her views. In her controversial article, 'Biosocial Perspective on Parenting', she argued that equality could not be achieved if the biological differences between men and women were ignored (Rossi, 1977). Although Rossi claimed to consider both the social and biological determinants of mothering, her arguments favoured the biological. She asserted, for instance, that women were predisposed to the mothering role because of their unique ability to give birth and lactate. Using neuro-endocrinology and bio-evolutionary theories, Rossi contended that the mother-child bond was hormonally regulated and crucial for the survival of the species. In Rossi's opinion, it was the devaluation of the biological role that minimised the mother's contribution to society and allowed men's intrusive technological interference in the birthing process. She concluded that women's unique propensity to be mother, as well as social conditioning from the media, schools and other institutions, meant that men could not share the parenting role. She appeared to revise this opinion in 1979 when she suggested that men should have special training to assist them in fatherly duties (Rossi, 1979).

Rossi was censured for her biological perspective of the mothering process. Her articles were depressing because of their restrictions on women's choices. According to Farganis (1996), Rossi's belief in the mother's prenatal hormonal response to her infant could not be authenticated. Farganis criticised Rossi's bio-evolutionary position, because its limited men's responsibility for childcare to the pecuniary. She noted that Rossi omitted to give data on the infant's connection to the father, which in some cases was equal to, or greater than, the mother's bonding experience. Rossi's belief that mothering came most easily to women was essentialist, as it ignored the variety of feelings women have toward their children and the nurturing capacity of some men. She did not allow for those women whose biological connection to their infant brought little nurturing response, or for women who adopted babies and had no biological connection, but great love and commitment (Farganis, 1996).

Psychoanalytic sociologist Nancy Chodorow blamed sexual inequality in society on the division of labour which allocated the primary infant care to women at home, while men were in the workforce in more highly valued occupations.

While her work was based on psychoanalysis, she moved away from Freud's concentration on the *libido*, instincts and drives, towards 'relational aspects of psychic development'. Drawing on the separation/individuation theories of

Margaret Mahler, Chodorow used 'object relations theory', which positioned the mother as 'an object' - the first and most important in the baby's life. According to Mahler, the biological birth of the child occurred on its release from the mother's body, its psychic birth occurred when it separated from its primary love object (usually the mother) and established its relationship to 'the world of reality' (Mahler *et al.*,1975:3). Object relations theory was characterised by its concentration on the pre-Oedipal experience where pre-verbal social relations had a critical influence on the baby's development. It explained that humans understood their existence by their connection to others.

Chodorow made the point that as women were responsible for mothering, daughters and sons were treated differently and in consequence, developed differently. The daughter, who shared a 'core female identity' with her mother, was encouraged to imitate her, while the son was expected to be separate and autonomous. During the Oedipal conflict, the daughter remained in an 'attached' relationship, which ideally suited her for adopting the caring and nurturing responsibilities in the domestic sphere. The son, on the other hand, turned away from the mother and moved toward the father, whom he saw as more worthy. He adopted, as a consequence, competitive traits which were suited to the 'powerful public sphere' (Chodorow, 1978:39-151). In addition, much like Dinnerstein, Chodorow concluded that the early memory of their powerful, omnipotent, mother left men, who struggled for ultimate control, with 'feelings of resentment and fear' (Chodorow, 1991:6). Chodorow strongly recommended the necessity for equal parenting in order to bring about social change. She maintained that it would be beneficial to women and girls as it would allow them subjectivity and autonomy. Additionally, the 'individualism and competitiveness' of boys would be reduced and their 'commitment to the group' increased (Lorber *et al.*, 1981:512).

Feminists in the 1970s, like Rich, Dinnerstein and Chodorow, introduced mothering theories which challenged, as Chodorow commented, 'nearly exclusive Freudian focus on the father and Oedipus complex' (Chodorow, 1991:6). Their revelations linked women's subordination in society to the gendered division of labour which allocated the mother total responsibility for childcare and restricted her to the domestic sphere. As a result of their writings, many women questioned the socialisation of motherhood as 'natural and inevitable' and decided that women's ultimate fulfilment in life should not necessarily be maternity (Chodorow and Contratto, 1982:54).

Motherhood: From the Perspective of Indian Feminists

Jasodhara Bagchi's book on motherhood is a significant contribution to a theme that resonates at many levels. Her insightful analysis looks at motherhood through gender lens and draws on feminists' responses to accepted notions of motherhood as the inevitable marker of the female of the species. The social construction of gender, builds on the biological division of roles between the human male as the sperm supplier to fertilise the egg the female carries, erects an elaborate signification of the primacy of the human male and consequent subordination of the human female.

Bagchi's contribution is an admirable approach on the joys of motherhood as against the agony of motherhood embedded in social structures. As she says right at the beginning that, the book emanates from the conviction that feminist understanding of motherhood is central to the unfolding of Indian society from the moment of its insertion into the global capitalist system.

A puzzle in the social construction of motherhood is the contradictory delineation: veneration on the one hand, and on the other hand, deprivation of actual living mothers of enabling conditions that would reward their dedicated service in bringing forth the regeneration of the human being. The *Jagatjanani* (Mother of the world) is only in temples of Mother Goddesses, in poetry and art. There is more than one kind of mother: mothers are women who inhabit or perform the role of bearing children or raising children, who may or may not be their biological offspring. Thus, women may earn the entitlement of being considered 'mother' by virtue of giving birth, by raising children, by supplying ovum for fertilising an embryo. We have the birth mother, the biological mother and the adoptive mother. These concepts are not exhaustive because much depends on how social, cultural and religious discourses define these roles (Bagchi, 2017).

Being made to represent the *Aryan* woman, however, and not a mere 'Hindu' woman nor 'Indian' woman, the ideology of motherhood in India got incorporated into a caste-race nexus that had consequences, however covert, of the strengthening the existing stratification of Indian society along gender-class-caste-ethnic lines. As Uma Chakravarti's extremely generative early essay analyses this trend of feeding motherhood into the retrieval of the Aryan Vedic past, it was Dayanand Saraswati who brought out this trend in his Arya Samaj. In order to maintain the pure quality of the Aryan race Dayanand had a lot of prescription for motherhood, which alone defined womanhood in his formation of the Arya Samaj. As Chakravarti says,

> Motherhood for Dayananda was the sole rationale of a Woman's existence but what was crucial in his concept of motherhood was its specific role in procreation and rearing of a special breed of men (Chakravarti, 2006:40).

Leela Dube's writings bring out what anthropologists have pointed out from findings made throughout India, the implications of the widespread metaphor of seed and field. Dube says,

> First, an essential unequal relationship is reflected in and emphasised through the use of these symbols, and second,

> the symbolism is utilised by the culture to underplay the significance of the woman's contribution to biological reproduction (Dube, 2001:136).

Dube goes on to expand the significance of this strengthening patriarchal control:

> While tying her down to the supreme duty of motherhood this symbolism is instrumental in denying her the natural right over her own children and in creating and sustaining the ideology in which strategic resources of both types - material as well as human - remain in the hands of man (*ibid*: 137).

Feminist historians have commented on the dynamic potential of the dialectical relationships between production and reproduction that is vital in understanding the gendering process of motherhood. Kumkum Roy points out, 'Focusing on reproductive relations may transform our understanding not only of the relationship of women to the economy, but of the economy itself' (Roy, 1999:22).

Colonial bondage produced a visible crisis in the masculinity of sons who had not been able to release the mother from bondage. Mrinalini Sinha has justifiably contested. Ashis Nandy's proposed binary between the coloniser's masculinity and the femininity associated with the colonised. For him, the question of colonial masculinity is a masculine one that involves crisis in masculinity at both ends of the divide and a complex interaction between the two (Sinha, 1995).

Throughout the world the study of motherhood creates major problematic among the feminists when they fight to replace the subordinate status of women. Women are the second sex considering their poor wages, denial of educational opportunity, poor security and facilities provided by government for maintaining their descent life. No doubt society advances with the changing status of women. But the real contradiction lies within the concepts and the contexts on which motherhood lies as mothers are also considered a 'category of women'.

Simone De Beauvoir also agreed that the mother is the poor half of the totality, so by virtue of her position she is considered as second sex. In general, the mothers develop more emotional attachments with their children. The children are protected, secured and nourished through their mothers in earlier lives so the roles of the mothers cannot be ignored.

Especially in Indian context, the mothers sacrifice their whole life for their children. Early socialisation teaches the daughters to become a mother in the future. So the roles of mother are socially constructed. Mothers are the role models of their daughters. As a result, through the development of their self the girls are indoctrinated to take the role of mother in future. But the social situations of mothers are not same.

Mothers' role in society is therefore unparallel as it is instinctual. But is it all? Motherhood is not restricted only to this particular domain. It is an institution and therefore it institutionalises mothers' role which is important in every society.

Sociologists and behavioural scientists, such as Rich, Rossi and Chodorow, have considered the actual experience of mothering. Challenging the notion that women must always be the primary care takers, they recommended instituting a system of shared parenting. They argued that sole responsibility for the child was unfair, and had the wider and potentially more important repercussion of keeping women in a subordinate position in society. Additionally, the biological viewpoint of sociologists such as Rossi implied an inherent and instinctual connection of mother and child. Societal pressure to mother has been criticised by the feminists like Beauvoir, Friedan and Firestone whose works are helpful in discerning representations of taken-for-granted notions of maternal bliss. Other feminists, such as Young, Flax and Rich promoted interest in the eulogising portrayals of motherhood which placed the mother on a pedestal as a chaste, virtuous woman. For them, the purpose of denying women's sexuality was clearly to benefit men.

Motherhood is culture specific and each culture has its own specific rules that define the role of motherhood through 'institutionalising mothers' role'. Apart from this institutionalisation of motherhood, the role of mothers is sometimes invisible. Behind the screen she enlightens her family which is generally observed in Indian culture. Motherhood and femininity are closely attached. Though feminists from different periods were highly impassionate as they think that women's oppression and subordination are partly due to motherhood.

Motherhood is a social construction. It varies according to the need of society. Patriarchy which enslaves the women is often puzzled if the denial of mothering comes in the front. Motherhood and pregnancy are the special domains of femininity. Throughout the history motherhood was described as the woman's basic mission, profession and an inseparable part of her nature. Women are supposedly drawn into motherhood by their instincts which at the same time guarantee their children's healthy growth and development.

References

Bagchi, J. 2017. *Interrogating Motherhood.* New Delhi: Sage Publications India Pvt Ltd.

Beauvoir, S.D.1953. *The Second Sex.* Paris: Vintage.

Chakravarti, U. 2006. *Everyday Lives, Everyday Histories: Beyond the Kings and Brahmans of Ancient India.* New Delhi: Tulika Books.

Chodorow, N. 1978. *The Reproduction of Mothering: Psychoanalysis and the Sociology of Gender.* Berkeley: University of California.

Chodorow, N. 1991. *Feminism and Psychoanalytic Theory.* United States: Yale University Press.

Chodorow, N. and Contratto, S. 1982. 'The Fantasy of the Perfect Mother', in B. Thorne and M. Yalom (eds.): *Rethinking the Family: Some Feminist Questions.* New York: Longman.

Dube, L. 2001. *Anthropological Explorations in Gender: Intersecting Fields.* New Delhi: Sage Publications Pvt Ltd.

Farganis, S. 1996. *The Social Reconstruction of the Feminine Character.* Maryland: Rowman & Littlefield Publishers.

Firestone, S. 1970. *The Dialectic of Sex: The Case for Feminist Revolution.* London: Bantam Books.

Flax, J. 1990. *Thinking Fragments: Psychoanalysis, Feminism, and Postmodernism in the Contemporary West.* Berkeley: University of California Press.

Friedan, B. 1963. *The Feminine Mystique.* London: Penguin.

Lorber, J. Lanb, R., Rossi, A.S. and Chodorow, N. 1981. 'On the Reproduction of Mothering: A Methodological Debate', *Signs: Journal of Women in Culture and Society,* Vol. 6(3): 482-514.

Mahler, M.S., Pine, F. and Bergman, A. 1975. *The Psychological Birth of the Human Infant.* New York: Basic Books.

Rich, A. 1981. *Of Woman Born: Motherhood as Experience and Institution.* London: Virago.

Rossi, A. 1964. 'Equality Between the Sexes: An Immodest Proposal', *Doedulus: Journal of the American Academy of Arts and Sciences,* Vol. 93:607-652.

Rossi, A. 1977. 'A Biosocial Perspective on Parenting', *Doedulus: Journal of the American Academy of Arts and Sciences,* Vol. 106:1-31.

Rossi, A. 1979. 'Considering a Biosocial Perspective on Parenting', *Signs: Journal of Women in Culture and Society,* Vol. 4(4):694-697, 712-717.

Roy, K. 1999. *Women in Early Indian Societies.* New Delhi: Manohar Publishers and Distributors.

Sinha, M. 1995. *Colonial Masculinity: The 'Manly Englishman' and the 'Effeminate Bengali' in the Late Nineteenth Century.* Manchester: Manchester University Press.

Weisskopf, S.C. 1980. 'Maternal Sexuality and Asexual Motherhood', *Signs: Journal of Women in Culture and Society,* Volume 5(4):766-782.

Young, I.M. 1990. *Throwing Like a Girl and Other Essays in Feminist Philosophy and Social Theory.* Bloomington: Indiana University Press.

Chapter - 2

Hermeneutics of '*Matritva*': A Study on Motherhood in Indic Culture

Sujit Roy

Motherhood in English is what can be transliterated as *'Matritva'* in Sanskrit and vice versa. The term *matritva* is composed of two words of '*matri*' means mother and '*tattva*' (or *tattwa*) means 'reality', 'principle', 'truth' or 'thatness' in Sanskrit. According to various schools of Indian philosophy, a *tattva* is an element or aspect of reality. Each and every culture provides its own way of understanding and interpretations of reality which connotes to a unique contextual meaning of the social world to its members. *Matritva* in Indic culture is not merely a concept, but it has been a reality with multi-ramifications in Indian society from time immemorial.

Hermeneutics in general refers to analysis, interpretations and understanding of texts, especially religious texts. Modern hermeneutics focuses not only on texts but also both on verbal and nonverbal communications as well as semiotics, presuppositions and pre-understandings. *'Bhashya'* in Sanskrit may be what is meant by hermeneutics in English. In Indian context *Bhashya* literally means 'speaking, talking, any work in the current, vernacular speech' (Monier-Williams, 2002) and any 'explanatory work, exposition, explanation, commentary' (*ibid.*) that brings to light something else. The root *Bhash* means 'speak about, describe, declare, tell' (*ibid.*). Then *Bhashya* is a commentary or exposition of any primary or secondary text in ancient or medieval Indian literature.

The present study has been an attempt to sketch out motherhood in Indic culture from the perspective of hermeneutical circle in respect of the word *matritva* with the reciprocity between text and context, which shifts the focus from 'interpretation' to 'existential understanding' by 'way of being' as a mother in the world than merely as 'a way of knowing' motherhood.

Indic culture here refers to the way of life of the people of the Indian subcontinent from the pre-historic time, which has been continuing in a sublime subtle way through the ages. Indic culture is an amalgamation of several cultures spanning across the Indian subcontinent. It has been influenced by a history that is several millennia old (Keay, 2011). Indic culture has been heavily influenced by *dharmic* religions (Mohammada, 2007).

Matritva has been one of the defining characteristics of the Indic culture. Mothers and motherhood have been continuously eulogised in Indic culture and tradition. Motherhood has bestowed a special status to Indian women who have been traditionally given insignificant socio-political space in a dominant patriarchal Indian society. It is no denying the fact that there are no clear-cut role models in *dharmic* scriptures for good motherhood. But, there certainly has been a cultural and ideological understanding of motherhood as a pre-eminent status and positional role in Indian society. Mothers have been depicted as sacrificing, loving women who, unlike the wife, have been in control of themselves and their children. The result is a whole body of oral tradition and literature that glorify motherhood, which influences, shapes and somehow transforms a natural role into a 'supernatural' one.

It is also no denying that motherhood confers Indian woman with a purpose and identity amid dismal poverty, widespread unemployment and the drudgery of child rearing. It has also been a point of worth that traditionally Indian brides enter their husbands' families not as wives but as daughters-in-law where intimacy with husbands has been consciously discouraged by the extended family. The daughter-in-law in her husband's family has been accepted and revered as *kulabadhu* (daughter-in-law of the family) who becomes a mother of the family. Thus, mothers have often been related best with their children. In Indian society, thus a mother is expected and traditionally encouraged to find emotional fulfillment primarily in her relationship with her children.

With the shared responsibility of parenthood and caring for the next generation, an Indian mother gradually develops later much intimation with her husband. Thus, it is only through motherhood that an Indian bride has traditionally come into her own as a woman. Motherhood role alone has given recognition of worth to an Indian woman in the family, in the community and in the life cycle.

Another important point is to be noted here that traditionally mothers have been held to be asexual. Indian society is very much unique in bestowing religio-cultural respect for mothers which has found expression in terms of increased safety and security for mothers in their interactions with other males. This concern has been translated into a relaxation of controls and an exercise of independence and power never before available to them as women.

This new found 'motherly' independence and power, along with their earlier preparations into the dual ideals of femininity as wife and mother, have been playing a significant role in the immense emotional investment in Indian mothers. All these make motherhood positive and satisfying for Indian mothers disapproving negative thoughts about their confinement in a humdrum role.

But, the question is whether eulogisation of motherhood in the Indian context has actually imposed a socially constructed role on women. Has it in reality gratified an essentially patriarchal society that gives little actual power to mothers, thus, making motherhood an emotional and ideational compensation for an otherwise exploited gender?

The fact is that there are biological differences between men and women as well as between women and mother. Then the 'mother-child unit' has been a 'natural' part of all cultures (Moore, 1988), which has assumed a particular significance in Indian socio-religious context. In India, all indigenous '*dharmic*' religions of Hinduism, Jainism, Buddhism and Sikhism have sanctified motherhood with tenets and ritualism which have made continuing Indic culture very distinctive since pre-historic time.

Now, the question arises whether there can be of any Indic motherhood i.e. '*Bharatiya Matritva*' that can be observed, measured and analysed from the perspective of social ontology. The answer probably lies in the resolution of 'big three' dichotomies: subjectivity and objectivity, structure and agency, and synchrony and diachrony (Archer *et al*, 2013). While the first deals with knowledge, the second with action, and the last with time. Again comes the problem of integrating or transcending the divide between micro, meso and macro-scale social phenomena of motherhood in Indian context.

The knowledge of motherhood in the context of Indic culture has to be gained through the resolution of subjectivity-objectivity dichotomy. The subjective here is the individual mother and her intensions and interpretations of the objective. The objective is then public or external action or outcome of a mother in discharging her mothering actions. Herein comes the paradox of a social researcher from the fact that a social scientist is part of the very object they seek to explain (Bourdieu, 1992). So, Indic motherhood should be analysed by taking into consideration the continuing cultural heritage writ large in Indian society influenced and shaped by pre-Vedic traditions through Vedic-Puranic continuum.

Now, the dichotomy of structure and agency, which forms an enduring ontological debate in social theory, is also relevant in interpreting and understanding Indic motherhood. While agency refers to the capacity of individuals to act independently and make free choices, structure relates to factors that limit or affect or shapes the choices and actions of individuals e.g. social class, religion, gender, ethnicity, and so on. Which one takes over other is the core of sociological epistemology, opening the debate over social reproduction: how are structures reproduced through the choices of individuals? If we consider motherhood in Indian society merely as a social construction by patriarchal dominance, then we have to deny any type of autonomy to Indian mothers which defies the basic logic of existence of human being. So we have to study Indian motherhood from a deeper as well as larger perspective. When a Hindu Shakta saint proclaims that *Kali Brahmn, Brahmn Kali*, the whole paradigm of motherhood gets transformed into the *divinity* which has been unparallel in any other organised religio-cultural society. This remains the basic source of agency of Indic mothers from time immemorial.

The dichotomy of synchrony and diachrony, or statics and dynamics (Lizardo, 2010) refers to a distinction of social reality with respect to time. While the former refers to an analysis of static social reality slicing moments of time, the later attempts to analyse dynamic sequences of social reality within the context of time-space relations inherent in the constitution of all social interaction (Giddens, 2006). Then synchrony considers social phenomena as a static concept like a *language* and diachrony would refer to unfolding processes like actual *speech*. These 'speeches' of Indic motherhood have to be sensed, understood and interpreted by analysing vast Indic texts as well as ways of life of mothers as *living heritage* in Indic land from the pre-historic time.

Then, the study of motherhood in Indic culture should be 'particularistic' in nature with the emphasis on the feelings of

Indian mothers in different social locations and their worldviews entwined with the quest for identity as mothers.

References

Archer, M. S. and Tritter, J. Q. 2013. *Rational Choice Theory: Resisting Colonisation*. London: Routledge.

Bourdieu, P. 1992. *An Invitation to Reflexive Sociology*. Chicago: University of Chicago Press.

Giddens, A. 2006. *Sociology* (5th edition). Cambridge: Polity.

Keay, J. 2011. *India: A History*. 2nd Ed. Revised and updated. New York: Grove Press/Harper Collins.

Lizardo, O. 2010. 'Beyond the antimonies of structure: Levi-Strauss, Giddens, Bourdieu, and Sewell', *Theory and Society*. 39.6: 651-688.

Mohammada, M. 2007. *The Foundations of the Composite Culture in India*. New Delhi: Aakar Books.

Moore, H. L. 1988. *Feminism and Anthropology: Feminist Perspectives*. Minneapolis: University of Minnesota Press.

Monier, M. W. 2002. *A Sanskrit-English Dictionary, Etymologically and Philologically Arranged to cognate Indo-European Languages*. New Delhi: Motilal Banarsidass.

Chapter - 3

An Exploration on Motherhood in Narratives of *Ramayana*

Anushua Roy

The *Ramayana* is a fascinating and absorbing repository embodying living traditions, myths and symbols. Delightful renditions recount varied characters and their exploits. Those are corollary to profound imagination. Centuries have passed witnessing several concoctions of Valmiki's epic (Brockington, 1998). Each dwelled with a subjective version of *Ramayana*; mainly laden with elaborate emphasis on valorising the protagonist Rama and Sita. However, beyond the horizon of their presence resides charming characters, invigorating alternative conjectures. Amongst, various facets that have been pondered, the present study is an effort on delineating the recurrent glorified construct of motherhood during the era of the *Ramayana*. Most of the deprecatory remarks employed with reference to Kaikeyi are responsible for evoking ire for her and several other women of the age. Comparing and condemning womanhood through these myopic lenses draw dismal images of vices. The brunt of being a mother is cumbersome, yet her contributions are merely discernible. Nurturing, rearing, and restoring are bestowed erroneously on a woman as she is an assumed-compassionate and sacrificing. The following reading will highlight the concomitant sensibilities and culpability associated with featured characters.

The entire gamut of existing interpretations and literature on the *Ramayana* relies on subjective conceptions while investing and exploring the varied condiments (Brockington, 1977). Each character champions as a father, mother, daughter, brother, son, wife, and so forth furthering their importance in the subsequent eras. Most of them in contemporary reiterations received accolades or reproach for their fictional dispositions. However, mélange of these colourful fictional characters are fragmented imaginations and are anachronistic. Namely, the patterns of behaviour and conduct as envisaged in the erstwhile epic are probably inadequate in contemporary era. In the changing texture of private and public sphere, preceding tenets are inconceivable. However, the *Ramayana* had stood for thousands of eons and will probably stand for infinity (Sankalia, 1982). Therein, further exegesis of varied *Ramayana*-s stands in prominence.

Deliberations of John Brockington, Sheldon Pollock, Wendy Doniger, Camille Bulke, A. K. Ramanujan (amongst several others) benchmark a genre of modern redefinitions. Their reflections have benefitted and engaged diverse academic discussions. Thus, a careful understanding of their literal eruditions is much appreciable. The present essay is an attempt to discuss the apparent glorification of identity and character as narrated in the epic.

Several former and contemporary scholars illuminated instances of character dimensions that were disconcerting or unfathomable in the epic. As mentioned earlier, centuries have passed entertaining and deciphering the epic and its luminaries. In light of which, Rama and Sita are archetypal of conjugal fidelity (Bulcke, 1950). Sita has been delineated more exceedingly and more independently in Valmiki's magnum opus than in later popular conceptions. She occupied a broader vista than in subsequent reiterations, which in itself, is an indication of the changing approaches towards her, in particular, and women, in general. In the epic, Sita is synonymous to Vaidehi, Maithili,

Janakatmaja and Janaki. While as, in later popular renditions, she is unabatedly mediated as Mother Sita (Buck, 1989). A self-determined and imperious individual later deemed pious. The changing texture of a character though often attributed to her miraculous birth to king Janaka is indistinct.

The cognisance of Sita as a cogent protagonist and mother though not an anew conception, yet it entails mounted disagreements. The epic has pellucid illustrations of binaries, engaging father, mother, son, wife, brother, husband, warrior, and a king adjacently. Dasaratha, as having three titled wives in addition to his numerous concubines juxtaposed to Rama as his son is enamored for his undisputable ardor for Sita. Alongside, beneficent characters such as Kausalya and Sumitra were posed against Kaikeyi. The formers portrayed were as submissive, docile, and abiding. Whereas, latter's intention to succeed her son to the throne was constituted as an act of vile deception. Simultaneously, Sita was posed as seemingly self-sufficient mother in rearing her sons in the wilderness relinquishing palatial pleasures. Mandodari stood firmly to her ground and unabashedly criticised Indrajit for being concomitant with his father's moral lapses. Subsequently, the contrast of sons is reflected in the illustrations of Rama, Angada (son of Sugriva), and Indrajit (son of Ravana). The former silently accepted his fate and retired to the wilderness for fourteen years. The latter two tried to avenge the defeat of their fathers. Additionally, as sons of Rama and Sita, Luv and Kush tried to discern their mother's reestablishment in Ayodha. Correspondingly, variant circumstances are featured to compare Rama with Bali, Sugriva, Kumbhakarna, Vivbhisana and Ravana.

Irrespective of its nativity, Rama narratives mostly deliberated in marking Sita's pre-eminence as a dotting wife. However, behind this garb stood a mother who might have been the first to be a single parent and survived in banishment. Discussions on distinct consideration of motherhood in the *Ramayana* though are in abundance therein; the present study aims to explore the stretch of such fervent constructs in Rama narratives. Since, time unknown motherhood construed as a concurrent achievement of every married woman. Most ancient texts had been prominently observant in delivering woman as either demure or brazen (Pollock, 2001). The composite ideation of motherhood has mostly been associated with the former; while as, the latter had been often depicted as withholding the responsibilities of rearing a child. Narratives had been instrumental in depicting importance of a woman bestowing on her relevance as a wife and mother. The *Ramayana* commences with Dasaratha yearning for an heir for his throne. With few ritualistic practices, he begets three sons who grew up to be the renowned warriors. His profound sterility thus provided gumption to the foundation of the *Ramayana*. Nonetheless, if his queens were incapacitated, the destiny of the *Ramayana* had been different.

Throughout centuries, motherhood is expected to render mercy, love, generosity, and charity. A woman giving a birth seemingly regenerates her husband (Richman, 2008). Thus, motherhood instate as a cherished imagination of every devoted wife. The *Ramayana* has glorified begetting son as a virtue. Although, most women in the epic had miraculous birth they were devoid of parental identity. Seemingly, they got validation through motherhood; localising importance as a mother to her son. This instated endorsement further attacked by curses of sterility. Balakanda recounts episode of Parvati and Shiva's union for progeny. During her period of expectancy, she irked and cursed several celestial beings with impotency. Likewise, she cursed *Prithvi* for not wishing her son, to inexperience the pleasure of having a son. Thus, can this accurse be synonymous to bearing a girl child? Contemporary expositions seek to explore the premises of woman far famed to be a competent wife and mother, but her birth and childhood are indistinct. Her identity is featured through her father or husband, masqueraded as both re-incarnation and operative to advance protagonists motives.

Consequently, fulfillment of maternity demonstrated through bearing valiant and intelligent sons. Accounts of mortal damsels engaging in sexual encounters with immortals and bearing sons matching the prowess and luster suggest the eugenic approach to urge for a superior species (Doniger, 2009). *Rakshasa* Sumali instructed his daughter Kiakesi to wait upon sage Visrava and beget sons, those splendid as the Sun and glorious alike Kubera; as an aid to replenish the *Rakshasa* race. Furthermore, Gandharvi Somada served sage Culi with all humility to be blessed with son endowed with Brahmanic luster. However, in spirit of sustenance and invigoration of a race, some episodes even demonstrated departure from fidelity. Vayu, violated the chastity of Anjana, wife of Vanara chief Keasri; the former's remonstration to it was soothed with the promise of a son with immense gallantry. Thus, Hanuman was born. Departure from procuring within the wedlock with occasional aberration glorified in the epic for son's rise to fame.

In this array of discussion, significance of a mother is bestowed with instilling personality on her child. Mothers are depicted to be casting protagonist's destiny. They are responsible for grooming and gearing for great sacrifices in the interest of family and probably humanity. The proverbial adage of sons takes after the father; daughters take after the mother as established in the epic. For instance, while Kaikeyi was sorting an empire for Bharata, he relinquished the throne for Rama. Sumitra mentions this act to be inherited from Dasaratha. Quite alike, Kaikesi (mother of Ravana) depicted as admonishing her son for the heinous act. She further insisted and urged Vivhisana and ministers in council chamber to restore Sita and bid peace with Rama. Ravana's refusal or resistance towards his mother clawed his identity as *rakhsasa* than his pious father. Evidently, nurturing and rearing do not affect the deportment of individuals. Although, descriptions of incompetent and unreasoned mothers hypothesised in the texts, Kaikeyi and Kaikesi draw notable attention. Both opinionated and thus manifested as being vile, the mothers goaded their sons to resist their stepbrothers. While Kaikesi prompted Ravana to outrival his stepbrother Kubera, Kaikeyi intended to isolate Bharata from his brothers. The interplay of binaries resurfaces with Ravana agreeing with Kaikesi in outrivaling his brothers; while Bharata remained fastened to Rama and Lakhsmana.

Before further introspection, an interesting inquisition lurks, as to who demands greater claims over women's solicitude, a husband, or the son? During Rama's preparation to retire to the wilderness, Kaushlya insists upon accompanying him leaving behind her husband. She expresses her agony and anger towards Dasaratha being responsible for her misfortune to banish Rama for an extensive period of fourteen years. She chides her husband for losing his wit to his youngest queen. In this episode of loss, Kaushalya not only narrates her fear to lose her son, but also being mistreated by Kaikeyi in absence of her son; thereby, demonstrating self-indulgence over benevolence of a mother. Simultaneously, Tara embraced the burning limbs of Sugriva on pyre than living with Angada. Nonetheless, Mandodori though lamented the death of her husband and sons; apart from cursing Rama, she also blamed her fortune. The instances capture the essence of a woman as a wife and mother. The ensemble of these three constructs constitutes a woman's recognition, validation of her maidenhood through marriage while virtue estimated through motherhood. The eminence of husband or son had riddled throughout the epic; while as, burdening the readers or listeners to have subjective interpretations. The relevance of aforementioned enquiry in the present debate may be located in transmission and transition of a prince to a warrior or king. The synergy of a character and identity enmeshes through parenting that incorporates conjoint participation of mother and father.

Tracing motherhood in other Rama-narratives

The ancient *Ramayana* enunciates quixotic parenting guidelines, depicting archetypal characters. In contrast, the wide stretch of colloquial narratives dismisses such illustrations. They challenge the self-compromising and accommodating notions of parenthood. Although uncertain of reliability, they uniquely conjure an esoteric rendering. A South Indian folk *Ramayana* narrates king Ravana (here named as Ravula) and Mandodari were childless and unhappy, followed by Ravula retiring to the forest to perform self-mortifications. Meanwhile he meets a mendicant who was none other than Shiva. The latter gave him a fruit and asked to share with his wife. Ravula assures that he will offer the sweet flesh of the fruit to his wife, while he will lick the seed. The *yogi,* skeptical about former's intention, warns Ravula of his impending doom if he disobeys. On returning to his kingdom, he arranged ritual prayers and was ready to share the fruit. However, he gobbled the fruit and left Mandodari the seed to lick. As she throws the residue in the yard, it sprouts and grows into a tall tree. Meanwhile, Ravula himself becomes pregnant advancing a month each day. Soon he sneezes out Sita; which means 'he sneezed' in Kannada. Subsequently, after consulting astrologers, he puts her in a box and leaves her in Janaka's field. The tale proceeds with birth and adventures of Rama and Lakhsmana. Followed by Sita's marriage contest, wherein, Ravula is humiliated and Rama marries Sita (Dharwadkar, 1999). The sequence of episodes is similar to the *Ramayana,* only with disparity of Sita not disappearing to the netherworlds. Here Sita's inorganic birth induces a new range of conjecture of Ravula's envy of Mandodari bearing the benefits of his austerities. It is an act symbolising male envy of childbirth. Procreation followed by nurture and sustenance yields potential authority. The intriguing endowment of conceiving and giving birth even ensnared the fierce king such as Ravula. Considerably, there is semblance in bearing child and power of creation.

Similarly, multiple arcane narrations have put forth parenthood of Sita to Ravana and Mandodari. In an episodic narration of the *Adbhuta Ramayana*, Ravana secured blood of *yogis*. Sage Gritsamada practised penance to acquire the goddess Lakhsmi as his daughter. Shortly, thereafter Ravana impeded sage's sacrifice infuriating Mandodari who resolved to drink the contents of the blood pot. She buried the daughter she bore, eventually ploughed by Janaka. Devi Bhagavata Purana recounts desire of Ravana to marry Mandodari though astrologers warned him about their progeny to be the destroyer of his clan. However, he buried the first-born, later grew as Sita. In Jain adaptation of the *Ramayana*, Dasaratha while performing sacrifice receives a rice ball. A crow took a bite of it and takes it to Mandodari who eats it and gives birth to Sita. A prophecy that his daughter will cause his death made him throw Sita into the sea, where the sea nymphs protect and take her to Janaka (Ramanujan, 1979). Apart from these, an interesting version of the *Ramayana* was the account of Candravati. In few similarities to the tales described above, Ravana deemed to be enjoying in his harem while Mandodari suffered in silence. Unable to bear the pain, she consumed a vial of poison. On a weird turn, she became pregnant. Soon, the news reached the king who assembled the council of ministers to determine the fate of the new born. Marking the girl born would be the cause of Lanka's downfall. None of Ravana's thousand sons will be alive. Thus, he ordered to build a casket, locked the child in it with golden clasps, and threw it in the sea. Eventually, a poor fisherman Madhava, rescued and took the casket home. Days later his wife Sata, dreamt a young maiden requesting to return the casket to king Janaka. Thus, destined predicament of Ravana followed. Apparently, in both the *Ramayana* and other Rama narratives, Sita is fated to be the agent furthering the end of Ravana.

Indeed, the above-mentioned allegories are delightful; however, none had appreciated the birth of Sita. Though parenthood had occupied a high pedestal in the epics, the anecdotes seemingly illustrate disheartening birth and abandonment of Sita. The king as a father disowned his daughter due to prophecy. Though none of the tales did mention about Ravana and Mandodari as the biological parents of the child, yet they simultaneously bore her in womb. Glaring iniquity to a daughter is worthy of exploring. Gradually, it may put forth whether a son born to them had encountered similar gruesome redressing. Certainly, the ancient poet had hazed description about Sita's ascendance, yet her path of life was no less than pathetic. Medieval poet Goswami Tulsidas redeemed her from antique misfortunes by withdrawing the trial by fire as Ravana abducted the illusory Sita. However, he also designated her as a universal mother. In the later years as few had effectively invested in reading the grand compositions, mostly the colloquial interpretations of Rama and Sita were on a spread. If narratives as mentioned above are prevalent then listeners will eternally perceive Sita as misfortune befalling on a family or clan. Even a reputed warrior king could not surpass impending doom by the birth of a daughter. Thus, one can reckon the challenge for a mortal. The passing several centuries have not ameliorated such popular opinions. Concurrent times still witness the abandonment of female fetus or new born. The fabrication of motherhood in the ancient tales garners appreciation, the same evidently receded with the birth of a daughter.

References

Brockington, J. L. 1977. 'Figures of Speech in the Râmâyana', *Journal of the American Oriental Society*, Vol. 97, No. 4, Oct., pp. 441-459.

Brockington, J. L. 1998. 'The *Ramayana* (3)', *The Sanskrit Epics*, Leiden, Brill., pp. 441-472.

Buck, H. H. 1989. 'The Role of the Sacred Book in Religion-The *Ramayana*', *The Ramayana Tradition in India*, edited by V. Raghavan. 2nd ed. New Delhi: Sahitya Academy, pp. 21-39.

Bulcke, C. 1950. *Ramkatha: Utpattiaur Vikas.* Prayag: Hindi Parisad Prakasan.

Dharwadkar, V. 1999. 'Three Hundred *Ramayanas*: Five Examples and Three Thoughts on Translation', in *The collected Essays of A.K. Ramanujan*, edited by Vinay Dharwadker. Delhi: Oxford University Press, pp.131-160.

Doniger, W. 2009. 'Women and Ogress in the *Ramayana* 400 BCE to 200 CE', *The Hindus: An Alternative History*. New York: The Penguin Press.

Pollock, S. 2001. 'Questioning and Multiplicity within the *Ramayana* Tradition', in *Questioning Ramayanas: A South Asian Tradition*, edited by Paula Richman. California: Unity of California Press, pp. 1-24.

Ramanujan, A. K. 1979. *'Tale and Teller in South India'*, 7th Congress of the International Society for Folk Narrative Research. Edinburgh Lecture.

Richman, P. 2008. 'Whose *Ramayana* is it?' in *Ramayana Stories in Modern South India: An Anthology*. Bloomington: Indiana UP, pp. 1-28.

Sankalia, H. D. 1982. *The Ramayana in Historical Perspective*. Delhi: Macmillan.

Chapter - 4

Motherhood of Kunti

Samita Manna

The *Mahabharata* is one of the most informative texts in ancient Indian literature indeed world literature too. In the epic story of the *Mahabharata* many women characters have drawn special attention to many academics for their different enlightening personalities of which Kunti was one of them. In Hindu mythology, Kunti was known as Pritha, the biological daughter of Shurasna. She was also the sister of Vasudeva, the foster daughter of her cousin King Kunti-Bhoja and the wife of king Pandu of Hastinapur. Kunti's motherhood was also successful as she became the mother of *Pancha Pandava*. In the *Mahabharata*, motherhood of Kunti possessed honoured and reflected brightening character as she played a virgin role for performing her excellent motherhood.

In ancient literature the names of five women- Ahalya, Draupadi, Kunti, Tara and Mandodari were personified with water, fire, earth, wind and ether respectively and commonly addressed as five *Satis* and were popular *aspratah-smaraniya* to the women folk. So among the five noble women Kunti was one of them who was also the queen of King Pandu. The then society's woman's position was no less important though Draupadi, the wife of *Pancha Pandava*, was greatly dishonoured by Duryadhana, the son of Dhritarashtra. Draupadi was dragged into the dice hall and insulted. There was an attempt to disrobe her which indicated the dominance of patriarchy.

Motherhood is not a monolithic. Understanding motherhood is a great task. Motherhood is social construction. In every society the nature of motherhood has been shaped and reshaped by its culture. Motherhood is a blessing for womanhood. Wifehood is glorified and made meaningful by motherhood. Popular local sayings like *Putrabati Bhaba* are often used by elders to bless married women. Motherhood brings profound changes in woman's life. Woman holds subordinate status as a wife, but her status changes when she becomes mother. Motherhood denotes security for the woman. So many situations affect the mother to becoming a perfect mother. In general, mother means who gives a birth of a baby. Within the family, motherhood is the source of integrity between husband and wife. Mother's role in any society is therefore unparallel as it is instinctual. Johnson and Ferguson (1990) suggest that motherhood is culture specific and each culture has its own specific rules that define the role of motherhood that is 'institutionalising mother's role'. With respect to the relationship between motherhood and marital quality, studies during the last two decades have shown that women's relationships with their children are richer and more complex than men's (Umberson, 1989). The pivotal role of being a mother is still the divine mission assigned to women alone. In a classic poem entitled 'What Rules the World', William Ross has said that rocks the cradle is the hand that rules the world. It illustrates the nature of influence which a mother casts on her child and in the long run on the society; a mother strives to nurture and teach a child, she explicitly makes the world a much better place. Women are actually given an opportunity and a privilege by god in giving life to another human being (Ghosh, 2016). In reality, mother has many and varied roles in society. Berger and Luckman's concept of the *social construction of reality* primarily focuses on how the world is constructed and created. The social construction of women, as being portrayed in the media and acted out by the majority in society, reinforces the stereotype that they will become mothers, whether or not that is their main desire (Billing, 2003). Each mother plays a distinct role toward their children. The calling 'Ma', 'Mother', or 'Mom' has some sort of emotional or devotional sound which creates an ambit with love, emotion, caring and everything. Indian society offers many examples of mothers like 'Ma' of Ramakrisna Mission, 'Sreema' of Pondicherry, 'Guruma' of different religious sects and so on. They are not natural mothers. On the other hand, when one is addressed as mother she feels the pleasure of heaven (*Swarga*). Married women are always blessed by the seniors to becoming mother. The concept of motherhood revolves around the idea of bearing and rearing the children. Bernard (1975) indicates that motherhood is an institution that lays emphasis on the duty of a mother in socialising girls to be mothers. Motherhood is a common but life changing phase in the life of a woman.

In the *Mahabharata*, Kunti being a mother of *Pancha Pandava* stood as a guardian like father figure to make her children as perfect sons of Kshatriya. In absence of lord Pandu she took all responsibilities to make her children like the sons of Kshatriya. She guided and advised her children for becoming honest, novel and perfect men of society by performing righteous work for the wellbeing of the people. In this context, Kunti played the role of biological mother, the wife of lord Pandu. But on the other hand, Kunti's motherhood during her maiden's time deprived Karna who was her eldest son and his father was God Surya.

This article 'Motherhood of Kunti' portraits a clear picture of society at that time of epic era of the *Mahabharata*. Motherhood is a special behaviour pattern of a married woman especially who bears a child. Motherhood is always glorified by some specific activities of a mother characterised her life for *tyaga* (sacrifice) and *seva* (service) for her children. It has its wider field. It is not homogeneous in nature. Every woman performs her motherhood according to the prescription of socio-cultural dogmas of the then society. Across cultures, the mother's role is a dynamic and powerful one. During the time of motherhood woman asserts her power which she imposes over her children. One may argue that this is a pyrrhic sort of power, exercised well within the long arms of patriarchy (Pramanick and Manna, 2010). According to Arendell (2000), mothering denotes as the social practices of nurturing and caring for people, and thus it is not the exclusive domain of women.

Finlay (2007) has said that discriminations against women may be viewed as arising from the generally ascribed status of 'female' and from specially ascribed status of 'wife', 'mother' and 'sister'. Dutta (2014) has explained that the role of the mothers and the meaning of 'motherhood' are not same in all socio-cultural contexts. In India, there is a religious and historical tradition of equating woman with 'mother'.

In this article, the author has tried to find out the changing role of motherhood of Kunti by following socio-cultural recognition to becoming a perfect mother. This study has also focussed on the dual roles played by Kunti as a mother of her five sons as well as the mother of her eldest son Karna whom she did not accept as a son due to societal norms.

Kunti was not an ordinary woman. Before her marriage she was blessed by Durvasa *Muni* (sage) and had a special boon which she obtained from the sage, Durvasa because of her kindness to him. She had a *mantra* that allowed her to acquire sons from the gods. After getting the special boon she became curious and applied her boon immediately; actually she wanted to test the *mantra*, so she called Surya, the Sun God. As per the blessings of Durvasa *Muni*, Kunti met with Surya and her first son was born and she became a mother of a son and his name was Karna. After birth of her son she became nervous and helpless as she was not married, so she did not want that the people might ask any question about her child (*Adi Parba*: 110). Due to social stigma, she put Karna in a basket and floated down in a river.

A *Suta* couple rescued him and they took care of him. She did not want to show her motherhood to the society as she was an unmarried mother and society did not accept unmarried mother to be a mother in a prestigious way.

In the *Mahabharata* it was known that Pandu was once cursed by one ascetic that he could not live conjugal life with his wives, if he did it, it would be the reason of his death. Pandu had two wives named, Kunti and Madri. But due to the curse he was unable to experience the happiness of being a father. Once he came to know about Kunti's boon and requested her for applying that for becoming a father. Using that boon Kunti gave Pandu three sons like Yudhisthira, son of *Dharma*, Bhima, son of God wind and Arjuna, son of the king of Gods, Indra. She also allowed Madri to use the boon once, and Madri cleverly called upon the twin Vedic Gods the Ashvini Kumaras, and gave birth to twin boys, Nakula and Sahadeva. These five brothers were known as the *Pancha Pandava* (sons of Pandu). After the death of Pandu and Madri, Kunti looked after all the children properly. There was no question that she was the best mother of her sons of Pandu in the epic story of the *Mahabharata*. She was also the symbol of motherly love. She brought up five *Pandavas* single handed after Pandu's death.

After floating Karna in a river, it was the first time Kunti saw Karna in a competition that celebrated all of her five boys who were graduated from Drona's academy. All of her sons were graduates. There she saw Karna and recognised exactly who he was. Kunti and Karna met again later in life. Unfortunately, it was at the time of war. He was fighting on the opposite side against her five sons (*Pancha Pandava*) and accepted Durjyadhana to fight against *Pandava*. Kunti went to Karna and told him that she was his biological mother. He was happy to know that his true mother was alive, but she was not ready to accept her as his mother because she abandoned him. Kunti begged Karna to switch over his sides in the battle. But Karna told it would never be possible as he got power and position just like king from them. But on her request, he promised her that he would not fight all of her sons together. He would only fight with Arjuna. He promised her that at the end of the war she would have five sons, but either he or Arjuna would be died. Karna kept his promise made to his biological mother. Karna died in battle while fighting with Arjuna.

She was happy that Arjuna was alive, but sad about Karna. Karna fought on behalf of his close friend Duryodhana against his own brothers during the *Kurukshetra* war.

Kunti was one of the most important personalities in the *Mahabharata*. She was a very intelligent, loving and soft mother who followed *dharma* and led her children's life with it. She was perhaps a support system of the *Pandavas* during the *Kurukshetra* war. As a mother, Kunti behaved differently towards her sons when she was recognised as a queen of lord Pandu then she appeared as an ideal mother for upbringing her children. But on the contrary, as a mother she did not recognise Karna as it was not socially approved and her motherhood was denied. Ultimately she was addressed as a coward mother by her son Karna (Narayan, 1978).

Basically, we found two important characteristics in Kunti's motherhood. All the *Pandavas* and Karna were the sons of various gods. All of them were talented in different spheres of their life. But throughout the story of the *Mahabharata*, it was seen that Kunti played a positive role as a mother in their life, but there was no positive role of Kunti in Karna's life. Though he was also a son of God Surya, but he was known as '*sutputra*' (lower caste) in his whole life. Due to his identity as a *sutaputra* society did not allow him to learn archery. The great archery teacher was Dronacharya who trained *Pandavas* and *Kouravas* but refused Karna as he was not a Khatriya. After his refusal Karna went to Parasuram and hid his real identity for learning archery. But after completion of his learning, Parasuram came to know his real identity and cursed him to forget his learning at the time of his requirement.

Similarly at the time of Droupadi's *sayambara*, Droupadi refused Karna, as he did not belong to upper caste. During the war of *Kurukhetra*, Karna was not allowed in the battle field with Bhisma. He entered in the field of the battle after Bhisma's *sarasojjya*. During the war, Indra, the king of the Gods came to Karna as a Brahmin and wanted his '*Karna Kundala*' (life saver of Karna which he had received from his birth). Karna knew the truth of Indra but he gave it to Him. For his kindness he was known as '*Danvir Karna*'.

So due to Kunti's selfish decision, Karna had to sacrifice his whole life, when Kunti as a mother took care of all *Pandavas*. She faced various hard situations with *Pandavas*. She was always there to guide them, nourish them and fight for the right of *Pandavas*. On the other hand, Karna was denied and ill-treated throughout his life as he was known as *sutaputra*, the son of a low caste and even finally he accepted his death for saving the life of Arjuna.

The stereotyped role of motherhood is a patriarchal construction which gives rise to gender narratives. Though women's role as 'child producer' or 'child nurturer' is widely acclaimed, they are assigned to secondary status in society. Women are considered as inferior, not fit for masculine jobs. In case of India, such a contrast is more revealing in rural areas though there are some perceptible changes occurred in family roles of urban India and particularly among members of Indian middle class. Beteille (1992) argues that the family among middle-class and upper-middle class Indian is changing its orientation away from lineage, sub-caste and caste to school, college and office. He, however, did not look into the intricacies of gender relation within such family (Ghosh, 2016).

Karna was saved and nurtured by foster *suta* parents named Radha and Adhiratha Nandana, the charioteer and poet by profession, engaged with the *Raj Sabha* of king Dhritarashtra. Karna grew up to be an accomplished warrior of extraordinary abilities, a gifted speaker and became a loyal friend of Duryodhana. He joined Duryodhana's side in the *Mahabharata* war. He was a key antagonist who aimed to kill Arjuna but he himself died in the battle field of *Kurukshetra* war due to his own desire. He sacrificed his life as Debaraj Indra as a Brahmin asked him to give his *kavach* and *kundala* having his life which he ascribed since his birth. He was a tragic hero in the *Mahabharata* but a great pious hero by which he did not refuse *Debaraj* Indra by giving the demanding alms. In this way he sacrificed his life.

Due to social stigma of unmarried mother, Kunti left Karna without thinking the future of her eldest beloved son. As a result, Karna had to face tremendous odds for sustaining himself in the structured society. Out of fear Kunti floated Karna in river Ashvanadi. Although he was saved but his life was deprived of social prestige, power, love and affection. On the other hand, hatred, false identity, loss of social status were his achievements. Karna was rejected as a son by his mother and the family members of his own family. But he became a man of exceptional abilities and extra ordinary qualities by which he sacrificed his life to perform *dharma*. When he met his biological mother Kunti, he discovered that he was the eldest brother of those with whom he was fighting in the battle field.

How does a mother behave towards her child is also determined by the prescription of societal laws. This particular type of ambivalent attitude towards her eldest son was only for the social taboos. Kunti was virtuous and knowledgeable woman. She took part in every side of state politics. At the time of war *Pandava* and *Kourava* she took decisions and took part in politics. Even before war she went to her eldest son and requested him to leave *Kourava* and join with his brothers as she knew Karna was a brave king. After all Kunti was the mother of her eldest son Karna. Her emotions, affections and love for

Karna never ended. On the other hand Karna proved that her mother was a coward and failed to perform her duty towards her son.

Kunti was constantly aware of the right from wrong and always endeavoured to follow the path of *dharma*; however, she was trapped in her life with different situations and had no choice but to adjust with her destinies. She did so with grace, dignity and showing unusual strength of character. Kunti led a checkered life and saw many ups and downs, but the humiliation of her daughter-in-law Droupadi at the hands of deceitful *Kaurava* brothers and in the presence of so-called keepers of *dharma* filled her with such wrath and a burning fire for revenge that she ensured her sons to avenge her insult.

Being subject to the patriarchal law of the Kshatriyas, Kunti as a mother sacrificed the possibilities of self definition and sexual independence. In Mahasweta Devi's writing Kunti had uncritically internalised the ideological dogmatism of the exclusivist or elitist cultural script of patriarchy. Julia Kristeva in her book *Revolutions in Poetic Language* (1985) spoke, Kunti's exile to the forest away from the domain of aggression and violence, signals her severance from the universality of the Law of the Father and entry into the domain of the Maternal, Feminine and pre-oedipal as she entered the womblike darkness of the aranya ruled by the mother. Hence, it is in the forest, that Kunti came to a halting discovery of the debt she owed to Karna as a mother. As Chodorow (1989) has theorised, the mother is both an object of the child's adoration as she lactates him or her as well as the object of revulsion and hatred as she can deny the child food, milk or love thus throwing the child in a perpetual state of want.

Society has led mothers to view themselves as un-maternal, unfeminine and guilty when they abstain from the maternal function to indulge their own desires. Kunti having internalised this phallocentrically constricted definition of maternity, rebukes herself for being a desiring being. Being subject to the patriarchal law of the Kshatriyas; Kunti as a mother sacrifices the possibilities of self-definition and sexual independence. According to Devi (2005), motherhood implies a cultural death of her sexual being; the woman who took Suryadev 'out of her own free will' is subsumed, crippled and forgotten so that she can acquire the predesignated identity of a child bearer. Kunti's submersion in motherhood which is the normalising script of social organisation, robs her of sexual autonomy (Devi, 2005). As a mother she only has a social value that accrues from her ability to gestate, conceive, reproduce and nourish the child; only through these social functions does she become serviceable. It induces a psychic split and disorientation in carrying out of her maternal function. Thus, in one hand, she has socialised her children with excessive protection, suffocating them with her overwhelming maternity like in the case of *Pandavas*. On the other hand, she has weaned away the child from her maternal protection, leaving it clamouring for her love and protection, as seen in her abandonment of Karna (cited in Bose, 2017).

References

Arcana, J. 1979. *Our Mother's Daughters*. California: Shameless Hussy Press.

Arendell, T. 2000. 'Conceiving and Investigation Motherhood: The Decade's Scholarship', *Journal of Marriage and Family*, Vol. 62 (4): 1192-1207.

Bernard, J. 1975. *The Future of Parenthood*. London: Calder and Boyars Ltd.

Billing, K. 2003. 'Questioning Motherhood: A Sociological Awakening in Human Architecture', *Journal of the Sociological of Self Knowledge*, Vol. 2 (2): 91-98.

Bose, A. 2017. 'Motherhood and Mourning in Kunti and the Nishadin. *Bharatiya Prajna: An Interdisciplinary Journal of Indian Studies*, Vol. 2 (2): 1-8.

Chodorow, N. 1989. *Feminism and Psycho Analytic Theory*. London: Polity Press.

Devi, M. 2005. *After Kurukshetra*. Trans. by Anjum Katyal, Kolkata: Seagull.

Dutta, A. 2014. 'Glorifying Motherhood: The Power of Identity', *Mainstream Weekly* LII (11).

Geetha, V. 2012. *Gender: Theorizing Feminism*. Kolkata: Stree.

Ghosh, A. 2016. 'Declining Child Sex Ratio: Crisis in Motherhood', in Manna, S. and Patra, S. (eds.) *Motherhood: Demystification and Denouement*. Kolkata: Levant Books.

Ghosh, B. 2016. 'The Institution of Motherhood: A Critical Understanding' in Manna, S. and Patra, S (eds.). *Motherhood: Demystification and Denouement*. Kolkata: Levant Books.

Hilt, C. 2017. *The Definition of Motherhood: It's looking into your Child's eyes and seeing nothing but love*. Published on now closed Huff post Contributor platform.

Johnson, K. and Ferguson, T. 1990. *Trusting Ourselves: The Sourcebook on Psychology for Women*. New York: The Atlantic Monthly Press.

Kristeva, J. 1985. *Revolutions in Poetic Language*, Trans. Roudiez, Leon. New York: Columbia University Press.

Narayan, R. K. 1978. *The Mahabharata: A Shortened Modern Prose Version of the Indian Epic*. Chicago: University of Chicago Press.

Pramanick, S. K. and Manna, S. 2010. *Women in India: Motherhood and Multiple Identities*. New Delhi: Serial Publication.

Umberson, D. 1989. 'Marriage as support or strain: marital quality following the death of a parent', *Journal of marriage and the family*, Vol. 5 (7): 709-723.

Chapter - 5

Decoding the Concept of 'Mother': Observations on Nadiara Incidence of Purulia, West Bengal

Soumyajit Patra

The concept of 'motherhood', or, 'mother' as a category should be looked at from the point of view of 'mother-child relationship'. In other words, 'mother' is relational. This relationship points to a set of responsibilities and obligations of the 'mother' towards her offspring(s). In this sense, 'motherhood' can be conceptualised as a social status and a role-set built around some socially-evolved expectations to be fulfilled by the incumbent of that status. The status-role set emerged out of this key position is a point of interest for those interested in understanding motherhood as a category. The cultural components in defining the said 'status-role set' are of prime importance that should also be noticed. It should be noted here that the connotations of motherhood have changed over time. During the fourteenth to the nineteenth centuries in England, the term 'mother' sometimes connoted the opposite of what today we actually mean: it was used to address 'an elderly woman of lower class' (Hansen, 1997:2). There was another and more derogatory usage: 'mother' denoted 'dregs or scum'. According to Hansen (1997: 3), 'this *mother* was associated with alchemy and used especially in the sixteenth century to refer to the scum of oils and subsequently to the dregs of fermenting liquids'.

Some believe that the term 'mother' was derived from the Dutch word '*modder*' that means mud or mire (*ibid.*). However, these meanings of the term 'mother' have almost been buried in the graveyard of history. Today 'mother' denotes '[a] woman who conceives, gives birth to, or raises and nurtures a child' (*American Heritage Dictionary*). No doubt the women celebrate the status even if motherhood is defined as a site of power-play and oppression by some feminist writers like Firestone (1979) or Chodorow (1978). Allen (2005) has rightly said that motherhood is a central concern not just of women, but of the societies in which they live as societies depend for their survival on women's willingness to bear children. Most of the women also take it for granted that mothering is an exclusive female activity and it is one of their moral duties to do it honestly (Geetha, 2002).

In this paper I would like to raise some questions on the construction of the connotations of the term 'mother'. If the notion of 'mother' is culture specific, the lower-middle class or average middle class Bengali urban families in which boys and girls are socialised or are indoctrinated should have a particular feeling or idea of mother or motherhood which may be different from the idea, an upper class family possesses. This notion of 'mother' and its associated process of mothering are neither absolute nor yardstick of making a universal image of 'mother'. The idea of 'mother' which, for example, I possess emerges out of my own life experiences. It consists of a few things. First, mother is home maker. She is the custodian of all domestic affairs. Second, she is the prime caretaker of the children and in some cases of the sick and elderly persons. Third, she is the role model in sacrificing everything for her family, including her parental family, career, talents and hobbies. Fourth, she is unsexed in the sense that the common perceptions around the idea of mother in lower-middle class or average middle class Bengali urban families place the mothers beyond all physical needs. This, imagery of mother, again to note, is not absolute, neither it is deductable from *conscience collective* as such. Rather the construction of the idea of 'mother' (and similarly of 'father') is a product of 'definition of situation' or, more specifically, of 'consciousness of kind'. The point is that this construction of 'mother' is situation-specific and so it is family-specific. It makes little sense when someone analyses the connotations of 'motherhood' of a particular society in a generalised format ignoring the peculiarities of the everyday life chores. From this point of view, a straight forward structural-functional analysis of the concept of mother would be partial, if not disastrous.

Murdock (1949) or Bowlby (1953) suggested that the role of the mothers was genetically ingrained and thus they essentialised motherhood as the destiny of the women. They deducted certain features of 'mother', which are biologically determined and so they thought of their ubiquitous presence. Such analyses are over-deterministic in the sense that they place peripheral importance on the cultural or economic variables, let alone the psychological ones, in the construction of the idea of 'mother'. It is possible that similar types of imagery are present in the minds of a number of different individuals, but variations in the role of mother, process of mothering and emotive elements in mother-child relationships are facts that need to be studied.

There are others, like Ann Oakley (1974) or Bruno Bettelheim (1969) who have put counter arguments and said that the role of mothers and the meanings attached to it are culture-specific and vary from one group to another (Manna *et al*, 2018). In this paper I would bank on the arguments of the latter camp and reduce the arguments to the level of the family, even, in some truest sense, to the level of individual. The idea of 'mother' may drastically vary among the siblings!

But before that let me tell you the story of little Supriya, which has made me realised that 'motherhood' should not be studied from one dimensional absolutist terms. I had the privilege to investigate the phenomenon directly from the accused mother of Supriya, as a member of an investigation team formed by the district administration. Let me narrate the incidence first.

Supriya was a three and half year's old girl of Nadiara village of Purulia of West Bengal. She lived with her mother Mangala and step father Sanatan. On 24 July 2017, Supriya was admitted to hospital with severe illness. She felt abdominal pain and started vomiting. She stopped playing with her friends and even stopped taking food. But her mother and step father at first were not willing to admit her to the hospital. When the villagers threatened Mangala of dire consequences if something happens to little Supriya, they were literally forced to admit their daughter.

After some investigations the doctors discovered seven small-sized needles from the abdomen of Supriya. After struggling a few days Supriya died. All primary investigations revealed that both her mother and step father murdered her. All national newspapers and electronic media covered the news. And the nation was shuddered. But when we met Mangala, who was under police custody, she confessed everything without showing any emotions and feelings towards her daughter who was murdered just a few days before. She was as usual. She said that they were poor and could not bear the burden of a girl child. One thing should be noted that if they were rich and if Supriya was a boy child this incident did not take place. Therefore, mother-child relationship is not given and absolute. It varies. According to Ann Oakley (1974), all 224 societies, studied by Murdock (1949), also had such variations.

In the incident, there is another story of mother-child relationship. This is the relationship between Mangala and her mother Madhuri. Madhuri was also arrested as an accused in the same case. We talked to her when she was in the police custody. Madhuri is a street beggar. When Madhuri's daughter Mangala got divorced from her former husband and started staying with her mother she felt burdened, and was relieved when Mangala got married with a completely unknown person named Sanatan. When the investigation team asked Madhuri why she allowed such marriage with an unknown person, Madhuri confessed that she could not run the family with her small income. She, almost without considering the consequences, allowed her daughter to live with Sanatan.

One more thing has been revealed from the study. Age is also important in mother-child relationship. When we say 'mother-child', the picture of 'smiling mother with a child in her lap' comes in our mind. But mother-child relationship take different forms when the child becomes adult or old. It further changes when he or she gets married. So mother-child relationship should not be romanticised. The variables such as income, sex and age have significant imprints on it.

A group of Western scholars have come to the conclusion that mother-child relationship is unduly romanticised and the glorification of motherhood is essentially middle-class construction. Ann Oakley (1974), for example, has observed that among the Mbuti Pygmies mother's role and father's role in rearing the children are not much different. Or in Alor, an island of Indonesia, the role and image of the mothers are quite different from the image we usually think of.

To conclude we can cite the study of Bruno Bettelheim (1969) on the children of the Kibbutz of Israel. The children of these Kibbutzes are collectively reared and so their relationships with their mothers are, to quote, Bettelheim (*ibid.*) is 'neither intimate nor intense'. And Bettelheim found that these children do not suffer from any mental illness or personality problems.

The meanings and symbols associated with motherhood are culturally constructed with a bunch of duties and obligations. As these are not biologically given, the manner we define or the manner we enjoy motherhood is different from the way a mother from the lowest economic strata enjoys motherhood. However, the physical attachment of the mothers with their children during the early childhood develops some kind of emotions but it wanes away under the impact of other factors. Mother-child relationship should be treated as a dependent variable having the influence of age, sex, income and many other factors.

References

Allen, A. T. 2005. *Feminism and Motherhood in Western Europe*. 1890-1970. New York: Palgrave Macmillan.

Bettelheim, B. 1969. *The Children of the Dream*. London: Thames and Hudson.

Bowlby, J. 1953. *Childcare and the Growth of Love*. Harmondsworth: Penguin Books.

Chodorow, N. 1978. *The Reproduction of Mothering*. Berkeley: University of California Press.

Firestone, S. 1979. *The Dialectic of Sex: The Case for Feminist Revolution*. London: The Women's Press.

Geetha, V. 2002.*Gender*. Calcutta: Stree.

Hansen, E.T. 1997. *Mother without Child: Contemporary Fiction and Crisis of Motherhood*. Berkeley: University of California Press.

Manna, S., Patra S. and Roy S. (eds). 2018. *Sociology of Motherhood and Beyond: Roots and Rejuvenation*. Kolkata: Levant Books.

Murdock, G. P. 1949. *Social Structure*. New York: Macmillan.

Oakley, A. 1974. *Housewife*. London: Allen Lane.

Chapter - 6

Diversity of Motherhood in the Animal Kingdom: An Explanatory Note on Rattle Snake (Crotalus SP)

C. K. Manna

Throughout history, motherhood has been described as woman's basic mission, obligation, and an inseparable part of her nature. A mother is someone who nurtures – someone who cares for the deepest places of your heart. Anyone can throw a meal at you or give you a bed to sleep on, but a mother makes a place for you. A mother not only cares for your hurts and fears, but also supports to fulfil your dreams and paves the way for your successes. She is a cheerleader, a coach, a trainer and a fan all at the same time.

Although maternal care is essential in many classes of vertebrates, it is most prevalent in mammals, since the care from the mother is essential for feeding and nourishing their young. Because the care exhibited by the mother plays such a large role in mammals, the role of the male is often very limited. Maternal care begins during fertilisation and pregnancy however, the most prominent arrays of maternal behaviours are exhibited by the mother after the birth of their offspring and until the offspring are capable of being independent. The duration that the offspring stays with the mother and receives care, and the types of care behaviour displayed by the mother varies amongst different species, forms of reproduction, and the level of development in the offspring at birth.

When we think of rattlesnakes, many of us think of them as being emotionless and heartless creatures. We tend to focus on the fact that they are venomous and capable of killing a person, or at least rendering them very ill. But the truth is that some species of rattlesnakes are actually nurturing and loving creatures that care for and protect their young. And contrary to the popular belief, many rattlesnakes are not capable of killing a healthy adult. They are also very unlikely to bite a human unless they are threatened. Rattlesnakes would never try to attack a person and would only strike defensively. The timber rattlesnake actually demonstrates the protective side of motherhood, which is existing among reptiles.

Naming of Pit viper

The Crotalinae, commonly known as pit vipers Mehrtens (1987), crotaline snakes (named for the Ancient Greek: κρόταλον *krotalon,* castanet/rattle of a rattlesnake's tail), or pitadders, are a subfamily of venomous vipers found in Eurasia and the Americas. They are distinguished by the presence of a heat-sensing pit organ located between the eye and the nostril on both sides of the head. Currently, 22 genera and 151 species are recognised: These are also the only viperids found in the Americas. The groups of snakes represented here include rattlesnakes, lance heads, and Asian pit vipers. The type genus for this subfamily is Crotalus, of which the type species is the timber rattlesnake, *C. horridus.*

Distribution

Viperines, *Causus,* and *Azemiops* are found only in the Old World (Europe, Asia and Africa), but crotalines inhabit in both the Eastern and Western Hemispheres. Australia lacks viperids, suggesting that this family evolved after the Australian continent became a separate landmass. The distribution of *Causus* is restricted to sub-Saharan Africa. *Azemiops* occurs in southern China, Burma (Myanmar), Laos and Vietnam. Viperines are distributed in Africa, Europe and Asia. Crotalines are found in North America, Central America, and South America as well as East Asia and Central Asia. One species (*Gloydiushalys*) enters Europe north of the Caspian Sea.

Classification/Taxonomy

Rattle snakes are pit vipers, in the same family (Viperidae) as cottonmouths, copperheads and other vipers. Rattle snakes are in the genus *Crotalus*, and are closely related to pygmy rattle snakes, which are in the genus *Sistrurus*.

The taxonomy of rattle snakes, according to the Integrated Taxonomic Information System (ITIS), is:

- **Kingdom**: Animalia
- **Subkingdom**: Bilateria
- **Infrakingdom:** Deuterostomia
- **Phylum:** Chordata
- **Subphylum:** Vertebrata
- **Infraphylum:** Gnathostomata
- **Superclass:** Tetrapoda
- **Class:** Reptilia
- **Order**: Squamata
- **Suborder:** Serpentes
- **Infraorder:** Alethinophidia
- **Family**: Viperidae
- **Subfamily**: Crotalinae
- **Genus:** *Crotalus*
- **Species:** *Crotalus horridus*

There are 29 species, including: Timber rattle snake (***Crotalushorridus***)

Structure of a Rattle Snake

Characteristics

Rattle snakes can range from one to eight feet, depending on the species (the big one is the eastern diamondback), according to the National Wildlife Federation. They are thick-bodied snakes with keeled (ridged) scales in a variety of colours and patterns. Most species are patterned with dark diamonds, rhombuses or hexagons on a lighter background.

There are some other peculiar physical features. These include producing venom, heat-sensing facial pits, hinged fangs and live births. Some other pit vipers such as the cottonmouth and copperhead also have these features. After the rattle, rattlesnakes' most distinctive physical feature is their triangular head. Also, they have vertical pupils, like cat's eyes.

Young rattle snakes do not yet have their rattles, though they are as dangerous as adults, according to the National Park Service at Yosemite. Furthermore, some adults may lose their rattles, so it is good to look for the triangular head.

*Fig. 1: Structure of an adult rattle snake (with rattle at the end of tail) (a) An adult Black-tailed Rattlesnake (*Crotalus molossus*) in the Santa Rita Mountains, Arizona (July 2015) showing a threat posture with its tail and rattle positioned near the head.*

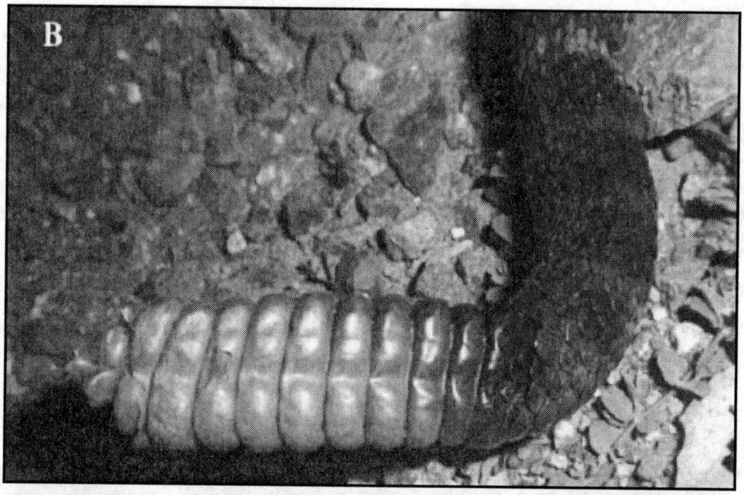

Fig. 1. (b) Close-up of the rattle of the individual in (a) showing the basic structure of interlocking, keratinous segments. Note the tear in the posterior-most segment, indicating a break in outer segments that exposed the internal lobes of the adjacent, complete segment.

Photos by Jesse M. Meik.

Reproduction

Most rattle snake species mate during the summer or fall, while some species mate only in the spring, or during both the spring and fall (Rubio, 1998).

Females secrete small amounts of sex pheromones, which leave a trail that that the males follow using their tongues and Jacobson's organs as guides (*ibid.*). Once a receptive female has been located, the male often spends several days following her around (a behaviour not common outside of the mating season), frequently touching and rubbing her in an attempt to stimulate her (Klauber, 1997).

The males of some species, such as timber rattle snakes (*C. horridus*), fight each other during the mating season, in competition over females. These fights, known as 'combat dances', consist of the two males intertwining the anterior portion of their bodies, often with their heads and necks held vertically. The larger males usually end up driving the smaller males away (Furman, 2007).

Although many kinds of snakes and other reptiles are oviparous (lay eggs), rattle snakes are ovoviviparous (give birth to live young after carrying eggs inside). The female produces the ova (eggs) in her ovaries, after which they pass through the body cavity and into one of her two oviducts. The ova are arranged in a continuous chain in a coiled section of the oviduct, known as the 'tuba' (Rubio, 1998). Male rattlesnakes have sexual organs known as hemipenes, located in the base of the tail. The hemipenis is retracted inside of the body when mating is not

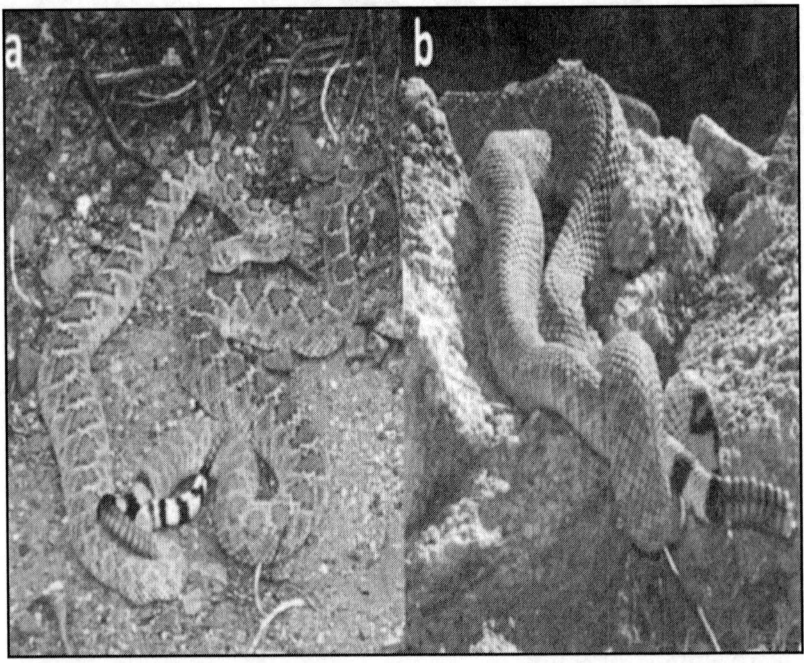

Fig. 2 (a & b). Sexual behaviour in Crotalus atrox. *(a) Pair of* C. atrox *in coitus. Unknown male (left) with female, September 13, 2001.*

(b) Pair of C. atrox *in courtship below a den site. The lower body and tail of unknown male is wrapped over and around tail of female (painted rattles), March 2012.*

Photographs by Roger Repp.

occurring. The hemipenis is similar to the human penis. Females can store semen for months in internal recesses known as spermathecae, which permits them to mate during the fall, but not fertilise the ova until the following spring (Rubio, 1998). The Arizona black rattlesnake (*C. oreganuscerberus*), has been observed to exhibit complex social behaviour reminiscent of that in mammals. Females often remain with their young in nests for several weeks, and mothers have been observed cooperatively parenting their broods (Melissa, 2011).

Rattle snakes generally take several years to mature, and females usually reproduce only once every three years (Geoffrey, 2004).

Hormonal level during breeding season in *Crotalus atrox*

The hormonal profiles of male and female *C. atrox* resemble those of many viviparous vertebrates. In females, maximum elevations occur in E2 (Estradiol) during vitellogenesis, P (Progesterone) during gestation, and B (Corticosterone)

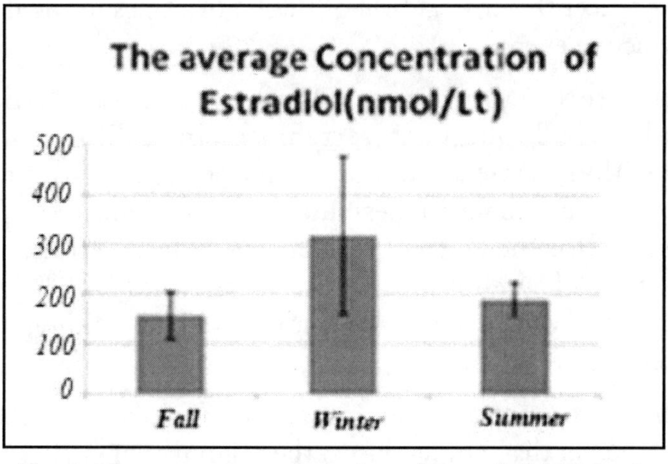

Fig. 3. The average concentration of Estradiol (E2) in the three seasons Fall, winter and summer in female Caucasian viper (± SEM).

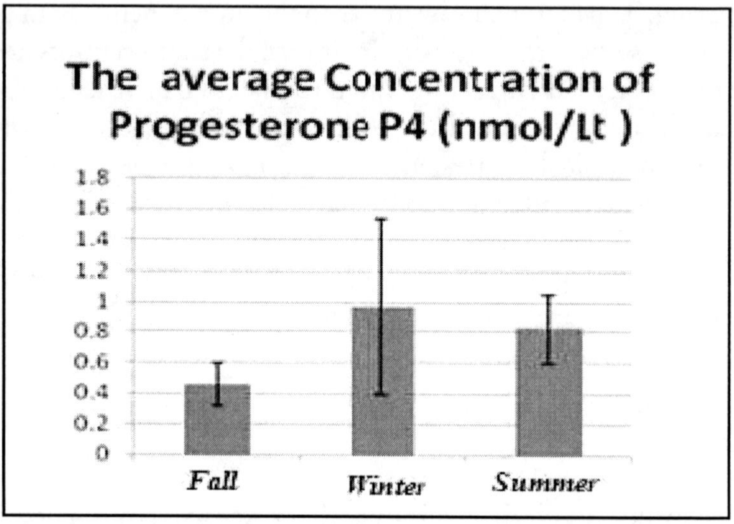

Fig. 4. The average concentration of progestron (P4) in the three seasons Fall, Winter and Summer in female Caucasian viper (± SEM).

immediately pre-parturition, while in males T (Testosterone) is maximal during the mating seasons. The strong similarities in seasonal levels of steroid hormones across broad taxonomic groups reflect the critical role of these hormones in regulating reproductive events.

The steroid hormones play an important role in reproductive biology of vertebrates including reptiles. The relation between steroid hormones and reproductive events in the female snakes shows that plasma E2 is high along vitellogenesis that reflects its role in stimulating production of vitellogenin by liver. The plasma P4 during pregnancy in viviparous snakes indicates its role in pregnancy maintenance.

The E2 concentration in female Caucasian vipers at the fall season is lower than winter, just at the beginning of vitellogenesis in snakes. Following of vitellogenesis the E2 hormone concentration is increasing in the winter that is similar to reproductive cycle of the Neotropical *Crotalus durissusterrificus* (Almeida-Santos, 2004a).

The concentration of P4 in female Caucasian viper of the Lar area was low in fall and higher at summer that is coincided with the pregnancy time and postparturation (Shakoori *et al*, 2015) that resembles to female rattle snakes of the North waters at East South of Brazi (Almeida-Santos, 2004a). Shakoori *et al* (2015) have reported birth of 3-5 young Caucasian vipers of Iran in the late summer.

Rattle snakes

Scholars like Van Hyning (1931), Meek (1946), and Wright and Wright (1957) found a large Eastern Diamond backed Rattle snake (*Crotalus adamanteus*) with 15-18 neonates in or near a Gopher Tortoise (*Gopherus polyphemus*) burrow. The last two reports specifically showed adult females with the young. An adult *C. adamanteus*, presumed to be a female, was found with a total of 10 neonates at Cumberland Island National Seashore, Georgia, on 14–15 September 1973, and that female retreated

*Fig. 5. A female Timber Rattle snake (*Crotalus horridus*) with her newly-born young.*

*Fig. 6. A mother Pigmy Rattle snake (*Sistrurusmiliarius*) with her brood. Because rattles are made of segments that form each time the snake sheds its skin, new born snakes have only one segment and cannot yet make sound.*

under boards when approached but did not appear otherwise disturbed by human observers. The neonates had obvious umbilical scars and cloudy eyes, implying they had not shed their natal skins (J. Cadle, in litt.). Butler *et al.* (1995) reported seven instances of litter attendance by unsexed adult *C. adamanteus*, including three at a tortoise burrow and one in a stump hole. The latter authors documented adults staying with babies until the latter shed, neonate dispersal within hours or a few days of first ecdysis, a tendency of aggregated neonates to retreat intruders, and wariness by an attending adult.

'The statement is frequently made in the literature that the mother snake leaves the young at birth, but [I have assembled] considerable evidence that females of Agkistrodon [contortrix] and Crotalus horridus remain with the young for several days' (Anderson, 1942:215). Service (1902:51) has written, 'I have year after year seen adders [Viperaberus] lying around their mother. As they glide out of sight beneath her she invariably lowers her head.'

It is a common statement that the Adder takes no interest in her family, but snakes in captivity are not always good guides on points of behaviour. The parental instinct is developed in many snakes (Smith, 1951:259).

'I once found a total of 22 [Agkistrodon contortrixand Crotalushorridus] ... in a six-foot hollow log. Here a mother copperhead had her young in one end of the log and a mother rattler had hers at the opposite end.... The log was a veritable nursery.' (Oliver, 1955:147).

'...there is no final evidence that young rattlers stay with their mothers for more than a day or so at most; if they are found together there is no proof that the young rattlers are more than a few days old or that their propinquity is caused by other than use of a common refuge.' (Klauber, 1956:737)

'...two adult females [Agkistrodon piscivorus] were found with 13 newborn young nearby .... This incident was so striking that I regard it as guarding behaviour ....Aggregation prior to and following birth could have survival value in repelling predators who could more easily cope with a lone female, even though the tendency may have originated in some egg- guarding oviparous ... [Old World pitviper].' (Wharton, 1966a:154–155)

'Obviously, reptiles are unlikely to teach us much about the hormonal control of parental care' (Moore and Lindzey, 1992: 77).

Discussion

Parental care is a behavioural and evolutionary strategy adopted by some animals, involving a parental investment being made to the evolutionary fitness of offspring. Patterns of parental care are widespread and highly diverse across the animal kingdom (Kokko & Jennions, 2008).

Parental care is seen among many insects, notably among the social insects such as ants, bees and wasps; among certain fishes, such as the mouth brooders; widely among the birds;

among the amphibians; some reptiles and especially widely among the mammals, which share two major adaptations for care of the young, namely gestation (development of the embryo inside the mother's body) and production of milk.

If we consider the case in reptiles and especially in rattle snake (Crotalus sp.), the picture is little bit different than other animal species. Mother rattle snakes have several babies per clutch, usually 8-10 at once. They are usually 10 inches long when they are born, and are already able to do most of the things that adult rattle snakes can, besides hunt.

Reptile mothers are generally very protective of their young, and take very good care of them. When the babies emerge from their egg sacks, the mother snake will protect and guard them, keeping them warm and out of danger. The first week of their life is spent in close proximity with the mother and their siblings, and after this first week the snakes will shed for the first time. At this point they are old enough to go hunting alone.

During this first week, mother rattle snakes will allow their babies to leave the den and explore, but will tap or nudge them if they stray too far.

Widespread presence of maternal attendance in pit vipers conforms to a theoretical prediction that parental care should characterise organisms that are especially capable of defence (Shine, 1988), but existing theory does not explain the apparent near restriction of that behaviour to crotalines within a larger clade of venomous snakes. Perhaps the costs of parental care are such that it is more likely feasible as part of a confrontational syndrome, a suite of pitviper innovations that also included infrared imaging organs (the better to assess enemies), aposematic sound production by the specialised tail tip, and increased reliance on camouflage and active defence rather than flight (Greene, 1992; 1997). We do not understand why delayed neonatal ecdysis (as opposed to shedding immediately after birth, typical of many snakes and some tropical crotalines) is associated with maternal attendance in temperate viviparous crotalines, but time to first shed is positively correlated with hatchling size in Australian pythons (Greer, 1997), so perhaps comparative studies of viperid life histories will inspire a solution to that mystery.

In mammals, the medial pre-optic area of the brain is responsible for the initiation of maternal behaviours. In a non-maternal female, this action in this area of the brain is inhibited by the medial amygdala but during parturition, the inhibition stops which cause the female to exhibit behaviours related to the maternal care of their newly born offspring. During the parturition, the paraventricular nucleus starts to produce oxytocin (along with other hormones) which aids in the delivery of the young, as well as the behaviours exhibited by the mother after birth Pascal (2005).

Prolactin and glucorticoides are chemicals that also play a role in the initiation of maternal behaviour in both birds and mammals. Prolactin is involved in the interactions between a mother and their offspring, while glucorticoides are released when the mother is expending energy and resources causing her to work harder in order to properly care for her young (Anne *et al*, 2006).

Considering the maternal behaviour of rattle snake with their snakelets, it seems that although the duration of care is for a very short period of time, still it leads to think that probably some important hormones (e.g. prolactin, oxytocin and glucocorticoids) might have some definite role in the mother individuals. For final conclusion, it requires some more investigations and necessary observations.

References

Almeida-Santos, S. M., Abdalla F. M. F., Silveira P. F., Breno, Y. N. and Salomao, M. G. 2004a. 'Reproductive cycle of the Neotropical *Crotalus durissusterrificus*: I. Seasonal levels and interplay between steroid hormones and vasotocinase', *Gen. Comp. Endocrinol.* 139: 143-150.

Anderson, P. 1942. 'Amphibians and reptiles of Jackson County, Missouri', *Bull. Chicago Acad. Sci.* 6: 203-220.

Anne, S. E.; Krista, D. M.; Donald, M.W.; Carolyn, W. J.; Sabina, W. I. 2006. 'Social and hormonal bases of individual differences in the parental behaviour of birds and mammals'. *Canadian Journal of Experimental Psychology*, 60 (3): 237-245.

Butler, J. A., Hull, T. W. and Franz, R. 1995. 'Neonate aggregations and maternal attendance of young in the eastern diamondback rattlesnake', *Crotalus adamanteus*. Copeia: 196-198.

Clark, R.W. 2004. 'Kin recognition in rattlesnakes', *Proceedings of the Royal Society of London B: Biology Letters*; 271(May 7): 243-245. Abstract.

Furman, J. 2007. *Timber Rattlesnakes in Vermont and New York: Biology, History, and the Fate of an Endangered Species*'. USA: University Press of New England.

Geoffrey, H. A. 2004. 'Connecticut wildlife: biodiversity, natural history, and conservation', *UPNE.* p. 328.

Graves, B.M. 1989. 'Defensive behaviour of female prairie rattlesnakes (*Crotalus viridis*) changes after parturition', *Copeia*; 1989: 766-769.

Greene, H.W. 1992. 'The ecological and behavioural context for pitviper evolution', pp. 107-117 in J. A. Campbell and E. D. Brodie, Jr. (Eds), Biology of the Pitvipers. Texas: S Tyler.

Greene, H. W. 1997. *Snakes: The Evolution of Mystery in Nature.* Berkeley: University of California Press.

Greene, H., May, P.G, *et al.* 2002. 'Parental behaviour in vipers', in *The Biology of Vipers*, G.W. Shuett, H. Hoggren, M.E. Douglas, and H. W. Greene (eds.) Traverse City, Michigan: Biological Sciences Press.

Greer, A. E. 1997. *The Biology and Evolution of Australian Snakes.* Chipping Norton: Surrey Beatty & Sons.

Klauber, L. M. 1956. *Rattlesnakes: Their Habits, Life Histories, and Influence on Mankind*, 2 Vols. Berkeley: University of California Press.

Klauber, L. M. 1972. *Rattlesnakes: Their Habits, Life Histories, and Influence on Mankind.* 2 Vols, 2nd ed. Berkeley: University of California Press.

Klauber, L.M. 1997. *Rattlesnakes: Their Habits, Life Histories, and Influence on Mankind.* 2nd edition. Berkeley: University of California Press.

Kokko, H. and Jennions, M. D. 2008. 'Parental investment, sexual selection and sex ratios', *Journal of Evolutionary Biology*, 21: 919–948.

Meek, G. 1946. *Creatures of Mystery.* J. W. Burke Co. [for] Gray Meek, Macon, Georgia.

Mehrtens, J.M. 1987. *Living Snakes of the World in Colour.* New York: Sterling Publishers.

Melissa, A., Jeffrey, S., John, S. 2011. 'Family values: Maternal care in rattlesnakes is more than mere attendance', *Nature Precedings*. doi:10.1038/npre.2011.6671.1.

Moore, M. C., and J. Lindzey. 1992. 'The physiological basis of sexual behaviour in male reptiles', pp. 70-113 in C. Gans and D. Crew (Eds.), *Biology of the Reptilia*, Vol. 18. Chicago: The University of Chicago Press.

O'Connor, D., and R. Shine. 2003. 'Lizards in 'nuclear families': A novel reptilian social system in *Egernia saxatilis* (Scincidae)', *Molecular Ecology*, 12 (March): 743-752.

Oliver, J. A. 1955. *The Natural History of North American Amphibians and Reptiles*. D. Van No Strand Co., New Jersey: Princeton.

Pascal, P. 2005. 'Mechanisms of activation of maternal behaviour in mammals', *Reproduction, Nutrition, Development*, 45 (3): 341-351.

Rubio, M. 1998. *Rattlesnake: Portrait of a Predator*. Washington, D.C.: Smithsonian Institution Press.

Shakoori, S., Todehdehghan, F., Shiravi, A. H., Hojati, V. (2015). 'The assessment of captive breeding in the Caucasian viper (*Gloydiushalyscaucasicus*)', *Iran Journal of Entomology and Zoology Studies*, 3 (2): 257-259.

Shine, R. 1988. 'Parental care in reptiles', pp. 275–330 in C. Gans and R. B. Huey (Eds.), *Biology of the Reptilia*, Vol. 16. New York: Alan R. Liss.

Smith, A. G. 1940. 'Notes on the reproduction of the northern copperhead', *Agkistrodon mokasencupreus* (Rafinesque), in Pennsylvania. Ann. Carnegie Mus; 28:77-82.

VAN Hyning, O. C. 1931. 'Reproduction in some Florida snakes', Copeia; 1931:59-60.

Wharton, C. H. 1966a. 'Reproduction and growth in the cottonmouth', *Agkistrodon piscivorus* Lacepede of Cedar Keys, Florida. Copeia; 1966:149-161.

Wildlife Guide - National Wildlife Federation. *www.nwf.org*. Retrieved 15 April, 2018.

Wright, A. H., and Wright, A. A. 1957. *Handbook of Snakes of the United States and Canada*. New York: Cornell University Press.

Chapter - 7

Consumerism, Gender Personality and the Reproduction of Mothering

Biswajit Ghosh, Kaushik Chattopadhyay

We take it for granted that motherhood is an instinctive propensity. As if any woman becoming a mother, is at the same time stands as the symbol of affection, sympathy, patience, love and nourishment. That is to say, she will rear her child with her milk, thus giving the child nourishment by waning herself on the one side, and on the other side, she will have to be conscious enough about emotional security and dependence she renders to her child in a larger way.

This is a form of universal mother. This is the real mother. From primitive society with savage culture to postmodern culture with global politics, such mother is present. Does any mother exist vis-à-vis this 'good' mother? If such a mother exists, it is perhaps right to hold that moral character, mental capacity, vitality of offspring and life are manifestly dependent upon the mother's mental attitude, character and strength.

The Sociology of Motherhood

This is not a post-Freudian perspective. But, for the idealisation and enforcement of women's maternal role, it may provide new rationales. However, before going into the sociological debate about 'Good mother-Bad mother' and analysing the character of the mother, it is better to be clear that motherhood is women's most sacred privilege (Cocroft, 1906). Only the women get the chance to be a mother. This is a peculiar sensation and realisation. Only women can go beyond this most beautiful reality. Here the meaning of sex-role and gendered-role relates to each other. Mother's sacrifice represents motherhood as a social reflection (Chodorow, 1978). This bondage of relationship extends through the birth of a new one. Therefore, if we treat physical motherhood as an accessory, mental motherhood is given the trust of a soul. It is expected that the debate about 'Good' mother and 'Bad' mother temporarily ends here.

One question may be raised in this context. Let us take the example of a capable woman who is not only physically fit, but also aware that during the period of pregnancy she will get mental support and all sorts of medical treatment available. Now if such an adult woman wants to stay away from pregnancy and enjoys a free married life with no kids, would she be labeled as a selfish woman who does not satisfy her reproductive duty as woman? Should we place her amongst those deprived women who have lost their opportunity of being a mother? A debate lies here also.

Sociologists explain motherhood from a socio-economic standpoint and from a cultural perspective. Broadly motherhood can be considered as a universal experience. Gestation of a menstruating woman is the precondition of motherhood. Every woman in any part around the globe when becomes a mother, holds the same expectations and experiences as others like her in some matters. The modern globalised world, with different expectations and experiences, enriches motherhood in different perspectives (Birns and Hay, 1988; O'reilly, 2001). A woman from Ghana when becomes a mother for the first time holds some expectations and gathers some experiences which are quite different from an Indian woman. Similarly, the hopes and knowledge of a Syrian or Iraqi or a woman from Libiya becoming mother for the first time are obviously different from their British or American counterparts. Consequently, sociologists claim that motherhood is differently patterned or shaped in different context.

Economy is considered as another important criterion in explaining motherhood. Here the class character may feature at the time of finding the issue. A woman from a low income group may become a mother at a very early age. A woman with tribal identity and leading a tribal life may also enjoy the privilege of motherhood at an early age. On some occasions, sexual enjoyment in some places ensures pregnancy and consequent motherhood. Such inconvenience or pullback is not prevalent in developed world. Use of contraceptives, extension of sex-education, extended medical facilities hold the everyday life in that concrete example where sexual intercourse is not essentially related to child birth. Self-management here indicates such a cultural flow for which the probability of mother's death while giving birth of her baby reduces. The risk of motherhood is turned down.

Motherhood is risky (Berry, 2010). Beyond physical risk, hazard is also there in socio-cultural field (Miller, 2005). In a society where joint families are predominant, conception by an unmarried girl is a misdeed. It is also negatively valued. Whereas in urban megapolis the physical contact is high with a contrastingly lower degree of social contact and here, the woman body is a bio capital and she utilises it as her source of income for survival. Consequently, frequent gestation breaks her health. This devalued condition, in the context of degeneration, labels motherhood as a sacrifice and marks it as a sociological variable.

Ideology of Mothering

This angle is established more through protagonist ideology. It is said that, it is immaterial whether a woman who is fit for motherhood, becomes mother or not, 'motherhood is central to the ways in which they are defined by others and to their perceptions to themselves.' (Phoenix and Wollett, 1991:13). Question on ideology arises through a biological deterministic comprehension. Sociologists do not fully support this ideological construct. They give emphasis on historical, cultural and social variations and claim that mothering, today, is not another instinctive performance. Like other socio-cultural organisations it is also a socially constructed form. Like gender, mothering is also a form which is socially bestowed by shifting of identity (Chodorow, 1978; Lawler, 2000). With the help of new reproductive technology, this special social category of 'mother' attains the ability to destabilise its inevitable presence.

So there is no scope to be under the opinion that mothering is something biologically inscribed. By the phase of time in different societies, there has been ideological shift. Working mothers have depended on the day-care institutes for nurturing their children. Post-industrial society has re-defined its role-structure. Paid 'mothering' has become a new concept and it is popular (Phoenix and Woollett, 1991). Full time employment with motherhood has minimised the probable role conflicts by developing some new organisational system in the social context.

This organisational development does not stand as alternative to family. The traditional family and motherhood worked as complementary to each other but, this is not altogether fulfilled in the new setup. Though maternity leave after child birth solves problems to a certain extent, some difficulties for working mothers still persist.

The helping organisations even though keep their frame flexible and women welfare policies even if pro-woman, the detachment of children from their parents and the punctuality in workplace create certain complications in local perspectives (Edelman, 2006). The following is a description of a typical morning rush: 'It was important for me to get to work on time, so I had to get the kid to day-care at a certain time. That was terrible. I had to be at work at seven o'clock in the morning, and so I would drag the boy out of bed and dress him even though he was old enough to dress him, but it was faster if I did it. They were always talking about how much they were doing for mothers with children, but when I had to race to nursery school with a child in tow and then race to catch the bus because my boss would carry on if I came five minutes late, that was bad. It would have been better if they had said that a mother with small children could get to work between seven and eight o'clock and make up the time another day. Sometimes when I came late to work it wasn't because I was lazy but because my son had wet his pants just before we left the apartment' (Dodd and Allen, 1992: 40).

On the basis of this description we can remember the form and content of 'The Captive Mother'. The Captive Mother is considered to be one of the masterpieces of modern sculpture. This was sculpted by a Norwegian-Danish Artist Stephen Abel Sinding. What does the sculpture signify? As a symbol, it expresses the supreme tragedy of modern society. In one word it stands for 'The Bondage of Motherhood' (Spargo, 1914). The consumer culture expects an ideological construction and there 'Motherhood' becomes 'Motherhood Triumphant'. This reverse explanation inflates the buying-selling market of motherhood.

The preachers of socialistic ideology in the middle of the 19th century have demanded that the major role of nuclear family is to supply continuously or keep on supplying labour to the capitalist system of production. The precondition for surplus value creation is motherhood. In analysing value, the anti-capitalist forum of the 21st century, talk about assisted reproductive technology (ART) and women's reproductive labour (Jordan, 1993). In capitalism, paying mothers directly challenge many assumptions about a mother's worth.

Capitalism does not appeal most strongly to the mother through its fundamental demand for the equalisation of opportunity. Within this society, where a mother does not differentiate between her son and daughter, the ideology she represents is quite peculiar because it wants to resist all sorts of political, social, cultural and economic incapacities which hinder women's progress. Therefore, the ideology construction of motherhood is a political-economic agenda.

The sociologists, though do not seek the continuance in the journey from tradition to modernity, and from there to the postmodern condition, but they surely inquire for the globalisation of mothering in the changing structural and functional perspectives of the family system. They try to understand and analyse. They uphold their views regarding sexual division of labour and sexual inequality within the family structure. Sociologically it has mentioned about the inequality within the joint family (Beteille, 1993). The feminist sociologists further introduce that women's mothering is a central and defining feature of the social organisation of gender and is implicated in 'the construction and reproduction of male dominance itself' (Chodorow, 1978: 9).

Globalisation of Mothering

Globalisation of mothering is indicating a new direction where gender role is reconstructing identity in a new array. It may be termed as the deconstructed form of identity. There lies a difference between child bearing and childcare (Edelman, 2006). It is stated that even if there are biological or instinctual basis of pregnancy, parturition and lactation, they cannot last throughout the childhood of the newborn. The associate male who is also the biological father of the newborn can also shoulder the responsibility of childcare (Miller, 2011). If the male is unable, single motherhood is inevitable.

The context of single mother has been discussed earlier while explaining child poverty. What is discussed in excess is that along with immigrant families, same-sex parents and feminist individualistic attitude are also debated (O'Neil, 2016). Where these are present, economic stability exists and in the same breadth high risk is also present. Single mothers can be a subject of sociological research. It may be observed how the single mothers will navigate the political challenge of transforming a new home and stepfamily.

A considerable portion of feminist sociology contradicts traditional socialisation theory (Fingerman, 2001). In this perspective it is stated that, the personality structure of a newborn develops in a multiethnic, multicultural environment, which is unlike dominant, single stagnant social structure. Hence parenting is a mutual responsibility. Mother's physical proximity is not exclusively necessary for the development of a newborn. The father should take up a role along with the mother (Simpson, 2009). A father should also take responsibility to satisfy the daily demands of a baby. 'Men don't rear children because they don't *want* to rear children' (Chodorow, 1978: 31). But why this happens in urban social frame? This is because parenting is an unpaid occupation outside the world of public power.

Thus, father works outside when mother is involved in regular household chores. Rearing of children secures parent's future, but it does not indicate higher status or higher capital control. It indicates less control of resource than paid work. So man imposes such duties on woman. Her relative powerlessness in society is clearly revealed. Gender social role gets a vitiated form (Backett, 1982). Mothering remains confined in a matrifocal aspect of society rather than keeping itself in a psychologically based role control. Lesbian motherhood confronts the same problem.

Sociologists speak about mental illness. They establish the theory of deviance. They enquire about the factors of family disorganisation. Simultaneously they demand that the reproduction of women's mothering is the basis for the reproduction of women's location and responsibilities in the domestic sphere, originally, new pattern of work organisation with new identities. This is a new dimension of the family of procreation.

Feminists and social psychologists talk about freedom of choice in the perspective of women's powerlessness (Chasseguet-Smirgel, 1986). Why the male members of a family do not establish themselves as eligible for child rearing? It is due to their unwillingness to perform the task. They have the choice of independence, but the women are devoid of such liberty. In our middle-class and also in low-income Bengali families one incident is occasionally prevalent. It is exposed that if a baby cries before the same aged girls and boy of the family, the senior family members direct the girl to cajole the crying baby. But the opposite is rarely possible. Therefore, it is evident that the action structure of the social system on which rests the gendered role structure depends on the social context.

Here we may mention about the role taking and social control. Socialisation theory always supports the restoration of existing role relationship of social order and power structure. But the concurrent time demands that social reproduction comes to be independent of individual intention and is not caused by it. Consequently, global reproduction of mothering directs to look into society's several aspects. Socio-economic role-relations, institutions, organisational values and ideologies are those facets whose presence is obvious in sociological analysis. Feminist sociology implores that when social practices take institutionalised form in regularised way, then they, in every case, construct social order. These practices are bound for direction as to if the agent of social control will shift or not, if anyone new can achieve the freedom of choice or not.

Capitalism does not only trade with woman body, but also usurp woman labours (Collins, 1994). Capitalism is aware that in the world-market, woman holds the first place in the consumer's list. A big portion of the sold out goods is bought by the women in a society. Woman controls a considerable part of household spending in developed, underdeveloped or developing world. Mother will not buy for herself but will spend for household stuff. It is noticeable in the advertisements for children for essential goods that even if mother does not buy anything for herself, she will surely buy for her child. Marketing techniques are designed in such a way that it increases the loyalty of the buyers to the goods on the one hand, and tries to encourage the buyers on the other hand so that they treat each other as objects. It may be seen as dehumanisation of consumerism.

Conclusion

New social practice is constructing new social structure. Here two things can be considered: firstly, single motherhood; and secondly, surrogate motherhood. Single motherhood is nothing new. But it can be considered as a newly accepted kind of mothering (Anno, 2010). It is now socially accepted in those corners, where tradition is deeply embedded. On the other hand, surrogate motherhood is a mythologically established fact and a conventional idea from the beginning of 20th century according to the aspiration of Haldane. But there lies a similarity between the realisation of such aspiration due to advancement of science and the present day socially accepted kind of mothering (Macklin, 1994). In both the cases the subject of alternative role performance is intertwined. In the first place, the father is absent. Therefore, the mother has to perform dual role in respect of her offspring. In the second instance, one woman gives birth to a baby for another woman.

The problem of infertility exists in all the countries. As overpopulation is a burning problem worldwide, the infertility of 8% to 12% couple is not considered as a serious issue. A surrogate mother renders service to bridge the gap of female infertility. Today's failing global economy is increasing the sales of surrogacy and In Vitro Fertilisation (IVF). Adoption may become another option and it benefits the state as the state thus may reduce its budget allocated for welfare activity.

It is not that there is no other resemblance. In all respect, the concept of market is strongly present. Economic sociology becomes more relevant in analysing the matter of family life in the context of consumer, consumer protection, etc. It attracts the caption: the motherhood business. It can be adjudged widely how the economy of culture justifies the subject. Let us go through it extensively. Suppose you bought sperm from a sperm bank, your consultant accepted a physical package and you succeeded in becoming a biological mother but, you cannot get all round guarantee. Again a surrogate mother from Thailand, inspite of receiving a huge amount of money as package, gives you a baby with Down's syndrome (Landsman, 2009). What will happen then?

If mothering is considered to be a paid service, then it is bound to have profit and loss accounts. There will also be over production according to the rule of capitalism. Consumer culture resulted in the globalisation of biocapital. Transitional surrogacy, with its 'Made in' logo has composed a new equation amongst motherhood, kinship, consumer acts and regulations and privilege. This is an unexpected and unpredicted unit of social reality.

Conventional feminists and social psychologists try to bring before us the different theoretical arguments. Socialisation theories present before us those concepts in varied propositional formats. But, can it always be true in social reality in respect of concrete social situation? Perhaps it does not happen so, and that is why the analysis of the sociologists becomes important. There is only one reason for this. Sociologists want to see women's mothering as a feature of social structure, where women's reproductive capability, gender personality, attitude toward their new born babies and overall the expression of motherhood can be explained and elaborated through social structure. And this is definitely dependent on existing social system.

References

Anno, K. 2010. 'Kim, Ellen, and Zack's Big Adventure: Lesbian Mothers Raising a Boy Steeped in His Masculinity', in Sheila Lintott (ed.), *Motherhood- Philosophy for Everyone: The Birth of Wisdom.* Oxford: Wiley and Blackwell.

Backett, K. C. 1982. *Mothers and Fathers: A Study of the Development and Negotiation of Parental Behaviour.* London: The Macmillan Press Ltd.

Berry, N. S. 2010. *Unsafe Motherhood: Mayan Maternal Mortality and Subjectivity in Post-War Guatemala.* New York: Berghahn Books.

Beteille, A. 1993. 'The Family and the Reproduction of Inequality', in Patricia Uberoi (ed.), *Family, Kinship and Marriage in India.* Delhi: Oxford University Press.

Birns, B. and Hay, D. F. 1988. 'Introduction', in Beverly Birns and Dale F. Hay (eds.), *The Different Faces of Motherhood.* New York: Springer.

Chasseguet-Smirgel, J. 1986. *Sexuality and Mind: The Role of the Father and the Mother in the Psyche.* New York: New York University Press.

Chodorow, N. J. 1978. *The Reproduction of Mothering: Psychoanalysis and the Sociology of Gender.* London: University of California Press.

Cocroft, S. 1906. *Motherhood: The Generative Organs, Their Purpose and Derangements.* Chicago: Physical Culture Extension Society.

Collins, P.H. 1994. 'Shifting the center: race, class and feminist theorising about motherhood', in E. Nakano Glenn, G. Chang and L. Rennie Forcey (eds.), *Mothering, Ideology, Experience and Agency.* London: Routledge.

Dodd, D. and Allen-Thompson, P. 1992. 'East German Women in Transition'. Manuscript, in Eva Kolinsky (ed.), *Social Transformation and the Family in Post-Communist Germany.* London: Macmillan Press Ltd.

Edelman, H. 2006. *Motherless Mothers: How Losing a Mother Shapes the Parent You Become.* New York: Harper Collins Publishers LLC.

Fingerman, K. 2001. *Aging Mothers and Their Adult Daughters: A Study in Mixed Emotions.* New York: Springer Publishing Company, Inc.

Jordan, B. 1993. *Birth in Four Cultures.* 4th edition. Illinois: Waveland Press.

Landsman, G. H. 2009. *Reconstructing Motherhood and Disability in the Age of "Perfect" Babies.* New York: Routledge.

Lawler, S. 2000. *Mothering the Self: Mothers, Daughters, Subjects*. London: Routledge.

Macklin, R. 1994. *Surrogates and Other Mothers Debate Over Assisted Reproduction*. Philadelphia: Temple University Press.

Miller, T. 2005. *Making Sense of Motherhood: A Narrative Approach*. Cambridge: Cambridge University Press.

Miller, T. 2011. *Making Sense of Fatherhood: Gender, Caring and Work*. Cambridge: Cambridge University Press.

O'Neil, M. K. 2016.'Single Mothers and Women's Autonomy', in Salman Akhtar (ed.), *The New Motherhoods: Patterns of Early Child Care in Contemporary Culture*. London: Rowman & Littlefield.

O'reilly, A. 2001. 'Introduction', in Andrea O'reilly (ed.), *Mothers and Sons: Feminism, Masculinity and the Struggle to Raise Our Sons*. London: Routledge.

Phoenix, A. and Woollett, A. 1991. *Motherhood, Meanings, Practices and Ideologies*. London: Sage.

Simpson, R. 2009. *Men in Caring Occupations Doing Gender Differently*. London: Palgrave Macmillan.

Spargo, J. 1914. *Socialism and Motherhood*. New York: B.W. Huebsch.

Chapter - 8

The Reproduction of Mothering: Portraying the Notion of Mothering as a Science

Soumya Narayan Datta

The word mothering is looked upon as a historically and culturally variable relationship 'in which one individual nurtures and cares for another.' Mothering occurs within specific social contexts that vary in terms of material and cultural resources and constraints. The ways mothering is conceived, organised and carried out are not simply determined by these conditions however. Mothering is constructed through men's and women's actions within specific historical circumstances. Thus, agency is central to an understanding of mothering as a social rather than biological construct (Glenn, 1994). The difficulties of theorising mothering in an individualist ideological context are well illustrated by the turn of the century in the debate between Charlotte Perkins Gilman and Ellen Key and these difficulties persist in contemporary feminist theory, given the continued hegemony of individualism in U.S. society and culture. Like Gilman and Key, contemporary feminist theorists have faced the challenge of analysing mother's situations and experiences, and theorising the significance of mothering in women's lives without recuperating essentiality of motherhood. This means that contemporary feminist theorists have encountered some dilemmas of difference and the paradoxes it produces, regardless of how they approach the issue of mothering. Accounts of the resurgence or 'the second wave,' of the women's movement in the United States in the 1960s often emphasise on its multiple origins and different kinds of feminism that developed at this time, but a focus on the issue of mothering leads to a different account of this period of feminism. From this perspective, second-wave feminist theory evidences two basic strategies for avoiding essential motherhood while negotiating the dilemma of difference. The first is to avoid essential motherhood by avoiding the issue of mothering as much as possible, either by minimising the significance of mothering in women's lives or by analysing mothering in overly simplistic, one-dimensional terms. This approach to mothering often relies on important elements of individualism, whether they are directly stated or implied. This approach involves feminist theory in all the difficulties of theorising mothering in individualist terms and risks misrepresenting both mother's situations and experiences and the significance of mothering in women's lives. The second strategy is to deal directly and explicitly with the issue of mothering, including all the aspects of the dilemma of difference that this entails. This approach to feminist theory usually requires a more or less explicit challenge to individualism. This second strategy thus involves feminist theory in the difficulties of representing mothers' and women's experiences, situations and interests in terms that are not consistent with the dominant ideology and risks the recuperation of elements of essential motherhood (Diquinzio, 1999).

Feminist debates on motherhood in India

In India, feminist engagement with motherhood surfaced in the context of the colonial state's intervention with the lives of women in different spheres. Quite a lot of the formulations came about through reaction to the challenges thrown up by colonial rule. The 'woman question' was the moot question with which the colonial rulers justified the 'civilising mission' of colonial rule. The alleged barbarism of the Indian male towards the womenfolk spawned a series of attacks on the 'natives' and the need to reform the organisation of the Hindu family so that women might enjoy greater equality and freedom. A complex interplay of a drive towards autonomy and collaboration with the hegemonic powers of the ruling elite produced the broad movements in colonial India characterised as social reform followed by the nationalist phase (Bagchi, 2017).

The paradox of motherhood in the context of feminist theorising in India was the potent contradiction between ideological glorification of motherhood as *Shakti* or power and the powerlessness faced by mothers in their everyday lived reality. Hence Indian feminist's theorising has had to take on board the complex process of the ideological use of motherhood to keep the family as the regulating and regulated social order, thereby confining women to the reproductive domain of 'home' and denying them access to the 'world'. For the mothers in the poor families, it meant denying women the scant privileges to which they were entitled within a limited and exploited role in the productive sphere. On the whole, however, the theorising has shown a bias towards the formation of the elite in India. Motherhood has been conceived as a culmination of the ideal womanhood. In Indian feminist literature on motherhood we find a spate of collective writings. The first was a collection of personal narratives contributed by twelve Indian feminists in the mode of an intergenerational testimony, 'A Space of Her Own'.[1] The essays contributed by some of the major feminists writing in India bring out their experiences of motherhood across three generations. Finally, there is a collection of essays on an authors' own experience of their mothers and of motherhood in a collection called 'Janani', edited by a feminist critic and documentary film maker.[2] The fact that needs to be registered is that motherhood exercised in woman the impulse to retrieve women's agency embedded in the experience of motherhood that Adrienne Rich talked about so eloquently.

An interesting offshoot of this trend in Indian feminist articulation was Bharati Ray's five generational narrative of mother-daughter succession.[3] Mother is the keeper of the social order upholding the upper caste/upper class Hindu family as a hegemonic instrument in keeping the public/private, productive/reproductive domains intact so that the boundaries of patriarchy are never crossed. This mother often makes appearance as a compliant daughter/wife/mother corresponding to the three different phases of her life as enumerated in the scriptural injunctions of the *Manusmriti*. As a chaste wife she was made to immolate herself on her husband's funeral pyre or as a life-long celibate widow often from her childhood she had to go through enormous social exclusions in food, clothing, entertainment and even the possibility of motherhood or be subjected to marital rape as child-bride leading to premature motherhood causing life-risks. This is the 'woman' in the Indian society who formed the subject of social reforms. Consequently, it was her powerlessness fostered by the *andarmahal* from which she was not allowed even to go to school which became the public discourse of women's 'powerlessness'. Since Personal Laws covering marriage, custody, inheritance, for instance, had been kept by the British rulers in the hands of the religious authorities of the religious communities in India, the 'Hindu woman' became the symbol of the normative order of the majority of Indian women, across the caste-class- religious divide (*ibid.*).[4]

The Notion of Scientific Motherhood

Scientific motherhood refers to a practice of mothering informed by expert knowledge. The practice evolved as medicine and science replaced other traditionally feminine domains of knowledge including practices related to fertility and birth. The movement to scientific motherhood redefined the childcare and child raising. The movement also altered women's identities from producers to consumers of mothering knowledge.

Industrialisation and urbanisation in the late 1800s reorganised the Western family from a site of production to a site focused on consumption. An educated, white, male upper class drove the rise of positivism and modern medicine. Women as the keepers of the private sphere were confronted with elevated expectations regarding household maintenance and child rearing. Before industrialisation, children were conceptualised as miniature, untamed adults. From an early age, each child made significant contributions to the family as she or he worked alongside siblings and adults. In the post-industrial period, the child became a project, a work site and a vocation for women. Scientific motherhood developed in parallel with the rise of domestic science. Although germ theory via domestic science education elevated the expectations for housework, science and medicine replaced a long history of women's knowledge in relationship to mothering. New levels of intensity developed around researching and enacting 'the good mother.' Expert knowledge became the domain of men in white coats. Psychology's efforts to be recognised as a science played an important role in transforming the field of raising children into a science. By the end of the nineteenth century, early psychologists, mothers' movement leaders and leaders in domestic science began to frame childhood as serious business requiring professional training. Research institutes and government conferences became centers for studying and doing something about the child. Women's magazines and child-raising books and manuals became central mechanisms for spreading the new behaviourist theories on the subject. The early tone was one of restraint and regularity. The orientation of the expert advice changed when Benjamin Spock popularised a child-centered approach with the publication of *The Pocket Book of Baby and Child Care.* Against the backdrop of behaviourism, Spock's ideas were revolutionary. The book went through seven editions, was translated into thirty-nine languages and more than fifty million copies were sold. Earlier parents had been told that holding a crying child only spoils him or her. Spock encouraged parents to go with their instincts, cuddle the crying child, be flexible, focus on individual needs and have fun parenting. The struggle between child-centered, permissive parenting and more restrictive parenting did not end with Spock. Parents today often find themselves caught between experts and the politics of gender and science. They might read attachment-oriented books such as *The Baby Book* by Martha and William Sears. This approach draws on non-Western child-rearing practices such as the family bed that emphasise on physical and emotional closeness between parent and child. At the same time, parents may refer to Richard Ferber's *Solve Your Child's Sleep Problems*, which emphasises on child-independence and self-comfort. This formula provides on for progressively increased lengths of letting the child cry to train the child to fall asleep on her or his own (Virnoche, 2009).

The politics of race, class and gender marked the discourses around scientific motherhood. Jacquelyn Litt in *Medicalised Motherhood* chronicled the experiences of African American and Jewish women born between 1894 and 1930. Socially respectable, good parents relied on physicians for expert advice on child health and education. Although the social networks of Jewish women afforded them multiple avenues to expert knowledge, African American women's access was restricted. As African American women continued to rely on informal networks and traditional knowledge, they framed their barriers to expert knowledge beyond gender stratification to issues of civil rights and although they advocated for access to medical expertise they remained wary of modern medical practitioners. Scientific motherhood is linked at an international level to the growth of the infant formula industry. Corporate marketing strategies manipulated the discourse of good mothering associating formula feeding as the new and improved method for caring for one's infant. In developing countries, where women do not have access to clean drinking water needed to constitute the powdered formulas and sanitise bottle products, millions of babies have died from diarrhea which is the leading cause of death for children worldwide. The politics and practices of motherhood weave through the intersections of race, class and gender stratification. Scientific motherhood, like parallel practices around fertility and birth was a Western masculinist project that displaced women's knowledge about mothering. It generated a space for intentionality and reflection concerning parenting. Yet the space was filled with knowledge external to the lived experiences of women. So scientific motherhood affected how children are raised and it affected the identity of women and their power in negotiating the development of their children into adults (*ibid*).

Reconstructing the notion of scientific mothering observed in a Bengali middle class family in Kolkata

In this section the author discusses some of his personal observations while emphasising on the process by which doctors specialised in the fields of homoeopath and allopath are shaping the process of childcare enacted by the mothers in Kolkata. Henceforth through such child caring process the author focuses on a completely different notion of scientific motherhood that segregates itself from the pre-established notions as developed by Rima D. Apple.

The author states two different situations in which he was undergoing allopathic and homoeopathy treatments. The first stage reflects on an important phase in the author's life which was a stepping stone towards moving to the next stage. It was the month of March and the mercury was rising towards thirty-six degree Celsius in Kolkata showing indications of excessive heat. The author appeared in the CBSE class X board exams. The day when the mathematics exam was over the author didn't have sufficient water to drink and he was not feeling well which resulted in dehydration after coming back home. Later on in the evening the author started vomiting and severe stomach pain occurred that became simply irresistible. Looking at the author's miserable condition everyone was worried. The author's mother called the general physician specialised in allopathic treatment and took an appointment to visit him so that he can diagnose the patient properly and prescribe some medicine. After examination the doctor prescribed some heavy doses of anti-biotic medicines like Pan D and Norflox TZ and advised the author's mother to apply the medicines for one month and five days respectively. Along with such medicines for a quick rehydration of the body the doctor also suggested for some oral rehydration powder that would provide some energy and prevent the body from becoming dehydrated in the scorching sun. Following the doctor's advice the author's mother with all her efforts took best care of the author so that the author could recover quickly and start preparing for the upcoming exam.

Ten years later another situation arose and surprisingly the coincidence was that it was again the month of March. Both the author and his mother were invited to attend an *upanayan* or the sacred thread ceremony. But this time a different situation occurred which was not felt ten years ago during the class ten board exams. The author forgot to drink water after having lunch and in order to quench the thirst and relieve him from the moisture and humid climatic conditions resulting from heat the author had some cold drinks. Later on it was realised that the author was not feeling comfortable which lead to increasing gastritis pain coupled with swelling of the stomach. As a result the author couldn't sleep well. In order to look that the health condition does not get worse any more the author's mother consulted a very reputed homoeopathy doctor based in Kolkata who was busy all the time dealing with some critical patients in his residential clinic located nearby. The doctor prescribed certain homoeopathic medicines which comprised of certain mixtures of lycopodium with aloe which could produce a quick curing effect. Along with this he also advised to take some homoeopathic globules that could bring certain comfort and increase digestive capabilities. The author's mother following the advice of the doctor started to take care of the author that helped towards a speedy recovery.

Conclusion

Doctors have played a significant role towards shaping the process of scientific mothering towards childcare. With the help of homoeopathy and allopathic treatment child care techniques performed by the author's mother created two different notions of scientific motherhood that don't bear any resemblance with the pre-existing notions of scientific motherhood as suggested by Rima D. Apple. The author through his observations has shown two different stages of scientific mothering that reveal two different ways of childcare. In the first stage scientific mothering depicts a picture which is framed according to the mode of care prescribed by the doctor through applying allopathic medicines. But while moving forward to the next stage a certain transformation in child caring by the mother occurs in accordance with the advice of doctors that suggests homoeopathic medicines after examining the patient and realising the symptoms behind the occurrence of certain diseases.

Notes

1. *A Space of Her Own: Personal Narratives of Twelve Women* is a book edited by Leela Gulati and Jasodhara Bagchi comprises of narratives demonstrating how each contributor established her own personhood through engagement with a wider kin group. Showing that women need not always be seen as victims, these are stories of women who found strength, success and independence from the inspiring lives of their mothers and grandmothers.
2. *Janani- Mothers, Daughters, Motherhood* is a book edited by Rinki Bhattacharya. Rinki Bhattacharya is a chairperson of the Bimal Roy Memorial Committee. She is also a well known journalist and documentary film maker based in Mumbai. She made a five-minute audio-visual capsule, *Janani* which is based on the same theme as this book.

3. Bharati Ray in her book *Daughters: A Story of Five Generations* demonstrates a chronicle of the lives of five generations of women in her family. Sundar-ma, Bharati Ray's great grandmother, was married into a conservative household at twelve. Ushabala, the author's grandmother, was the proud wife of a college lecturer and a consummate homemaker while Kalyani, Bharati Ray's mother, was the first woman in the family to get a college degree but she gave up her studies and career to raise her children. Bharati Ray's daughters, Khuku and Tista, both extremely bright, lead busy, fulfilling lives as academics.
4. Prabhati Mukherjee's book *Hindu Women: Normative Models* seeks to answer the contemporary question of how and why women came to lose their position in society by making an incisive study of the role of women and the position accorded to them in the religious and secular Hindu texts.

References

Bagchi, J. 2017. *Interrogating motherhood: Theorizing feminism*. New Delhi: Sage Publications.

DiQuinzio, P. 1999. *The Impossibility of motherhood: Feminism, individualism and the problem of mothering*. NY: Routledge.

Glenn, E.N. 1994. 'Social constructions of mothering: A thematic overview', in E.N. Glenn, G. Chang & L.R. Forcey (Eds.) *Mothering: Ideology, experience and agency* (pp. 1-32). NY: Routledge.

Virnoche, M.E. 2009. 'Scientific Motherhood', in Jodi O' Brien (Ed.), *Encyclopedia of gender and society* (Vol. 2, pp. 739-740). Thousand Oaks, California: Sage Publications.

Chapter - 9

Challenges of Single Motherhood

Pankaj Kumar

In the age of freedom and democracy, it is not astonishing that women, both married and single, should wish to breathe the pure fresh air of emancipation like men. Though the Constitution of India guarantees equal rights and opportunities to women in India, in reality the life of women is steeped in misery and subjugation (Shikha, 2009). This is especially true of single women who are further exploited and victimised. Women have been the victims of male tyranny for centuries, as a result of which their talents have not been allowed to bloom. It has been rightly said that women are perhaps the largest underprivileged group in the world (Swarup, 1985). The first slavery in human history began with the subjugation of women within the family; gradually they are pushed out of productive roles and relegated to the domestic role.

Singleness is a socially and culturally constructed category, wherein the disadvantage is manufactured by the virtue of the patriarchal societal setup. In this way gender is constructed as 'singleness'. Women who choose to remain single owing to a range of circumstances find themselves in locations of multiple disadvantages as a result of social and cultural, legal and administrative constructions of singleness. This has been exemplified further with the aid of case studies that attempt to bring to report the voice and the lived realities of women who are single.

Single parent family may be defined as 'A family comprising of a single mother or father having their own dependent children' (Kumar, 2018:167). The single parent family is created in a number of ways like death of one parent, divorce, separation and so on. In some societies, widows, divorced or abandoned women may be subjected to social exclusion, isolation and harassment, so it is very difficult for them to maintain a healthy livelihood for themselves or for their children. Women heads of household with young children may face great time constraints and may have to limit their working hours. Even though female headed households are a relatively small proportion of households, evidence shows that in the last 20 years their number is increasing in most regions of the world.

Though single women accept spinsterhood as an alternative lifestyle, society still devalues spinsterhood, and considers it as a personal failure of the women. Kins, neighbours and office colleagues couch stereotypes of single women in derogatory terms, such as lack of attractiveness, arrogance, deficit in personality, inability to develop intimate relationship with another person, lack of parent's interest in daughter's career and so forth. It is this attitude of society which creates stresses and problems of adjustment for single women. This calls for in-depth study of the problems of the single women.

Indian society is experiencing widespread and dramatic change in traditional gender and family roles. The major gender role change has been a substantial increase in the number of young women engaged in paid employment outside the home. Employment is now the norm for young women. A majority of young women now expect to get job after completion of their education and the more highly educated women the more likely they are to be employed. Though women's educational and occupational options have greatly been expanded, there has not been as great an increase in the number of women planning to forego motherhood since the role of mother also is a highly valued one for women. However, Nautiyal (1994) has stipulated that incidence of single women in India is likely to increase due to education and employment of women.

Indian single mothers always try to prove how good or worthy they are as mothers. This is not only for their children and family but for the society around them at large. Being a single mother her qualities are to be examined and judged by people whether she is fit enough to bring up a 'good' child without a man. These people, from the larger society, do nothing to support her, do not give her due dignity or space, but their sense of entitlement gives them the license to scrutinise and pass judgments on her life.

Since many decades, single women have showed up themselves as sign of power, freedom and courage in this men-dominated society. They have been surviving by facing all the obstacles in this cruel society. Ginny Shrivastava, the founder of the National Forum for Single Women's Rights, in his study, conducted in 2013, noted the stories of single women which narrated about human cruelty, wicked superstition, systemic corruption, age-old cruel customs. In his work single women were discarded, abandoned or murdered. But generally, women were survived, and brought up their children, through the sweat and blood of their labour. They were strong women, not weak women. Nussbaum (2000) has mentioned that women are treated as mere instruments of the ends of others-reproducers, caregivers, sexual outlets, agents of a family's general prosperity. A study conducted by Salaff (1981) has highlighted the problems of single women in Chinese families. It shows that their life-styles differ from of their mothers. He has listed seven overlapping images of singles. They are seen as following:

(a) Deviant or abnormal;

(b) Immature or unable to experience life;

(c) Sexually deviant;

(d) Over-concerned for being free, or unwilling to accept responsibility;
(e) Either very happy or very lonely;
(f) Affluent, and
(g) Devoted to their careers and workaholic.

Some social scientists have empirically examined the phenomenon of singlehood as an emerging lifestyle and an alternative to marriage (Stein, 1973,1976; Duberman, 1974). These studies, based on responses from both males and females, reveal the following positive reasons for remaining single: scope for freedom and enjoyment, opportunities for variety of experiences, sexual availability, self-sufficiency, career opportunities, sustaining friendships, freedom to change and experiment, nobility and availability of supportive groups. As regards the negative reasons, the following can be pointed out: suffocating one-to-one relationships, obstacles to self-development, boredom, unhappiness, lack of friends, isolation, and loneliness, limitation on mobility and available experience, influence of and participation in women's movements.

Single Women: Diverse Spectrum

A single woman is defined and her role in society, particularly within the larger context, is delineated, in terms of the social and psychological problems encountered by the members of this minority group.

It is said that all round development of a nation depends upon the development of women. The Constitution of India ensures not only opportunity for women but also empowers the state to adopt effective measures in favour of women for neutralising the cumulative socio-economic, educational, political disadvantages faced by them. The Government of India is pushing for special dispensation for single women, particularly those who are single by choice, under various government schemes in the 12th Five Year Plan. In addition to reserving a certain percentage of jobs for single women under centrally sponsored schemes, the plan panel has proposed to promote and strengthen federations of single women at the block and district levels. Government hasn't responded to their existence as they are not performing their voting rights properly.

In the beginning of the 20th century, a lot of women were devoting their energies in reshaping the nation. Indian single women are no way less than their counterparts across the globe, that redefined spinsterhood. The number of single women in India is increasing rapidly. According to the Census of 2011, there are 71.4 million single women in India, which is about 12% of the female population. It was 51.4 million in 2001, and was increased by 39% in a decade. Single woman was defined then as those who never got married, as well as divorcees, separated from husbands, and widows (Dasgupta, 2014).The greatest percentage of single women are widows. Uttar Pradesh has the highest number of single women, i.e., 12 million; followed by Maharashtra at 6.2 million and erstwhile Andhra Pradesh at 4.7 million.

The focus of the study has been on single women who choose to remain single, widows, divorced or abandoned in Asansol, Raniganj and Muradi of West Bengal. This area comes under Paschim Bardwan district of West Bengal. A purposive sample of 50 households has been selected for interview. The sample drawn from rural and urban areas represented the families from upper class, middle class and lower class. The interview schedule has been divided in different sections - personal profile, family profile, position of the children in the family and the intra-family relations. Field survey has been done in 2017-2018.

Educational Qualification of the Respondents

Education is one of the most important characteristics that might affect the person's attitudes and the way of looking at and understanding of social phenomena. In a way, the response of an individual is likely to be determined by his educational status and therefore it becomes imperative to know the educational background of the respondents.

Table 1: Educational Qualification-wise Distribution of the Respondents

Sl.No.	*Qualifications of the respondents*	*Total*	*Percentages*
1.	Literate	7	14%
2.	Class I to V	5	10%
3.	Class VI to VIII	4	8%
4.	Class IX to XII	6	12%
5.	Intermediate	15	30%
6.	Technical education	2	4%
7.	Graduation	8	16%
8.	Post-graduation	2	4%
9.	Illiterate	1	2%
	Total	50	100%

Source: Field survey.

Table 1 describes the educational qualification-wise distribution of the respondents. It reveals that 14% of respondents are literate, 10% of the respondents are in the category of class I-V, 8% of the respondents are in the category of class VI to VIII, 12% respondents have educational level of class IX to XII, 30% respondents belong to Intermediate, 4% of the respondents are technically educated, 16% respondents are graduate, 4% respondents have completed their Post-graduate education and 2% respondents are illiterate. So majority of the respondents have completed their intermediate courses.

Economic Independence

Socio-economic status of an individual is indicative of his/her lifestyle and the pattern of his/her behaviour. In general the persons from low socio-economic background have some peculiar social and psychological characteristics which in turn might be reflected in their responses to a particular problem.

Table 2: Nature of Economic Dependence of the Respondents

Sl. No.	*Dependence*	*Total*	*Percentage*
1	Yes	18	36%
2	No	32	64%
	Total	50	100%

Source: Field survey.

Table 2 describes the nature of economic dependence of the respondents. It reveals that 36% of the respondents are economically dependent and 64% respondents are economically independent.

Categories of Singleness of the Respondents

Indian society is one of the closed societies in the world. It is also characterised by the uniqueness of endogamy, where in the marriages outside of one's social group is not permitted. This has been one of the reasons for continuation of the social disability of many downtrodden people. But with the spread of education the situation is changing day by day and people are becoming socially liberal. Taking this into consideration, it is necessary to know the attitudes of the respondents towards the category of singleness.

Table 3: Category of Singleness

Sl. No.	*Categories*	*Total*	*Percentage*
1.	Unmarried	4	8%
2.	Mutual separation	3	6%
3.	Widow	15	30%
4.	Divorce	13	26%
5.	Deserted	12	24%
6.	Others	3	6%
	Total	50	100%

Source: Field survey.

Table 3 describes the category of singleness. It reveals 8% respondents are unmarried, 6% respondents are in mutual separation, 30% of them are widow. It has also been found that 26% respondents are divorced and 24% respondents are deserted. So majority of the respondents are widows.

Social Responses

Indian society is traditionally compartmentalised and stratified. The channels of communication among the relatives are not open and hence exchange of ideas and views is not possible. With the passage of time and the educational advancement of the people, followed by modernity, the attitudes of people are expected to change and become more liberal. In this context, it is essential to investigate the nature of the relations of the respondents with the relatives.

Table 4: Attitude of Relatives

Sl. No.	*Attitude of the respondents' Relatives*	*Total*	*Percentage*
1.	Supportive	10	20%
2.	Not supportive	15	30%
3.	Indifferent	13	26%
4.	Not clear	12	24%
	Total	50	100%

Source: Field survey

Table 4 describes the attitudes of the relatives towards single mother. It reveals that the 20% respondents' relatives are supportive and 30% respondents' relatives are not supportive. 26% respondents' relatives are indifferent and 24% respondents' relatives have not expressed any opinion.

Legal Awareness

Legal awareness, sometimes called public legal education, is the empowerment of individuals regarding issues involving the law. Legal awareness helps to promote consciousness of legal culture, participation in the formation of laws and the rule of law. Taking this into consideration, an attempt has been made to know the knowledge of law and rights of the respondents.

Table 5: Knowledge about the Laws and Rights

Sl.No.	*Knowledge about the laws and rights*	*Total*	*Percentage*
1.	Having awareness	13	26%
2.	Having awareness but reluctant to go to the court	10	20%
3.	No awareness	27	54%
	Total	50	100%

Source: Field survey.

Table 5 describes the knowledge about the laws and rights. It reveals that 26% respondents are having awareness, 20% respondents are having awareness but reluctant to go to the courts and 54% of respondents are not at all aware. So, most of the respondents do not know about legal rights.

Social Hardships of Single Mother

The role of single parent is challenging one especially when the family is headed by a woman. Problems of single mother are linked with the upbringing of children, their future and settling down in life. Till the children get married and/or get jobs they are dependent on the single parent. Single mothers reported that they felt lonely, helpless, hopeless, lack of identity and lack of confidence. In social sphere, majority of the single mothers tried to avoid attending social gatherings and had changed their dressing style due to depression. Majority of the single mothers found it hard to maintain discipline among the children due to absence of male members. The mothers complained about loneliness, traumatic feelings and depression and found it difficult to handle all the responsibilities of childcare and to establish a routine for her children (Puradkar, 2014).

Some of the main hardships faced by single mothers are:

- *Single mothers seen as 'socially unacceptable':*

  Single mothers experience negative attitudes and lack of support from her peers and society. She is looked down upon and pitied and seen as immoral. Single parents, especially the unmarried or separated women, are silently suffering from discrimination in many aspects of life. Moreover, this discrimination passes down to their children. Even with the fast growth in the number of single parents in India, society still cannot grasp the fact that there are women today that would choose to bring a child into the world alone. Single mothers are just waiting for the recognition which they deserve for child rearing. But unfortunately they are yet to be recognised and they are being looked down upon as immoral women by the rest of the society.

- *The need of fatherly advice and guidance:*

  This problem is common for the single mothers with sons as when their sons reach puberty the mothers are unable to relate especially in the matter of sex and the changes in his body. A young adolescent boy going through puberty is often in need of a fatherly figure to find his own identity as a man. When the father is absent, the child faces difficulties in developing his own personality. This is when the need for a father figure must be recognised back into the family or in the rearing of the child, in the event that there is no father figure to guide the child, alternative models of men of good moral and good stature can be a substitute to help the child in finding his identity.

- *Social pressures of getting married:*

  Indian society always keeps putting pressure on single women to get married. People often overlook or conveniently ignore the complex family bond that they are trying to create. The remarriage proposal may or may not work. Sometimes, it does work; at other times, it miserably fails (Kantilal, 2014).

- *Financial Security:*

  When upwardly mobile women from progressive families may have been imparted a good education and have been encouraged by their families to pursue lucrative careers, there are also millions of single women in India at grass roots level who have sadly been denied requisite qualifications. As a result, they have had no option but to go on to take on low income jobs. Worse still, there are some conservative families where women aren't allowed to work. Indian women have always been disfavoured as far as inheritance of property is concerned, more so in traditional families. Because of all these reasons, the majority of Indian women are in weak position. Single women don't enjoy the benefit of living in a double income family or being solely financially supported by their husbands. So, financial problems hit them hard if they aren't earning well or haven't inherited property.

- *Safety:*

  As many single women live in a joint family, the safety and security issues of them are predominant there. However as nuclear families are gaining in popularity, many women do face problems with respect to safety; especially single women who travel to other cities for work become more vulnerable.

- *Sexual Harassment:*

  Men often prey on single women, as far as sexual harassment cases are concerned. Though women of all relationship status are the victims of sexual harassment, men erroneously think that single women may more easily yield to their advances as they are to be assumed that they are starved of a relationship and will therefore even be ready to be with an unattractive obnoxious married man who is old enough to be her father or grandfather.

- *Absence of Caring Husband:*

  Though many single women may not readily admit it, quite a few of them do, miss the presence of a romantic partner in their lives. Some women settle for no-string relationships, but the more traditional kind avoids doing so.

- *Loneliness:*

  Many single women face issues of loneliness, though there are many married women who may face the same, if single women feel confident of themselves and are psychologically strong; they are less likely to feel lonely. Socially they face a lot of problems and are not given a high place in the society which makes them feel insecure and experience various mental conflicts and the agony of a lonely life, finding it difficult to live in a society dominated by men (Kumari, 1987).

Future Ambition for Single Mother

Single women are divided on the question of increasing the phenomenon of singlehood in Indian society. Most of them have developed the feelings of social insecurity which ultimately results in the fear of old age or prolonged illness. Single women have emphasised on the need for establishment of social institutions for them like women's clubs, single women's associations, social service centre run by NGOs, special hostels, special old age homes and multi-purpose information and awareness centers. The future plans of single women include their fight against social stigma attached to singlehood. They want to serve the people by associating themselves with NGOs to fight for their just status in society.

They have underlined the need for developing positive attitude towards single women and understanding their problems through empathy. Single women who feel well adjusted with their state of singlehood aspire to do something for the betterment of their fellow women.

Conclusion

To conclude, it may be said that the incidence of permanent singlehood is a type of a social phenomenon which defies a simple explanation. Most women who choose single parenthood are strong-minded, independent, and creative problem-solvers in many aspects of their lives. They possess all excellent traits to pass along to their children. It is said that raising a family is difficult enough, but it is even more difficult for single women to meet the expectations of the society. They don't need more obstacles but need more opportunities. In India, there are hardly any support groups or communities for single mothers. Due to the judgments directed at them most single parents have to keep a low profile. Time has come to change the situation. For a single woman, a parent life is not only full of struggles, but also a journey to be strong. The best thing single mothers are doing for their children is to inculcate among them a sense of responsibility- for taking control of their own lives, for understanding their obligations to others as well as for giving them an open door to avail possibilities that gives them a love of learning and exploration of spirituality. Indian society has to change its attitude towards single parents.

Mass media— print, audio and audio-visual-should make purposeful attempts to negate the prejudices that exist against single mothers. They should help in creating a sympathetic and humane approach towards the problems of the single mothers. They should not feel alienated from the society. They should not think that they are women who are more vulnerable than others and are misfits in society. They need not necessarily subject themselves to a variety of mental torture. They should develop a positive approach towards life.

References

Dasgupta, J. 2014. *'Problems and Challenges faced by Single Women in India Today'*, unpublished proceedings of the workshop on 'Issue of Single Women' organised by Ramniranjan Jhunjhunwala College of Arts of Science and Commerce, Mumbai.

Duberman, L. 1974. *Marriage and Other Alternatives*. New York: Praega.

Jethani, U. 1994. *Single Women*. New Delhi: Rawat Publications.

Kumari, K. N. S. 1987. *Status of Single Women in India: A Study of Spinsters, Widows and Divorcees*. New Delhi: Uppal Publishing House.

Kumar, P. 2018. 'Single Women and Motherhood in Indian Society' in Manna, S., Patra, S and Roy, S (eds.) *Sociology of Motherhood and Beyond.* Kolkata: Levant Books.

Kantilal, S. P. 2014. 'Single Mother: Problems and Challenges of Parenting in India', unpublished proceedings of the workshop on 'Issue of Single Women' organised by Ramniranjan Jhunjhunwala College of Arts of Science and Commerce, Mumbai.

Nautiyal, K. C. 1994. 'Single Women- A View Point', in Neshla (ed.) *Single Women in Indian Perspective*, Kurukshetra: Nirmal Book Agency.

Puradkar, R. A. P. 2014. 'Single Parenthood by Choice: A Challenge?' unpublished proceedings of the workshop on 'Issue of Single Women' organised by Ramniranjan Jhunjhunwala College of Arts of Science and Commerce, Mumbai.

Salaff, J. W. 1981. *Working Daughters of Hongkong: Filial Piety or Power in the Family.* Cambridge: Cambridge University Press.

Shikha, D.2009. *Single Women: Problem and Challenges*, Ph. D thesis in Sociology CCS University, Meerut, Shodhganga.inflibnet.ac.in/bitstream/10603/114235/16.

Stein, P. 1973. *Single in America*, Unpublished Manuscript, Rutgers University.

Stein, P. J. 1976. *Single*. Englewood Cliffes, N. J.: Prentice-Hall Inc.

Swarup, H. 1985. *Women must be trained for scientific society*, in *The Statesman*, 27 December.

Additional Sources:

http://journals.sagepub.com/doi/pdf/10.1177/0265407515607647

https://topyaps.com/7-common-problems-faced-single-ladies http://shodhganga.inflibnet.ac.in/bitstream/10603/114235/16/16_synopsis.pdf https://www.naaree.com/living-single-woman-in-india/

Chapter - 10

Rights of Motherhood for Maintenance under the Hindu Personal Law: A Critical Analysis

Sadhna Gupta

> *"Why can't a woman take charge of her destiny?*
> *Why does she have to wait alone by the roadside?*
> *Head bent, eyes forlorn, waiting for a miracle in the morrow?"*
> **- Rabindranath Tagore**

'All history attests that man has subjugated woman to his will, used her as a means to promote his self-gratification, to minister to his sensual pleasures, to be instrumental in promoting his comfort; but never has he desired to elevate her to that rank she was created to fill. He has done all he could to debase and enslave her mind; and now he looks triumphantly on the ruin he was wrought, and says, the being he has thus deeply injured is his inferior.... But I ask no favour for my sex.... All I ask our brethren is that they will take their feet off from our necks and permit us to stand upright on that ground which God designed us to occupy.'- **Sarah Grimke**[1]

Introduction

The issue of gender justice has been a concern for all, connected and concerned with equality and liberty, in many nations and for some centuries. Though laws enacted profess and mandate formal removal of institutionalised discrimination, yet the mind-set and the attitude ingrained in the subconscious and society have not been erased. Women still face all kinds of discrimination and prejudice. The days of yore when women treated as fragile, feeble, dependent and subordinate to men, should have been a matter of history, and effaced but it has not been so, as it seems. Gender equality and women empowerment are the call of the day and attempts are to be made to achieve satisfactory results. Everybody should be prepared to fight for the ideal and actualise the conceptual vision in practice[2]. Women have a unique position in society as they play different roles as daughter, wife, mother and sister. Inspite of her contribution in the life of every individual human being, she still belongs to a class which is in a disadvantaged position on account of several social barriers and impediments. On the one hand, she is held in high esteem by one and all, worshipped, considered as the embodiment of tolerance and virtue; on the other hand she has been the victim of untold miseries, hardships and atrocities caused and perpetuated by the male dominated society (Reddy, 2011).

In India, almost half of the population is women who have been always discriminated against and suffered in civilised as well as primitive society. Even though self-sacrifice and self-denial are their nobility and virtue, yet they have been made the victims of all inequalities, indignities, inequity and discrimination from time immemorial. One of the problems is maintenance as the woman has not been traditionally a bread winner, though more often than not she has been put to hard and even harsh works. The concept of maintenance could provide safety within a feudal property structure where property is inalienable. The history of women's right is not linear with the religious and customary laws. The rights are not only constrained by a uniform set of patriarchal norms but are also shaped and moulded by several social, economic and political currents. So, more accurately, within this complex framework, it has been a case of 'gain some, lose some' (Agnes, 2011). Mother includes being wife and no special law has been made so as to the rights of for maintenance. In order to live a stable life and support she requires maintenance for herself and her children. Various provisions have been made under the Hindu personal laws to get the maintenance and mother also can claim for maintenance under Section 125 of Cr. P.C. This paper attempts to examine the role of woman in motherhood and the rights of motherhood to maintenance under Hindu Law at various stages of life as wife, as divorced and as single mother[3]. The paper specifically highlights on the rights of mother who are Hindus and who can claim for the rights of maintenance under the Hindu Personal Laws.

Nature and Obligation of Maintenance

Marriage is the very foundation of any society for maintaining family peace and stability. It is to be considered as socially sacred institution. Marriage, according to the Hindu Law, is a holy union for the performance of religious duties. Marriage is not a contract but it is a *sanskar* or sacrament.[4] Hindu marriage protects a woman by guaranteeing her legal rights for restitution of conjugal rights in case of desertion[5], legitimacy of children and relief in case of cruelty[6], adultery[7], impotency, claim of maintenance and alimony[8] etc. Various statutes have been enacted to empower married woman under Hindu Laws to provide her protection through maintenance.

The right of maintenance arises from the concept of undivided family. The head of such a family is bound to maintain its members, their wives and their children. Maintenance includes food, clothing, shelter, as well as things necessary for the comfort and status in which the person entitled to be maintained can reasonably expect to live. The Hindu Adoption and Maintenance Act[9] defines maintenance as provision for food, clothing, residence, education and medical attendance and treatment[10]. The Act deals with the maintenance of wife under

Section 18, maintenance of widowed daughter-in-law under Section 18, maintenance of children and aged parents under Section 20. The term 'dependents' under Section 21 includes mother, widow, unmarried daughter, widowed daughter son's widow and minor illegitimate daughter etc.

The Parliament has passed The Hindu Adoption and Maintenance Act to amend and codify the law relating to adoptions and maintenance among the Hindus. Hence mother is entitled too for maintenance under such act by the husband and children as they are regarded to be dependents within the ambit of Section 21. Under the old Hindu Law a person was under personal obligation to maintain the wife, aged parents and minor children and under moral obligation to maintain other dependents of the family. The Act is not the only law that provides for maintenance but the Hindu Marriage Act provides for maintenance *pendent lite* in Section 24 and permanent alimony and maintenance under Section 25.

Nature and extent of the right to maintenance under the Hindu Adoption and Maintenance Act, 1956

(i) Maintenance of wife: Section 18 of the Act deals with the maintenance and separate residence of a wife. Prior to this Act the Hindu married women's Right to Separate Residence and Maintenance Act, 1946 was in force but this has now been repealed by Section 29 of the Hindu Adoptions and Maintenance Act, 1956 (Agarwal, 2006).This section confers statutory right on a Hindu wife to claim maintenance while living with the husband or living separately from the husband in certain cases.

- A Hindu wife whether married before or after the commencement of the Act shall be entitled to be maintained by her husband during her lifetime.
- A Hindu wife shall be entitled to live separately from her husband without forfeiting her claim for

maintenance: (a) if he is guilty of desertion, (b) if he has treated her with such cruelty as to cause a reasonable apprehension in her mind that it will be harmful to live with her husband, (c) if he is suffering from virulent form of leprosy, (d) if he has any other wife living, (e) if he keeps a concubine in the same house, (f) if he has ceased to be a Hindu by conversion to another religion, (g) if there is any other cause justifying her living separately.

The obligation of a Hindu male to maintain wife is personal and depends upon the relationship of the parties. The husband is liable to maintain his wife if he is capable of earning. He cannot plead that he is unable to maintain her due to financial constraints.[11] If the petition of the husband filed under the provisions of Section 9 to Section 14 of the Hindu Marriage Act 1955[12], no alimony can be granted to the wife under Section 25 of the Hindu Marriage Act. However, maintenance can be claimed by her under Section 18(1) of the Hindu Adoptions and Maintenance Act, 1956 or under Section 125 Code of Criminal Procedure[13].

(ii) Maintenance of widowed daughter-in-law: According to Section 19 of the Act, a Hindu wife is entitled to be maintained after the death of her husband by her father-in-law. It is immaterial whether her marriage took place prior to this enactment for availing this benefit. However, her right is not absolute and it depends on the following factors:

- She must not be able to maintain herself out of her own earnings or other property; or
- She has no property of her own; or
- She is not able to obtain maintenance either from estate of her husband or her parents or her children.

In fact, it was moral obligation of the father-in-law to maintain the widow daughter-in-law under the old law. Later this was made as a legal obligation under Section 19 of the Act.

She forfeits her right to maintenance either on her re-marriage or either she obtains a share in her coparcenary properties. *Raj Kishore Mishra vs. Meena Mishra*[14], was an appeal case where it was held that liability of the father-in-law to maintain daughter-in-law arises from statutory provisions contained under Section 19 of the Act. It has also been said that obligation of father-in-law shall not be enforceable if the father-in-law has not the means to do so from any coparcenary property in his passion out of which the daughter-in-law has not obtained any share.

The object of this section is to make it clear that the widowed daughter-in-law can claim maintenance from her father-in-law only where she is unable to maintain herself out of her own property or from the estate of her husband, father, mother, son or daughter. It is also provided that the father-in-law shall be under no obligation to maintain his daughter-in-law except in cases where there is some ancestral property in his possession from which the daughter-in-law has not obtained any share.

(iii) Right to maintenance of wife/mother of Joint Family Property: It is important to note that the right to maintenance of a wife or mother cannot be exercised in respect of the husband or son's share in the joint family property. The Supreme Court of India emphatically declared that, that neither under the customary Hindu law, nor under the Hindu Succession Act, 1956, nor under the Hindu Marriage Act, 1955 nor under the Hindu Adoption and Maintenance Act, 1956 is there any provision which gives a share to a wife in the joint family property held by her husband nor to the mother in the joint family property allotted to her son in the partition.[15] Thus, the right of the mother or wife to maintenance is a personal right.

The Hindu Succession Act, 1956 was amended in 2005 [The Hindu Succession (Amendment) Act, 2005 (39 of 2005)] conferring coparcener property rights in favour of the daughters under the Hindu personal laws. The earlier Law (HAS) has conferred coparcener rights upon the male members only. This has altered the fundamental framework of *Mitakshara* coparcener and a daughter is now inter alia capable of acquiring an interest in the coparcener property, of demanding a partition of the same, and to dispose of the same through the testamentary disposition[16]. The HAS, 1956 conferred limited rights upon those members of joint family who entered into it through marriage, whereas the 2005 Amendment confers coparcener rights upon those members who are born in the family and, therefore, they enjoy coparcenary property rights by birth. Those members who enter into joint family through marriage enjoy rights which are restricted to maintenance out of the funds, rights of residence in the family house etc[17].

Maintenance under Section 24 of HMA Alimony, *pendent lite* and expense of proceedings:

> The rational behind this section is to enable the wife as the case may be who has no independent income to provide the other so that the proceedings may be conducted and she may be maintained the pendency of the proceedings may not be handicapped[18]. Alimony is the financial provision to a wife from her husband while she was obliged to live apart from him. It might be awarded temporarily *pendent lite*, pending the outcome of the matrimonial cause between the spouses. The amount is at the court's discretion. After the decree of judicial separation alimony became a permanent allowance which continued for the whole period of separation. A wife's allowance is now called maintenance and is a permanent financial provision (Walker, 1984).

After reading Section 24 it becomes clear that the section empowers the court to grant two specific reliefs to the petitioner.

They are:

(a) Expenses of the proceedings in respect of which the relief is sought, and
(b) Monthly maintenance allowance during the proceedings.

The relief of maintenance is available during the pendency of substantive proceedings under this Act and it comes to an end when the proceedings are over. While awarding maintenance *pendent lite* the court has to see the following as required by Section 24 of Hindu Marriage Act:

(a) status of the parties;
(b) reasonable wants of the claimant;
(c) income and property of the claimant;
(d) number of persons to be maintained by husband;
(e) the amount required by the wife to live in a similar lifestyle as she enjoyed in the matrimonial home keeping in view food, clothing, shelter, education and medical needs of the wife and the children, if any, residing with the wife; and
(f) paying capacity of the husband.[19]

Section 25 is welfare legislation and provides for permanent alimony and maintenance. Maintenance would include right to residence. Wife cannot be denied right of residence in the matrimonial home. On the application of either spouse, the court may pass an order for permanent alimony and maintenance:

(a) at the time of passing of the decree granting the petition, or
(b) at any time after the passing of the decree granting the petition[20].

When a claim of permanent alimony and maintenance is made after the passing of the decree, it should be done by a petition in the court which granted the petition.

Rights of maintenance to father/mother through Code of Criminal Procedure (Amendment) Act, 2001: The Code of Criminal Procedure, 1973, a secular code, provides a comprehensive scheme for the maintenance of wife, children and aged parents. The provisions are contained in Sections 125-128 Cr.P.C. The proceedings under this section are not punitive but of civil nature. The remedies provided under the sections are in the nature of civil rights. The objective is to provide speedy justice. This provision for maintenance of mother or father who may not be able to maintain her or himself is new. A father is entitled to maintenance if he is unable to maintain himself. This is a statutory obligation and cannot be defeated by pleading that the father had failed to fulfill his parental obligation towards children during their minority.

After the conflicting opinions of various High Courts it was held in *Karodiben vs. Rajubhai Mahendra Singh*[21], that a stepmother is not entitled to claim maintenance. But where a mother stays with one son it was held, in *Shanmugam vs. Potiammal*[22], that she is entitled to maintenance from the other son who is in possession of the joint family property.

Role of Indian Judiciary as to Maintenance

It is clear from the forgoing discussion that though, over a period of time, improved rights are bestowed upon Indian Hindu women, the rights available to them do not match with the rights required (Parashar, 1992). In this context Indian judiciary is found to be ambivalent. This conclusion is fortified in *Masilamani Mudliar vs. Idol of Sri Swaminathswamithirukoli* where the Supreme Court came to the conclusion that the personal laws, to the extent they are in violation of the fundamental rights, are nothing but void[23]. The High Court of Calcutta in *Sisir Kumar vs. Sabita Rani*[24] showed the strict behaviour of judiciary toward the aggrieved spouse. In the matter of implementing the provisions of the Act, the technicalities of the provisions must be left to some extent.

Another case *Amit Kumar Sharma vs. VIth Additional District Session Judge Bijnor*[25], pointed out whether the wife can seek maintenance for husband's mother who needs to be taken care of under the same application for maintenance under Section 25 when mother is staying with her. Here the court has taken very rigid and technical view and ordered the old mother to file separate claim under Criminal Procedure Code, 1973 or under Section 20 of the Hindu Adoption and Maintenance Act, 1956.

Conclusion

A woman in our country belongs to a class of society which is in a disadvantaged position on account of several social barriers and impediments. The existing maintenance statutes in India are disparate, chaotic and scattered (Sivaramayya, 1999) and are not based on the concept of equal economic partnership of the husband and wife but on the concept of maintenance as gratis or at the best an act of compassion[26]. On the contrary, it is the wife who sacrifices her future career and serves the husband, their children and sick and infirm parents-in-law. There should be no bias in favour of the money-earner against the home-maker and the child-carer. Today there is greater awareness of the value of non-financial contributions to the welfare of the family, that is by being at home and having looked after young children a wife may lose forever the opportunity to acquire and develop her own career. Understanding the rights of motherhood under the above backdrop it is realised that a wife is mother and that she is entitled to the rights of maintenance. She is entitled for the maintenance during the pendency of the proceedings and also has sufficient fund to defend and carry on the litigation so that the spouse does not unduly suffer in conduct of the case for wants of funds. The plight of the mothers in the house of their sons is sometimes miserable. What was once their home is taken over by the sons where the daughters-in-law rule over them. The mother ends up as cooks, *ayas* and caretakers.

At times she is separated too. Therefore, the Personal Law of Hindus helps these helpless mothers to claim for the maintenance which is brought in consonance with our social needs. Under the concept of motherhood a mother is entitled for maintenance under Section 125 of Cr.P.C. where the primary objective is to provide social justice to women.

Notes

1. Sarah, M. Grimke. *Letter on the Equality of Sexes and the Condition of Woman*, Boston: Issac Kanapp, 1838, reprinted by Source Book Press, New York, p. 10ff.
2. Nyaya Deep, *The official Journal of NALSA*. Volume XVI. Issue 2 April 2015.
3. Reddy, Dr. G B. "Women and the Law", 2011, Gogia Law Agency, Hyderabad pp. 3-8.
4. Agnes Flavia, *Law and Gender Inequality*, 2011, Oxford University Press, pp. 203-204.
5. 125 of Cr.P.C. and section 18 of Hindu Adoption and Maintenance Act 1956.
6. Desai, Satyajeet Atul, Sir Dinshah Fardunji Mulla, *Principles of Hindu Law*, Volume I (20th ed.), New Delhi, Lexis Nexis Butterworths, 2007 at pg. 9.
7. Section 9 of Hindu Marriage Act, 1955.
8. Section 13(1) (ia) of Hindu Marriage Act, 1955 and 498A of Indian Penal Code 1960.
9. Section 13(1)(i) of Hindu Marriage Act, 1955.
10. Section 24 and 25 of Hindu Marriage Act, 1955.
11. The Act received the assent of the President on December 21, 1956 and therefore it shall be deemed to have come into force on that date.
12. Section 3(b) of the Act.
13. Agarwal, R. K. "*Hindu Law*", edn. 2006, Central Law Agency, pp. 110-119.
14. Kirtikant, D. Vadodariavs. State of Gujrat, (1996) 4SCC 479-A.
15. Section 9 to 14 of the Hindu Marriage Act 1955 deals with the provisions of –Section 9(- Restitution for Congugal Rights), Section 10 (Judicial Separation), Section 13 (Divorce), Section 13B (Mutual Divorce), Section 14(No petition of divorce to be presented before expiry of one year of divorce).

16. *Chand Dhawan vs. Jawaharlal Dhawan,* (1993) 3SCC 406.
17. AIR 1995 All 70.
18. A.G. *Varadarajulu vs. State of Tamil Nadu* (1998) 4SCC 231.
19. Ms. Indira Jaisingh, "Mapping Women's Gains in Inheritance and Property Rights under the Hindu Succession Act, 1956", Lawyers Collective Women's Rights Initiative, p. 35. Available at http://www.lawyers collective.org/files
20. http://lawcommission ofindia.nic.in/reports/on rights of the Hindu Wife to Maintenance: A relook at section 18 of the Hindu Adoption and Maintenance Act, 1956pdf.Para 3.2
21. *Rukhmanibai vs. Kishanlal Ramlal*, AIR 1959 MP 187.
22. Walker, D. M. *Oxford Companion to Law*; pp. 48-49.
23. *Alok Kumar Jain vs. Purnima Jain,* 2007 SCC Online Del 561(2007).
24. *Mummuswami vs. Hansa* (1974) 2 MLJ 237.
25. 1997(4) Crimes 259 (Guj).
26. 1996 Cri L J 2984 (Mad).

References

Agarwal, R.K. 2006. *Hindu Law.* Kerala: Central Law Agency.

Agnes, F. 2011. *Law and Gender Inequality*. New Delhi: Oxford University Press.

Parashar, A. 1992. *Women and Family Reform India*. New Delhi: Sage Publications.

Reddy, G.B. 2011. *Women and the Law*. Hyderabad: Gogia Law Agency.

Sivaramayya, B. 1999. *Matrimonial Property Law in India*. New Delhi: Oxford University Press.

Walker, D.M. 1984. *Oxford Companion to Law*. Cambridge: Cambridge University Press.

Chapter - 11

Queering Motherhood: Beyond the Biological Interpretation

Reshmi Chakraborty

Motherhood is not uniform all over the world. Human life starts within the womb of a mother. Mother plays of crucial role in a child's life. Mother is the only person who cares for the child not only after the birth of the child rather she cares before the birth also. In our Indian society motherhood is a glorification of mother-child relationship. At the same time motherhood is very much related to the womanhood. Every society has some mind-set about social phenomena; motherhood and gender are not the exceptional. It is thought that motherhood is a special domain of woman. The status of a married woman has been highlighted by the society depending on her capability of child bearing. But mother and motherhood are not confined to the binary of gender. Rather it is beyond gender, it is all about care, nurture, love, affection and sense of responsibility towards children.

If we go through our Hindu mythologies, there are ample references of queer personalities with their distinct stories which break the socially constructed stereotyped design. One of them is the story of Ayyappan. Ayyappan is very popular in Kerala and recently controversial for the 'Sabarimala' incident. He is the Hindu god of growth. He is the son of Lord Shiva and Mohini- the female avatar of Lord Vishnu. Ayyappan is also referred to as Ayyappa, Sastavu, Hariharaputra, Manikanta, *Shasta* or *Dharma Shasta* (Chandra, 2001).

Another famous character of Hinduism is the Goddesses Parvati, the wife of Lord Shiva. They have three children namely, Kartikeya, Alokasundari and Ganesha. She is not the biological mother of their children. Every child has unique story related to his or her origin. One of the famous stories is the birth of Ganesha. Once, at the time of taking bath Parvati created an image of a boy out of turmeric paste which she prepared for cleaning and purifying her body and inculcated life into it, and thus Ganesha was born (Brown, 1991).

Not only in mythology at the same time in the long trajectory of human civilisation the concepts of mother and motherhood have also been changing along with its nature, context and connotation. Now motherhood is not confined only for woman or biological mother rather it extends its wings beyond the gender identity and biological limitations. Today we are talking about lesbian motherhood, adoptee motherhood, foster motherhood, transgender or *Hijra* motherhood; all of which depict the queer nature of mothering.

Generally sex and gender are two related concepts we always jumble but both have their distinct meanings. Sex is a biological instinct and a child takes birth with some physical characteristics and through the process of socialisation his/her gender identity gets a shape in the name of masculinity or femininity. Gender is a socially constructed phenomenon and there are some stereotype idealisations about gender roles in a society. At the same time some people also spend their life crossing the boundary of male-female binaries. *Hijra* is one of them.

Queer theory was developed in mid-1980s through the work of Michel Foucault. This theory has tried to analyse the usefulness of gendered binary distinctions and re-examines the issue of the centralisation of heterosexuality (Pilcher, 2009). Indian society is patriarchal in nature and it approves heterosexuality where homosexuality has been treated as a deviance. But there are many people who enjoy their sexuality in their own ways beyond the binary division of gender and queer theory also focuses on them.

The word 'queer' denotes the displacement of sexual identity from its gender identity. Butler describes it as '...sexual crossing, mixing up multiple or at least more than one identity pathway...' (Butler, 2008: 105).

In this paper the writer has used the term 'queering motherhood' as a disjunction of the context of motherhood from the concept of womanhood. Motherhood is not a static phenomenon. It has cosmic connotations all over the civilisation. At the same time it is not limited to gender identities. The famous Indian transgender activist Gauri Sawant expresses her views on the notion of motherhood as, 'Motherhood is beyond gender, motherhood is a behaviour'.

Hijra is an Indian professional group of transgenders who have a distinct way of life. This group is also seen in Bangladesh and Pakistan. Basically a *hijra* is considered neither as a man nor as a woman. They born as a male, but their feminine attitudes make them different. They are also known as transgender. It is an umbrella term including many other sexual minorities like lesbian, gay, bisexual, and transsexual. It is known as LGBT community. But there is a sharp difference between the *hijra* and transgender. All *hijras* are transgender by nature. But all transgenders are reversely not *hijra*. The *hijra*s are the few transgender who sustain their livelihood depending on *hijra* profession.

Hijra identity may lie closest to the western transsexual identity. Many of them consider themselves of having born in the wrong body with the wrong sex (Kalra, 2012).

The original meaning of *hijra* in Urdu and Hindi is eunuch or hermaphrodite. The word *hijra* implies a sort of impotency and an inability to perform a male sexual role (Nanda, 1999; Rehan, 2011). A *hijra* is someone who is feminine but not a complete woman, masculine but not a complete man, remaining beyond the dichotomy of man and woman. The person follows the rigid rules and regulations of the community, having a *guru,* lives in feminine attire, may or may not be castrated (Chettiar, 2015).

Guru Maa plays a vital role in *hijra*s' life. She is the teacher and the philosopher who guides the new *hijra*s. *Hijra*s learn the behaviour as well as the ways of sustaining life from their *Guru Maa*. In Indian philosophy '*Guru-Sisya*' tradition is not a new one. It is an age-old traditional system of learning where *guru* gets honourary position in society.

The Western mind finds it difficult to submit with total and unquestioning surrender to the *Guru*. That is why generally it is advised to find the guidance and the presence within themselves; it is true that this process is very often open to uncertainty and self-deception, mistaking some voice of the ego in disguise for the Divine's guidance.... When the two meet, he who knows and he who wants to know, there springs up a new hope in the world, and a little light penetrates the prevailing darkness (Collected Works, 2004).

II

Motherhood talks about mother-child relationship. The attachment between mother with her child is something which is impossible to depict in a single word. The divineness of this relationship is a universal one.

The present paper is trying to analyse the motherhood experiences of the *hijra*s as foster mothers in their everyday life beyond their existence in community. At the same time the researcher refers to a case study on the 'Vicks' advertisement about motherhood and discusses the life story of Gauri Sawant based on her various interviews available in social media. It is purely a qualitative study emphasising on a few case studies.

The paper also focuses on the caring attitudes of the *hijra*s towards their parents and other family members with all of their hardships. All fifty data have been collected from various parts of North 24 Parganas, Nadia and Hooghly - three districts of West Bengal. Samples are selected by using snow-ball sampling method.

In this study, 58% respondents belong to several places of North 24 Parganas, 34% respondents belong to three different places of Nadia and 8% respondents belong to Hooghly district.

III

The *hijras* refuse the 'socially set identities' of genders and create a new one which is mixture of multiple identities. They have to face a long struggle throughout their life to know their identity in this stratified complex social panorama. They live their life in a different way. Here the writer has focused on three cases where the *hijra*s are acted as foster mothers.

According to Child Welfare League of America:

> 'Foster family care offers the child who otherwise lacks adequate parental care and who cannot remain in his own home a closer approximation to normal family living than other types of substitute care, and is particularly adapted to meet the child's normal developmental needs in a family-centred society. Foster family care should provide, for the child whose parents cannot do so, experiences and conditions which promote normal maturation (care), which prevent further injury to the child (protection), and which correct specific problems which interfere with healthy personality development (treatment)' (cited in Fanshel, 1966: 3-4).

Now in this 21st century social media creates a great impact on society. Media has the power to articulate social massages towards the mass. Recently an advertisement of 'Vicks' makes a new essence of mothering where a teenage girl speaks her feelings about her mother. The advertisement shows one girl is travelling and thinking about her mother who wants to make her a doctor. The mother takes care when the baby girl becomes ill and nurtures her with love. The three and half minute's advertisement depicts the beauty of mother-child bond. But the mother is not her biological mother. At the same time she is neither a man nor a woman rather a 'transwoman' (who changes herself from male to female through SRS) named as Gauri Sawant.

Gauri Sawant was born as a male child in a middle class Maharashtrian family. He had an elder sister and his parents were happy to have a son after a girl. But at very little age he lost his mother and after a few years his father noticed that the boy was not behaving like a boy. He did not understand the reason and kicked out him from his family. Basically he was a male child biologically but mentally he was feminine. He came to Mumbai from Pune and joined in a *hijra* community for earning. But he liked to identify himself as a transgender not as a *hijra* and he changed himself from male to female following medical procedures known as SRS (Sex Reassignment Surgery). He had to face lots of trouble, stigma and harassments in his life for his feminine behaviour. In this paper the writer has addressed Gauri Sawant using feminine terminology, though earlier Gauri Sawant was born as a male in his family. Gauri Sawant is her new name adopted after changing himself from male to female.

Being a transgender, she worked for female sex workers regarding their health issues under a NGO. One day at noon one sex worker asked her to bring some pickle to her and she gave it to her. After five years of this incident one day she came to know about the death of that lady and about the little girl child she had. Immediately Gauri went to their clumsy house. There she saw that after the death of her mother, the local pimp of that area wanted to sell the girl child at 'Sonagachhi', popular redlight area of Kolkata. Suddenly Gauri felt mother like emotions and took that girl with her. When she returned her *Khol* (a house where *hijras* live together) with the child, her *Guru Maa* rebuked her but she determined to keep the child with her. The mother-child bonding started from that day and now the child named as Gayetri is known as the daughter of Gauri Sawant, first transgender mother of India.

According to Gauri, motherhood is not only limited to giving birth to a child rather it is an emotional transmission of love and care to her baby. This state of condition changes her life and since then a new journey starts for her. During that period one of his well wishers has wrote an article on her. Her life got a paradigm shift in the year 2014 when she was approached for the advertisement of 'Vicks'. That advertisement changed her life, people started to recognise her and she came into the limelight and got the acceptance by the society. This adopted child changed her life and she became a mother slowly beyond her profession, beyond her sexuality.

After that, one day when she was working in a redlight area in Mumbai named as Kamatipura, she saw a lady was engaged with sex work in front of her child. The child was playing with mother's *Aachol* (a part of cloth). Gauri was speechless and shocked. Immediately she took the child and returned home. She interacted with her *Guru Maa*.

It is a common belief that the children of sex workers generally become sex workers in future. But she understands the harsh truth of her life that a red light area is not the safe place for the upbringing of the children. So she convinces her *Guru Maa* to understand the fact that they are not only feminine in nature but they also wear feminine clothes outwardly and biologically they want to be females. It is the great opportunity to them for fulfilling their femininity and to build a separate place 'Aaji ka Ghar' a place for the abundant children. There the old transgender persons are trying to give a safe shelter and secure childhood to the abundant children. This home makes them happy to becoming mother and they enjoy the emotions of motherhood.

This picture has also seen in the study done by the writer where three *hijra*s acted as foster mother. They try to give them good education and a better social life which they never achieved in their life. They cannot adopt children legally but they nurture children and the children live with them. One of them is Bobi *Hijra* (70 years old) who has adopted (socially) a girl by taking care of her. She has made her educated and finally arranged her marriage. Another case is of Basanti *Hijra* (55 years old). She has also adopted (socially) a boy and now the boy is going to complete his masters degree. Another is Puja *Hijra* (60 years old). She has adopted (socially) a girl child. The child lives with her in her *Khol* and reads in class IX. When all *hijra*s come to Puja's house in the evening and they have fun in the first floor of the house, and during that time the girl is not allowed to come. Otherwise throughout the day she lives freely with them.

Not only as foster mothers but as biological children of their families these *hijra*s are continuously playing their role towards their parents and members of the families with their own adversity and struggle. Motherhood speaks about mother-child relationship. Early descriptions are all talking about the role and duty of the mothers towards their children. But we cannot deny the role of the children towards their parents.

There is a widespread belief that male children take all liability of the parents in their old age. They are the future support of their parents. Culturally male children get some extra advantages from the society. They enjoy the right to perform the funeral rituals and to gain *Mokhsha* (salvation). But being a *hijra*, these males are treated differently by the mainstream society. They have to face lots of adversity throughout their life. But still they are supportive to their parents. They play feminine roles and cook for their parents, take care of them, clean their houses and clothes and at the same time take all economic burdens (according to traditional thought). They also take care of their brothers, sisters and other family members.

Table 1: Nature of Relationship of the *Hijra*s with their family

Sl. No.	*Nature of Relationship*	*No. of Respondents*
1.	Good	10 (20.00)
2.	Medium	05 (10.00)
3.	Bad	03 (06.00)
4.	No relation	04 (08.00)
5.	Initially bad but now good	16 (32.00)
6.	Initially bad but now medium	12 (24.00)
	Total	50 (100.00)

All the figures in parentheses indicate percentages.

Table 1 depicts the nature of relationship of the *hijra*s with their family. It has been seen that majority of the respondents i.e., 56% have a bad relation with their family previously. But when they started earning they could help their family financially and gradually the relationship turned into positive direction. 32% respondents have said that they have a good relation now and 24% respondents have opined that they have a relationship which is not so good but medium with their family members. Table 2 also shows that there are 20% *hijra*s who have a good relationship with their family from the beginning, whereas 10% *hijra*s have a medium relationship with their family. At the same time 8% *hijra*s have no relation with their family and 6% *hijra*s have a bad relation with their family.

But it is surprising that from these 6% *hijra*s, one *hijra* gives money to her father every month and her father takes it for sustaining the livelihood but does not accept her in his family.

She is not allowed to get entry in her father's house. She lives in a rented house. Her father gave all the property to her elder brother and after that the elder brother kicked his father out of his house. Now father lives with his sister and the resopndent regularly gives money to fulfil all the needs and medical expenditure for her father.

The study also reveals that 88% *hijra*s take all the responsibilities of their parents and other family members. They like to take care of their old parents. They arrange their sisters' marriage. Many of them help their brothers in their family expenses. But at the same time, these *hijra*s are not well accepted in their families. On the other hand the family members do not take care of them and feel embarrassed for them. It is an irony.

In this study few cases are there which can reveal this caring attitude more accurately:

- Mina *Hijra* has brought up her brothers. Now her brothers are all married and their children are very close to Mina. They live with Mina and she takes all responsibility of their education.
- Another is Keya *Hijra*, who lives with her mother. She has one elder sister. She arranges her sister's marriage with dowry and other demands. But after marriage she gave birth to a girl child and due to this, her in-laws murdered her. After her death, now Keya nurtures that girl.
- Nita *Hijra* lives with her brother. Her parents died few years ago. Her brother loves to play football and she supports him.

Other *hijra*s have their own life history also. In this way, these queer persons spend their life and perform all duties towards their family.

Actually the society does not accept the *hijra*s. The society creates pressures on the families. Due to the continuous pressure of the kin groups and neighbours, the parents and the family members become impatient to the concerned *hijra*s (transgender also).

IV

Birth of a child is an important and glorious occasion of family life in India. If the child is a male child then the happiness becomes more as the society is patriarchal in nature and till today male child is more desirable than a female child. Generally a *hijra* is born as a male. But as he grows up, his behavioural pattern changes. These male children are biologically male but they think and pretend themselves as females.

Their feminine attitudes make them caring and develop the courage to become mother. They cannot deny the impulse of motherhood within themselves. It is beyond their professional role, beyond the *hijragiri* or shamelessness which they do for their profession for earning and create a stereotyped image within the community. But they have some instinctual unconditional love and affection for the children which they miss throughout their life. Mother-child relationship is the most lovable relationship which exists in their community to get relaxation in their life.

In recent years, transgender people around the world have made tremendous strides toward achieving legal recognition. The right to get recognition as a person before the law is guaranteed by numerous human rights treaties which are fundamental aspects of affirming the dignity and worth of each person.

The unique lifestyles and typical behaviour patterns of the *hijra*s are not accepted in the prescribed and perceived gender norms which become the source of discrimination, harassment and violence in their life. Hence they are socially ostracised and become identified as 'others'. They claim to be neither male nor female and are placed at the extreme boundary of social exclusion because of various socio-economic factors.

This study reveals that mother-child relationship is beyond the gender identity. Even 'trans' (*hijra*) performs all the duties towards his/her parents and family. So this mother-child relationship and the duties of the children towards their parents are very common and worldwide. The *hijras* are not an exception. They are the part and parcel of the society being a human being. So gender should not be restricted only to the earlier binary concepts. They should be recognised as human beings with worth and love by others.

References

Brown, L. R. 1991. *Ganesh: Studies of an Asian God.* Albeny: State University of New York Press.

Butler. W. 2008. 'Queering Gender/Queer Feminism', in Beasley, C. (Ed.): *Gender and Sexuality: Critical Theories, Critical Thinkers.* New Delhi: Sage Publication.

Chandra. S. 2001. *Encyclopaedia of Hindu God and Goddesses.* New Delhi: Sarup & Sons.

Chettiar, A. 2015. 'Problems Faced by *Hijras* (Male to Female Transgenders) in Mumbai with Reference to Their Health and Harassment by the Police'. *International Journal of Social Science and Humanity.* Vol. 5, No. 9.

Collected Works. 2004. *'The Mother: Words of the Mother'*, Second Edition. Pondicherry: Sri Aurobindo Ashram Publication Department.

Fanshel, D. 1966. *Foster Parenthood: A Role Analysis.* Minneapolis: University of Minnesota Press.

Kalra, G. 2012. '*Hijras*: the unique transgender culture in India', *International Journal of Culture and Mental Health*, Routledge Publication, Vol. 5: 121-126.

Nanda, S. 1999. *Neither Man Nor Woman.* Canada: Wadsworth Publishing Company.

Pilcher, J. & Whelehan, I. 2009. *Fifty Key Concepts in Gender Studies.* New Delhi: SAGE.

Rehan, N. 2011. 'Socio-sexual Behaviour of *Hijras* of Lahore', *Journal of Pakistan Medical Association*, Vol. 61.

Chapter - 12

Experiencing 'Motherhood' and the Challenges of the Eunuchs

Dibakar Bera

Motherhood has been crystallised as a social institution from the beginning of civilisation and the mothers are all in all of it. A new born is reared in this institution and becomes an individual member of the society. Mother as the supreme commander plays a vital role in this accomplishment. So motherhood completes the claim of femininity. The study explores how motherhood is perceived by the eunuchs who cannot be biological mothers owing to their distinctive physiological features. Does motherhood in this marginalised group bear the same meaning as to the others? In Indian society there are a bunch of socially marginalised groups, suffering from a lot of social and economic problems. The eunuchs are marginalised section of population who are not allowed to participate in the social affairs of others. Sometimes they are also labeled as vulnerable communities due to their sexual ambiguities. In the relationship between *Guru* and *Chela*, *Gurus* are often equated with mothers of *Chelas* but *Guru Ma* is not the biological mother of her *Chelas*. Because of the absence of womb they are unable to give birth to a child. But they want to overcome this challenge by embracing the notion of motherhood with a bit of different connotations.

In sociology it is perceived that the difference between the East and West is mainly based on culture including customs, values, education and so on. The major difference between the East and West is that people in the East are considered as more conservative and traditional than the people in the West. It can be noted through their behaviour and attitudes. People of the East are more customary in following traditions, clothing, and rituals. They are inflexible in their beliefs and ideologies and unwilling to challenge their customs and traditions. For example, Indians pay regards to their parents by touching their feet.

The people of the Western countries are more liberal and open. They are more free to express their feelings. A person there is more flexible and free to take decisions on his own. For example, topics like sex, birth of a child are openly discussed in Western society. Markas and Kitayama (1991) argue that people in different parts of the world tend to construe themselves in two different ways. Western cultures generally do not construct an independent view of the self as bounded, unitary, stable and separate from the social context, whereas cultures in other parts of the world portray interdependent view of the self as closely connected to others, fluid, and contextually embedded.

The parenting style is also different. In the West, independence of a child starts from very early age. Children do not sleep with their parents from the early days. A separate room is marked for them. Meals are usually placed in the front of the children to allow them to interact with others. But in some other parts of the world the scenario is a bit opposite. Parents in the East follow what they have learnt from their parents, which are reflected to bring up their children. They generally see the need to feed their children, teach them to adhere to stricter routines. For that, they do not get opportunities to develop their motor skills. The mothers do not allow their children to play in the dirt or mud. They meet and chat while their children play in a home or outside the home. But in the era of globalisation, family interactions are constantly changing by education, media and technology, which affect the eastern parenting styles. Some parents opt to raise their children liberally and have sent their sons and daughters to study in the Western schools.

Motherhood as a social institution

The history of social institutions cannot be traced from their very beginning. Sociologists agree that institutions arise and persist because of a definite felt-need of a society. Like family, marriage and kinship, motherhood also serves a vital role as a social institution. This institution constitutes mother and their children. Mother has some functions or duties to perform for their children which are prescribed by society.

Motherhood has been crystallised as a social institution from the beginning of civilisation. The main functions of this institution are to give birth of the children and nurturing them in the best possible way. The mothers are all in all of it. The word 'mother' is a small one. In Bengali, it is '*ma*' that constitutes only two letters but its significance is wide. According to Mead, mother is the most significant among the significant others.

If motherhood is like a laboratory, mother is a researcher doing research on different challenges. They are busy to nourish their children. She does not know when she would sleep. From feeding to bathing, clothing to sleeping - all are done by the mother. Let us quote here the famous remarks of Sanjib Chottopadhaya, a Bengal Novelist '*Banyera bone sundar, sisura matri crore*'. It should also be noted here, the famous remarks of former President of India Dr. A.P.J. Abdul Kalam to a question asked by BBC World: what is a birthday? The answer given by Dr. Abdul Kalam was 'The only one day in life, your mother smiled when you cried...otherwise whenever you cry your mother also cries'.

If we consider it as a job, then how much salary is paid to the mother? But it is interesting that their salary is not paid. Nancy Chodorow in her book *The Reproduction of Mothering* explores why women choose to be a mother. She rejects the idea that mothering is an innate, natural instinct, and equally discards the idea that it is merely the result of social conditioning, that means women has a free choice in the matter of whether to be a mother. At this juncture, we can say that a woman becomes a mother on her own will. So a woman rejoices to become a mother. It is true that when a woman develops some problem to conceive a child and cannot become a mother she suffers from mental deprivation.

Is motherhood in crisis today?

Now we are in a post-modern era. In this post-modern society, we are busy to fulfill our own needs and desire following the patterns of the consumer culture. We can say that it is a schizoid desire. Social scientists tried to highlight the changing nature of the society. According to them, traditional social forms, such as kinship systems, customs, and religious beliefs and so on swept away. They refer to this process as 'deteritorialisation' of social codes.

Here, the study highlights the desire of the mothers in this post-modern society. It is schizoid in the sense that now-a-days most of the women are reluctant to obey their duties as a mother. Some women are not interested to become a mother. While some women become mothers but are not interested in raring and caring of their children. They appoint a caretaker for raring their children or send their children daycare centres. Even some women want to stay unmarried to avoid these troubles.

In the case of working mothers it is quite considerable. Because in this highly expensive world it is necessary to earn money by both father and mother. That does not mean as a mother she evades her duties to their children. The children face several cognitive and behavioural effects for maternal employment during their childhood or early development. This affects their school performance, participation in extracurricular activities and normal behavioural practices. Even in some cases it might be positive. Because with increased financial earning families are able to provide much more such as healthcare, nutrition, educational opportunities and so on for their children.

But now-a-days in most of the cases, women are busy with their passions such as to join parties, attend social occasions and go to long trips leaving their children. They forget that she is a mother and has a child or children. 'Scary Mother' a Hollywood movie, directed by Ana Urushadze, highlighted a 50 years old housewife who struggles with her dilemma between her family life and passion (writing). She is repressed for years and decides to follow her passion and plunges herself into writing, sacrificing to it mentally and physically.

Here, this study also highlights examples of mothers who behave in rude ways with their children. In recent time, an American mother went to a long trip leaving her four children in a closed home (*Eisamay*, 1 Oct, 2017). Some mothers killed their children due to extra marital or illegal relationships (Nadiara, Purulia, 2014, *Anandabazar Patrika*, 19 July, 2017). Even in some cases, mothers are not interested to take their children to a party or to a trip. Very interestingly, their logic is that child is very naughty. Children are always naughty. It is their natural instinct. Then, why and how does a mother claim this? Even some mothers do not give breast feed to their children because of their misconception is that they would lose their beauty. It is also found that some mothers behave badly with their girl child although she herself is a female.

In this post-modern era, we are dependent on modern technology such as mobile network, social media etc.

We are busy with social media throughout the day. Mothers also remain busy with social media and forget their responsibilities of their children. There is a joke that such a child wants to be a mobile. Because he feels that his mother loves her mobile more than him. He feels that his mother at once runs to receive the call when mobile rings. For that some children had died due to lack of responsibilities of mother to their children. Children fell into a pond or well or hot water at the time when mothers were busy with social media or mega serial.

Reverse also occurred there. Children also behave with their mothers a rude way. It is questionable that how a child behaves to their mothers by whom they become an individual of society. Mother is our first teacher from whom we learn and know about the world. The study also highlighted some example of son's /daughter's rude behaviour to their mother. In recent time, a policeman threw his aged mother from the home (*Sangbad Pratidin*, 14 Oct, 2017). It is unimaginable when a son raped his own mother. A 45 years old son raped his 70 years old mother regularly (ABP Ananda, 18 Sept, 2017).

Notion of Mother in Eunuch Community

Unity in diversity is the most prominent feature in India. Gender diversity is also present there. There is a bunch of gender categories. Eunuchs are one of them, known as the third gender. They are marginalised because their identity is not clear. In Indian context as well as in South Asia, eunuchs are known as *hijras*. Eunuchs have the unique gender identity and have a long history in Indian subcontinent (Nanda, 1986; Reddy, 2003). Therefore, they are uncomfortable being identified as males or females, but want a separate category as a '*third gender*' (Herdt, 1993; Nanda, 2000; Reddy, 2003). They are facing a lot of problems such as identity crisis, poverty, illness and so on due to their sexual ambiguities. They are known as intersex, neither men nor women.

There is a popular perception that they have a different type of sex organ. But the truth is different. There are three types of eunuchs: (a) Those that are born with sexual ambiguities. But the exaple of such persons having genetic root of the problem is very rare. (b) Castrated males (the number of castrated females is very few). (c) Physiologically normal males but just playing role of eunuchs. In fact, there are many eunuchs who are neither physiologically hermaphrodites not castrated. They are normal males just playing the role of a eunuch.

The present study is an empirical micro-level study. The study area was selected purposively taking into consideration the size of the eunuch population in the concerned district of West Bengal. The study has been conducted at Golbazar of Kharagpur municipality of Paschim Midnapore district of West Bengal in India. An exploratory-cum descriptive research has been conducted on 22 *hijras*. They are living in the same *Dera*. All the respondents have been taken for this work. A multi-tool approach was used for data collection which was based on interview and focus group discussion (FGD).

Is the concept of the mother present in the *hijra* community? Is there any role of the mother in this community? What are the roles they are playing as a mother? Is the role of the mother significant one? The concept of mother is present among the *hijra* community. Mother is the significant among them on two reasons. The first one is the absence of fatherhood among them and second one is that their lifecycles revolve around the notion of mother.

Hijras have a different kinship relation. They are not related to each other by blood ties; it is neither consanguine nor affinal, it can be called called fictive. The eunuch kinship alignment is not normative familial arrangements. This relationship is derivative and therefore devoid of specific symbolic value. The *Guru-Chela* relationship is the cornerstone of the eunuch kinship network. It is a hierarchical obligatory relationship, as evidenced by the nature of the duties and responsibilities towards one another. It is a reciprocal bond that entails responsibilities and obligations as well as rights and benefits on the part of both *Guru* and *Chelas*. Without a *Guru*, a eunuch's identity is questioned. She is treated as *gandu* or orphan. Similarly without *Chelas*, a *hijra* does not have *izzat* in the community.

The kin relationship between *Guru* and *Chela* is made by two ways. One is nursing ritual and another is gift ritual (dowry). The nursing rituals refer to the nurturing bond between mother and daughter symbolised by the milk that a nursing mother feeds her daughter (milk daughter) - milk that is shared by sisters, as daughters of the same mother, called as milk sister. In case of gift rituals, the mother sometimes gives gifts (dowry) to her daughter (anything she might need such as pots, pans, mattress, a few good saris, some jewellery and so on, just like a new bride), as parents give a dowry to the bride on the occasion of her marriage.

The dramatic resonance between the consanguinal mother-child bond – symbolised by breast feeding— and the eunuch's nursing ritual makes the parallel apparent. Love and affection are the significant components of these relationships. Their existence is significant, not only intrinsically, but also because they highlight the centrality of affective (mother-child) bonds in eunuchs' kinship network.

The relationship between *Guru* and *Chela* is mutually favourable. In Indian society eunuch's community has a hierarchical structure. The relationship between *Gurus* (teachers) and *Chelas* (disciples) is like mother and daughter. All the rules and regulations of the community are dictated by *Guru ma* and she plays various roles for maintaining their sacred tradition. *Chelas* are obedient, respectful, and loyal and they serve their *Gurus* well by catering to all their domestic needs. Like mother, as the first teacher of child, *Guru ma,* takes care of her *Chelas* and trains them for their society.

Even when a *Guru* suffers from serious illness, *Chela* looks after her *Guru*, cooks and cleans for her, bears all the expenses. They [*Chelas*] never rebel against these responsibilities and are always respectful and considerate of her *Guru*'s well being. Similarly *Guru* treats her *Chelas* with same consideration, giving her gifts of saris and even gold jewellery on some occasions (Reddy, 2005).

Though, they are not related to blood ties or affines, they are bound together through unconditional care, love and affection. As a mother of *Chelas*, *Guru ma* plays a significant role in the socialisation of its members as well as in taking care of all the *Chelas*. Respectively *Chelas* are also responsible to their *Guru ma*. As a mother, *Guru ma* takes care of her daughters and daughter also takes care of their *Guru ma*.

Challenges faced by the Eunuchs in becoming mothers

Motherhood is characterised by womanhood. Motherhood is often seen as gender norm required to achieving authentic womanhood. Womanhood depends on what gender roles are expected out of a woman. The identity of being a woman becomes a stereotype, based on a repeated performance of gender and sexual norms. Eunuch's motherhood challenges heteronormativity of the family as a social institution. Because the concept of womanhood is absent among them.

Every woman has the right to become a mother; that does not mean only who has the capacity to conceive a child would be a mother. A woman who adopts a child also becomes a mother. Normally, a woman becomes a mother when she gives childbirth. The word 'mother' is related with femininity (presence of womb). But the eunuchs do not fall into this category. They do not have the capacity to conceive because of absence of womb. For that they never become a biological mother. But they can adopt a child and become a mother.

The question is why they adopt daughters rather than *Chelas*? They adopt daughters to extend their kin relation. Daughters would more likely be *Chelas* of other *hijras* with whom they could form an alliance. Such relationships also serve publicly to strengthen ties between *hijras*. Each *hijra* is able to establish relationships with other *hijras*; thereby not only they widen the kinship network but also strengthen ties. This is made for an extended, interconnected network of relationships between eunuchs living together.

Eunuchs have emotions and want to be mothers like other women. But due to absence of womb they are not able to conceive. So sometimes they adopt child and bring it up as an adoptive mother. Adoption in eunuch families has always been the norm. It was only through cases of child adoption that *hijra* motherhood came into being. It is unclear whether the adoption by eunuchs is legal. They have faced some legal barriers to adopt a child. The formalities of adoption by eunuchs are not clear in law and large sections of the population do not accept it easily. Teenagers and adults who want to become members of the *hijra* community are adopted by the *hijragurus* through an initiation ceremony, which is sanctioned by arbitrary councils within *hijra* community known as the *hijra* panchayats or *jamaats* (Goel, 2016). Information regarding adoption by 'third gender' is also not available in the Central Adoption Resource Authority (CARA) under the Ministry of Woman and Child Development (MWCD).

Conclusion

To overcome the challenges of the eunuchs, there is need to redefine the notions of adoption and motherhood beyond the gender-sex binary. The changing role of the conventional institutions of family, marriage and kinship is important. There is need to decriminalise adoption for the third gender, who are yet to get marriage and adoption rights. There is also need to intervene at the policy level to scrutinise the adoption rights beyond the gender and sex, in that way making the process of adoption more accessible and transparent. The traditional mechanism of reproduction has been broken and now it is possible to have virgin birth and make human reproduction sexless. The eunuchs' community offers an alternative lesson towards a future, where it will not be necessary to identify motherhood by gender-sex binary.

References

Goel, I. 2018. 'What Does it Mean to be a *Hijra* Mother?', *Economic and Political Weekly*, Vol. 53, Issue No. 8.

Herdt, G. H. 1994. *Third Sex Third Gender: Beyond Sexual Dimorphism in Culture.* MIT: Zone Books-MIT.

Markus, H. R. and Kitayama, S. 1991. 'Culture and the Self: Implications for Cognition, Emotion, and Motivation', *Psychological Review*, 98, 224-253.

Nanda, S. 1986. 'The *Hijra*s of India: Cultural and Individual Dimensions of an Institutionalised Third Gender Role', *Journal of Homosexuality*, 11 (3-4): 35-54.

Nanda, S. 1990. *Neither Man nor Woman: the Hijras of India.* Belmont, CA: Wadsworth Publishing.

Reddy, G. 2005. *With Respect to Sex: Negotiating Hijra Identity in South India*. Chicago: University of Chicago Press.

Additional Sources

1. Magazines and Media.
2. BBC World, 18 Jan, 2010.
3. *Eisamay*, 1 Oct, 2017.
4. *Anandabazar Patrika*, 19 July, 2017.
5. *Sangbad Pratidin*, 14 Oct, 2017.
6. ABP Ananda, 18 Sept, 2017.

Chapter - 13

Role of a Mother in Shaping the Life of a Child with Special Needs

Kaynat Kenukhan

Mother is a term referring to 'a woman in relation to her child or children' and motherhood can be defined as 'a state of being a mother' (*Oxford English Dictionary*). Motherhood is not just a quality but also a spirit, a spirit of being a mother and accepting the challenges coming on her way along with motherhood. A mother does much more than just giving birth. She plays a crucial role in a child's overall development and has immense contribution in shaping a child's personality.

Every child is unique in its own special way but there are some children who need special care and attention while growing up. There are children who are mentally and physically challenged, these children are little under-developed and they lag behind in the race of overall development compared to a normal child.

The present paper is an attempt to look through the challenges and struggles that a mother faces in shaping a life of a child with special needs.

Motherhood marks its beginning from the moment a woman conceives a child. Today's world has become too much competitive in terms of career and education. Women are struggling their way out to match steps with men and are achieving their own positions in the society. For the sake of career and higher education more and more women are delaying their marriage and later delaying pregnancies. Women planning for their baby after their thirties fall in the category of high risk pregnancies. Birth defects are more common among the children of older women. Even older men are more likely to reproduce faulty batch of sperms. The stressed lifestyle, drinking and smoking habits effect the behaviour of sperm cells (Lewis, 2013).

Sociologist Ernest Groves declared that even typical mothering needs scientific improvement. Too much affection and too little attention both could impair development and he encouraged parents to seek professional guidance to maintain a right balance. He further argued that only through professional guidance mothers could save their children. Correct 'mothering' practice was prescribed. Psychologists argued that proper motherly actions would lead to hard-working, self-disciplined, law-abiding adults and any inconsistency would create weak-minded, badly behaved, abnormal adults (Waltz, 2015).

A child's disability may burden his/her family members in multiple ways. Parents of such child are the worst sufferers. A child with disability may impact his parents' quality of life. Parents might need to spend a good amount of time in taking care of them, and they do not get enough time for themselves to engage in any recreational activities. It also limits their social life thus affecting their quality of life. The more severe the disability the more poor his/her parents' quality of life (Leung & Li-Tsang, 2003).

Hastings and Brown (as cited in Barnes and Dia, 2008) found that parental self-efficacy, the relationship between children and parental stress are significant.

There are many ways in which parents of disable children can transform their bitter experiences into a positive one. Studies reveal that, parents have reported their child's disability has given them an increased sense of purpose and personal growth, increased spirituality and tolerance as well as sensitivity. A positive view on childhood disability correlates with less anxiety and pressure. Assisting families in finding a positive meaning to their child's disability may prove to be an important intervention in alleviating parental stress (Barnes and Dia, 2008).

Caprio (2019) describes her personal experiences as a mother of a special child by stating that at a very young age of 23 years she had a daughter who was diagnosed with developmental disability, Caprio thought her life was over, but her family and her husband supported and helped her overcome the emotional and mental turmoil, and take care of her special child. Today she is a happy mother and recalls a saying 'If you think you can do it, you can. And if you think you can't, you're right'.

The present paper is based on in-depth case studies collected using face to face unstructured interviews. The mode of the case study is totally qualitative in nature. Through the case study an attempt is made to map and gauge the actual scenario which is provided by the respondents. In a homely atmosphere the stories narrated by the respondents are analysed and observed. Their in-between informal behaviour is also taken in account.

For the present paper four special case studies are selected. By taking four contrasting case studies an effort is made to understand the importance of the mother as well as proper parenting and guidance of both mother and father in order to shape the life of a differently-able child and to pave his/her path in the right direction.

Case Study - I

Dipayan is a boy in his early twenties. His family consists of his mother, father and two sisters. They live in a village. His father works in a local court and mother is a housewife. Their monthly income is Rs 6000 to Rs 7000 per month. Dipayan was normal at the time of birth but after two months he was affected by typhoid, and when he reached at the age of one year his parents realised that he was not normal like other children of his age. After consulting a local doctor they came to know that he was deaf and mute and his mental growth was slow. Dipayan never visited a therapist, due to the unavailability of therapist in his village and they were unable to arrange one from the city. His parents could not afford a hearing aid for him. Since childhood his only close companions were his mother and elder sister. All his basic needs were fulfilled by them.

He is very much loved and adored by his mother but still he always feels the absence of his father; he could never connect with his father. After an interaction with his mother it has been found that they are poor and Dipayan's disability frustrates his father, he feels that Dipayan is adding to their misery. His father's indifferent behaviour has made Dipayan more aggressive. His only comfort is his mother and he loves to interact with her through drawings. When asked how does he interact with his mother, his mother says that he interacts through drawing. This is how he expresses his feelings to her. In this case it is very much clear that how much a mother is caring towards her mentally and physically challenged child, even she understands that he will never be able to support them and carry out the responsibility of a son but still she loves him and cares for him, on the other side his father is extremely indifferent towards him. Financial stability also plays a vital role in taking care of children with special needs. Dipayan's family's financial issues are big obstacles between him and his treatment. His condition is worsening because his parents could not afford proper treatment. Although he never got medical help but his mother always provided him all the love and care that he deserved, she never treated him as a burden. Only the spirit of motherhood has kept her going.

Case Study- II

This case is about Abhirup (a 8 years old boy). He lives with his parents and elder sister. He was a premature baby. When his mother was six months pregnant his growth suddenly stopped and the doctors had to carry out a caesarean surgery eighteen days before the scheduled delivery date. Abhirup is an autistic child and he suffers from speech impairment. His mental growth is slow with an IQ level of 50%. And he behaves very violently sometimes. Presently he is undergoing speech therapies and other medical treatments from NIMH, Kolkata. His treatments are affecting him positively. He is totally dependent on his father for all his basic needs. He doesn't even bathe or go to toilet alone. His elder sister helps him a lot and he is very close to her. But he loves his father most and enjoys spending time with him. His father usually shares his difficulties. When asked about Abhirup's mother his father has told that Abhirup is not comfortable with his mother; she finds it difficult to take care of him or understand his words. His violent behaviour disturbs his mother and she becomes nervous. Although she loves her child but she feels really uncomfortable in dealing with him. She is very worried about his future and curses her fate for having an abnormal child.

The information found in this case is very contrasting with Case-I and this compels the researcher to think that not only a mother but father is also very important in shaping the life of a child. Here Abhirup is neglected by his own mother but his father has taken all his responsibilities. His father is playing exactly the role usually a mother plays. He is struggling for his child and is never giving up.

The next case study has also some shocking revelations.

Case Study- III

Aarna is 4 years old; both her parents are government employees. Aarna is their only child and she is born ten years after her parents' marriage. She was a normal baby without any complications. On her first birthday her father gifted her Kindle e-book. Her parents gave her Kindle because they wanted her to learn all rhymes by her own with the help of that gadget. Her parents have a busy schedule and they do not get much time to spend with their daughter. Aarna is looked after by a baby sittter. She never wants her parents to be with her because she is always busy with her Kindle. And she never feels their absence. Aarna rarely talks to anyone and she only interacts with a world that is so unreal (her Kindle e-book). Her mother narrates that one year ago Aarna was sick and they visited a local physician. The doctor observed that Aarna behaved in an abnormal manner and advised them to seek medical help. She is diagnosed with partial autism, her mental growth is slow and her brain development is lacking maturity. The doctor believes that Aarna has developed this problem because of the Kindle e-book, as she is introduced with the gadget at an early age. She is detached from the real world around her and she is only aware of the characters and language that she sees in her e-books. Her parents do not give her required time which has also resulted into her detachment from everything around her. She talks in a robotic manner. Aarna only talks and understands English language. She does not even understand Bengali which is her mother tongue. She rarely shows emotions like happiness or sadness. But when her parents try to take away her e-book she gets angry. She is very hyper-active and is on regular nerve medicines. By talking to her parents it has been observed that they are not much concerned about her health issues. In fact they believe that this is not any form of illness. They believe that their daughter is very moody that is why she does not interact with anyone. Her parents believe that she will be fine when she will grow up. When asked why Aarna lacks emotional attachment with her parents, her mother has explained that she is very understanding and knows that her parents are busy in their respective professional life. Her mother thinks that she is not at all emotionally detached, rather she helps her parents to concentrate on their work, and does not throw any kind of tantrums. Here in this case study it is clearly observed that how both the parents are busy in their life and do not pay attention to their own child which is affecting her mental and physical health. Although they are financially well to do still they are unable to cure their child. Their reluctant attitude towards her proves that neither the mother nor the father is playing an appropriate role in shaping her life.

Case Study- IV

This last case study discusses about a family who are moving ahead in their life with a unique challenge. This case is the most ideal case found in the present research. This is about Arpita who is 11 years old. She lives with her parents, uncle, aunty and cousin. They belong to a lower middle class family. Her father has a small photography business. Arpita is deaf and mute by birth, her mental development is also very slow. Her mother came to know about her child's problem when she was only 2 months old. She was 8 months old when her parents first visited the specialist doctor. The doctor declared her as deaf and mute. Everyone in their house were shattered but her parents were determined that they will not lose hope on her. They are still struggling. Arpita is on therapies from the last ten years and she is improving. Her special hearing aid helped her a lot. Although it is expensive her parents never fails to manage money for her hearing aid. Arpita goes to a normal school— when asked why, her mother replied 'it was not an easy decision. Everyone around us opposed our decision but we were determined, because we believe that after completing her schooling Arpita will have to face the real world. Being in a mainstream school she will be more able to deal with everyone around her'. Arpita also takes Karate coaching. She visits the therapist twice a week with her father. She is very close to her parents and enjoys being with them. Her mother describes their experience: 'after being in a state of shock for months we consoled each other and promised that we will try every possible way to cure our daughter'. She believes that Arpita is their fighter and all three of them are fighting a battle with her disability and they are determined that one day they will win.

This case study clearly tells us that it is important for a couple to work together in order to overcome the challenges faced while nurturing a child with special needs. When both parents work as one, then it is possible to shape a child's life in the best possible manner.

Conclusion

Through the case studies it has been found that every child requires love, attention and care in their childhood to cope up with the challenges they are facing in life.

In Case-I it can be observed that how much a mother is important for a child; no matter whatever be the situation, she never fails to take care of her child. Although financial crisis caused Dipayan to remain untreated till now his mother's care remains unaffected by any factor. Even though Dipayan gets his mother's attention but his father's negligence is affecting him adversely. Through this it can be concluded that although mother is important for a child but the role of father is equally essential for the wellbeing of a special child.

In Case-II, Abhirup is completely dependent on his father; his father is his only solace. In fact, a mother who is considered as a universal caregiver is found to be playing a less important role in Abhirup's life. His mother is unable to understand his own child's expressions and feels nervous in his company. This case clearly states that a mother is not the only shelter for a child; sometimes father also plays an equally important role.

In Case-III, we can observe how reluctant attitude of the parents adversely affects a child. Although Aarna's parents are very well to do they do not give the child the required time and attention and their negligence is the main cause of her mental disability. Even if money is important for the treatment and nurturing of a special child, but sometimes money also fails, because along with money attentiveness of parents is equally important for childcare.

Case-IV is the most ideal case so far. Arpita's parents are working together in shaping the life of their child. Neither fatherhood nor motherhood alone is effective for nurturing a child with special need. Instead of that if they both work together then that would be more helpful. For many years society has approached motherhood as an over glorifying part of a woman's life. But now it is the time for a redefinition where we should proceed for a more fruitful concept called parenthood.

References

Barnes, S. L. N. & Dia, D. A. 2008. 'Families of children with disabilities: A review of literature and recommendations for interventions', *Journal of Early and Intensive Behavior Intervention*, 5(3): 93-107. Retrieved from https//eric.ed.gov

Caprio, T. L. 2019. 'A Mother's Story: Raising a Special-Needs' Child', *The Rainbow Connection*. Retrieved from http://www.rainbowguardian.orgon12-04-2019.

Leung, C.Y.S. & Li-Stang, C.W.P. 2003. 'Quality of life of parents who have children with disabilities', *Hong Kong Journal of Occupational Therapy*, Volume 13 (1):19-24. Retrieved from https://pdf.sciencedirectassets.com

Lewis, J. 2013. *'Are older parents putting our future at risk?'* Retrieved from https://www.telegraph.co.uk/news/health/news

Waltz, M. M. 2015. 'Mothers and Autism: The Evolution of a Discourse of Blame', *AMA Journal of Ethics*, Volume 17(4): 353-358. Retrieved from https://journalofethics.ama-assn.org

Chapter - 14

Anxiety of Mothers about their Children's Education Primarily in English Medium Schools

Soumik Bhattacharjee, Abhra Chanda

The term 'Motherhood' means a state of experience faced by a woman after giving birth to her child. We are all aware about mother's role in a child's life. The overall development of a child is mainly supervised by the immense activities of his/her motherhood. A child is helpless without a mother because motherhood is a socially constructed phenomenon. Naturally in the present day especially the mothers those who are residing in urban places having at least one child are in dilemma. Often, they are over anxious and worried about their children's education starting from pre-school education (Gar and Hudson, 2005; Hudson, 2016).

For this study fifty mothers having one child each have been selected purposively from Kalyani, a municipality area in the district of Nadia, West Bengal. In Kalyani, a good number of educated mothers are worried about the education of their children and they prefer to admit their wards in different English medium schools. This study mainly deals with the nature and extent of anxieties faced by the mothers for growing up their children in English medium schools.

Two English medium schools are selected purposively from Kalyani Municipality area. 27 sample mothers from Springdale and 23 sample mothers from Julien Day School have been selected for this study.

Distribution of the children's mothers in different classes:

Class	*Frequency*
Class V	16
Class VI	11
Class VII	08
Class VIII	14
Class IX	01
Total	50

Ever since a woman becomes a mother, faces a lot of anxiety. Child feels helpless without mother's emotional and psychological assistance and guidance. Motherhood is a socially constructed phenomenon which assigns different socially expected roles which a mother must perform. Anxiety is defined as a painful or apprehensive uneasiness of mind usually over an impending or anticipated consequence. Anxiety is a complicated condition which is difficult to explain.

After the birth of a child it is the duty of the mother to ensure proper care which includes nutrition, socialisation, education etc., which may be challenging for a mother and that may cause anxiety. Since the paper is based on the anxiety of mothers of English medium school going children, it is important to know a little about the origin of English medium schools and the subsequent culture created by it. English as a medium of instruction traces its root back to English medium institution which was established because of British colonial interests. Three important agencies were responsible for spreading English medium education in colonial India: British government, Christian missionaries and progressive Indians. In present time the need and relevance for being educated in English medium institutions have achieved different level of significance. English as a language has attained world-wide popularity for which it has been termed as the 'lingua franca'. In a globalised world, the connectivity and mobility of the people has increased manifolds. The participation in different private firms and multinational corporations demands fluency in English to enable better communication. This is one of the main reasons for which mothers feel a pressing need to educate their children in English medium institutions (Desai, 2000).

No effective relationship in Indian family is warmer or more intense than that of the relationship between mother and children which has been continuing throughout the Indian civilisational history up to the modern times. While father is the supreme authority for outer world, the mother is the centre of the domestic chores of which the education of the child is a crucial part taken care by his mother. The probable reason behind the anxiety of the mothers towards education of their children is due to the responsibility of looking after the education of their children along with everyday domestic chores. (Lannoy, 2012).

> 'There is some evidence that the parents' behaviour, especially mothers', can increase the level of anxiety in the children. Moreover, it is reported that changes made to the family including the death of a parent, divorce, and the birth of a new sibling are among the common causes of anxiety in children. One of the important family factors is the parents' aggressive behaviour, especially mothers', which can disrupt the child's sense of security and be a cause of stress and crisis leading to anxiety in the child. Anxiety prevents the child from doing the age-appropriate activities and participating in school assignments' (Rostami *et al*, 2017).

It is important to identify the factors affecting children's education resulting from the anxiety of mothers and its effects on children from different psychological, physical, and social dimensions. There is scanty of study on the physical and mental health of English medium school going children and the anxiety of their mothers.

Objectives

The main objective of this work is to find out the anxiety of mothers of English medium school going children. The authors chose to conduct a survey on 50 respondents purposively selected from two different English medium schools. The interviews are done through semi-structured survey schedule following face to face interactions and non-participant observation (Krishnaswami and Ranganatham, 2011).

The area of the study selected for this research is Kalyani of Nadia district (West Bengal). As this town has a lot of different educational institutions, the researchers have selected it for this work.

The limitations encountered during the field work include-

- Reluctance to answer during the interview.
- Not being able to give ample time during the interview.
- Avoiding certain questions which they felt personal in nature.

Observation and Analysis

The first stage of anxiety that mothers feel at the outset of their children's academic life, is during the process of getting admission or securing a place for their children in a good English medium institution. It has been observed that many of those institutions also demanded that the parents, particularly mothers, be trained in several important life skills, because they often coach and guide their children.

Another important source of anxiety of the mothers originates from their concern about their children's health and well being. However, it has come to the notice of the researchers that though the mothers are well aware of the nutrition and other bodily requirements of their children's physical well being and good health, they often neglect the mental health of the children by exposing them to cut throat competition for academic success.

The study reveals that all the respondent-mothers are educated in Bengali medium of instruction. They think that these often create many challenging and difficult situations in their career. So they have felt the need of English medium schools. This decision-making process involves the participation of both parents where the role of mothers is also praiseworthy.

In the process of educating a child, the mother plays a very important role. The mother has to perform all the assigned traditional roles of a typical Indian housewife and also at the sametime she looks after the child's academic domain which includes activities like feeding, making ready the child before going to school, taking them to the school and back and helping in their home works etc.

It has also been found that the level of satisfaction of the mothers in their wards' academic performance is very low. Mothers always feel that their children would be constantly under pressure to perform their academic venture which in turn keeps the mothers engaged to do a lot of extra work load and study hour on their children to overcome this. This also results in the deteriorating state of the mental health of the children.

The mothers feel that now-a-days the children are gradually developing their inclination to electronic gadgets for the purposes of entertainment and refreshment of the mind. They suspect that this type of dependence on modern technology possibly in the long run would put a detrimental effect on the well being of their children.

Lastly, the mothers also acknowledge the fact that there is an academic competition among the children in the walls of the educational institutions which in turn creates a lot of competition among the mothers too. But the mothers always dodge the possibility of this competition to have any ill effect on their children.

Conclusion

The data collected from this study highlight various anxieties faced by mothers. Mothers play a substantial role in the early academic years of their children. In finding out the nature of various form of anxieties, this work has unearthed both positive and negative impacts of anxiety on mothers. Positive impacts include things like ensuring good health, better education and a bright future. Right from the birth of a child, socialisation, nutrition, maintenance of good health and educational needs of the children are looked after by the mothers. Hence, it can be safely assumed that certain anxieties of mothers do play a positive role.

However, certain negative aspects have surfaced as well. The present society is full of competition in different spheres due to lack of sufficient resources. This leads to a condition which necessitates the 'survival of the fittest' mindset. Due to this rampant competition, there are certain negative impacts on both the mothers and children. The negative impact is reflected in more and more cases of mental disharmony and depression.

In some cases mothers' demand for excellence puts constant performance pressure on the children, who often feel suffocated in such an environment and resort to the virtual world for some relief. Now-a-days the child is facing the problem of isolation which was not prevailed (this is uncharacteristic of the children) in the previous eras where the child indulged himself with others in various outdoor games and activities to keep healthy body and mind. Some of the erstwhile agencies of socialisation are being replaced by certain virtual agencies and this is a matter of concern for many parents.

Lastly, despite mothers' anxieties regarding their children and their future and the positive and negative impacts, the role of a mother is irreplaceable and undeniable. Motherhood is such an emotion which is omnipresent across different species.

References

Desai, A. R. 2000.*The social background of Indian nationalism.* New Delhi: Popular Prakashan.

Gar, N. S. and Hudson, J. L. 2005. *Family factors and the development of anxiety disorders.* Psychopathology and the family. New York: Elsevier Science Journal.

Hudson, J. L. 2016. *Threat interpretation and parental influences for children with asthma and anxiety.* Melbourne: Centre for Emotional Health, Melbourne University.

Krisnaswami, O. R. and Ranganatham, M. 2011. *Methodology of Research in Social Sciences.* Delhi: Himalaya Publishing House.

Lannoy, R. 2012. *The Speaking Tree.* New Delhi: Oxford University Press.

Rostami, S., Banaeipour, Z. and Zarea, K. 2017. 'Relationship between the General Health of Mothers and the Anxiety of School-Children', *International Journal of Pediatrics,* Vol. 5 (10): 5863-5870.

Chapter - 15

Motherhood: Working Mothers' and Grandparents' Role in Child Care

Tania Upadhaya

Motherhood is not just a word; it is an experience of raising a child. Today the horizon of motherhood is defined on two vital levels- conceiving and caring a child. Childcare is not only limited to the biological mother but the role of other family members is also important. In this case grandparents are examples of extensive motherhood. Now-a-days it is expected that a woman should engage herself in the outer world for better living. In most of the families both husband and wife are seen to be involved in economic activities. In such families the role of the grandparents becomes important for nurturing of a child. Dewey (1916) emphasises that education in its broadest definition, is the means through which habits of a group of people are sustained from one generation to the next. Generally, it occurs through experience that has a formative effect on the way one thinks, feels, or acts.

Our realisation about grandparents raising grandchildren continues to evolve, particularly as we learn more about how they compare with other parenting groups (Whitley *et al.*, 2015).

But the major queries that arise are: Is the role of grandparents enough for a child? Can they take the place of a child's biological parents? The present study is an attempt to explore how much importance does extensive motherhood has in today's world.

Background

Indian joint family system has an age-old tradition of taking care of the children. But due to several factors like employment opportunities, modernisation, needs of privacy etc., the traditional joint families are now turning into nuclear families. However, it is noticed that many parents want to keep their child with their grandparents for the sake of proper education, protection and affection. Grandparents' involvement can serve as an important source of emotional, financial and instrumental support that can save the parents from adverse psychological consequences (Gordon *et al.*, 2004). Many of these grandparents are filling the parenting gap: attending school meetings, helping in homework, advising young people about careers (Tan, 2010).

In our Bengali culture we find many vernacular stories and proverbs like *thakurmar jhuli, golpo dadur ashor, than didar thole, dada moshayer thole, asholer theke shuder daam beshi*, etc., which help to realise that grandparents have played an important role in a child's life since the very beginning. By taking care of the grandchildren, grandparents could ease the mothers' dilemma in their dual roles as mothers and employees. Mothers who work get more childcare support from their parents (Gray, 2005; Vandell *et al.*, 2003).

The relationship between a child and his grandparents is very interesting, sometimes they play the role of game partners and sometimes the role of a teacher and a student. Grandparents can inject positivity into the life of a child.

Motherhood means not just being a mother. It is also about socialising the children, encouraging them, educating them to be the best versions of themselves. Now-a-days most of the women are working women. Besides work, they also have to look after the baby. So the importance of grandparents in childcare is immense. Though the main focus of the present paper is to find out the importance of a mother who has given birth to a baby, it also points out the importance of other family members in the physical and mental development of a child. Descriptive method is used to examine the experience of motherhood. This paper makes some important contributions to understanding the influence of family on children.

For the present study, the district of North 24 Parganas has been selected purposively. Survey method has been applied to collect information. The present paper has focused also on in-depth interviews with case study method. Through the case study an attempt has been made to map and gauge the actual scenario provided by the respondents. Some parents, grandparents and children have been selected purposively for this study. Details are given below.

Case Study- I: Asad Ali Khan

He is a 5 years old boy and studies in KG II. He stays with his parents and grandparents. His aunties stay in another house near his own residence. Asad is the only child of his parents. Both of his parents are working. His mother is a nurse in a government hospital. She has a rotational duty and sometimes works in a night shift. Sunday is Asad's favourite day of the week, because on Sunday he gets time to spend time with his parents. During the week days after returning from school, Asad spends his day at his granny's place. He is comfortable with his grandparents. He loves playing video games and ludo with grand *pa*. His grand *ma* teaches him to make chains with beads. He is friendly to everyone around him. After talking to him personally, it has been observed that he feels hesitations in sharing his minor problems with others. May be this is because he is too young to realise it. He is involved in extra curricular activities, such as recitation, drawing and marshal art. Asad enjoys his stay with grandparents, but if he is given any option, he always chooses his parents. After having an intense conversation with Asad's grand *ma*, it is seen that his parents had a love marriage, and his grand *ma* even today feels uncomfortable with his parents. Asad is very close to her mother. The void in their relationships has affected Asad, and he sees that his parents are little indifferent towards his grandparents. Even he finds it difficult to be emotionally connected with them. Parents do play the role of a mirror. A child always loves to perceive his surroundings through the eyes of his parents.

Case Study- II: Oli Mandal

She is 5 years old girl. She stays with her grandparents because her mother is a working woman and also doing her Ph.D. She spends little time with her daughter. Oli's parents have a good relationship with her grandparents, and they love each other as well. She is extrovert, over active and bubbly, and loves to play virtual games. She is involved in extracurricular activities such as dancing and singing. She is very close to her grandparents. She loves to play with them. Her grandfather takes her to dance class or singing class. She shares all her stories with her grandparents. They spend time together during holidays. She too loves to play with her parents in weekends. Her demands are limited and she is well behaved, obedient and fond of her family members.

Case Study- III: Subhankar Modok

He is 15 years old and a student of class X. His parents run their family business. His parents and grandparents live in different houses. He lives with his grandparents. He adores his grandparents more than his parents. He loves playing cricket and does not have much interest in studies, though he is very intelligent. When Subhankar was in class V his grandparents thought he was not getting proper attention, so they took steps for rectification. But from his childhood he was interested in cricket. So, his grand*pa* gifted a cricket bat to him. But his father was against his love for cricket. Grand*pa* understood his passion for cricket and took him to cricket academy. He continued for few years, later his father discontinued his cricket training because he thought that cricket would affect his studies. But his dream was to become a cricket player. Parents always pressurised him to do well in study. He was a little bit introvert since his childhood and faced difficulties in expressing his feelings to anyone. He used to share his problems with his grandparents and parents.

He respects his grandparents a lot but due to generation gap he feels that they are unable to understand him much. All his school related activities are taken care of by his father. He never shares his minor problems with anyone because he thinks that no one is capable of understanding his problem.

Case Study- IV: Ananya Banerjee

She is a 9 years old girl. She is a student of class V. There are five members in her family- parents, grandparents and Ananya herself. Both of her parents are working – they are teachers by profession. They have to spend a fixed time for their job. Ananya spends five to six hours every day with her parents, mainly in the evening or at night. But she spends rest of the day with her grandparents. Sometimes she plays indoor games with grandfather, goes for a walk with him or listens stories from grand*ma*. They take care of her. Her tutor, parents or sometimes grandparents help in her studies. She has joined in several kinds of extracurricular activities such as recitation, painting, dancing etc. Mainly her grandfather takes her to attend different classes and to the school as well. Sometimes other members also accompany her when they get time. Her mother or grand*ma* prepares dinner for her. In case of any problem in the school her mom goes with her as a guardian, because she is the teacher of the same school. Ananya loves spending her free time by reading story books and watching cartoons. Sometimes she plays alone with her dolls or practises recitation. She either shares her problem with one of her cousin brothers when he comes at her place to meet her or she writes it down in her personal diary. But she is more comfortable in staying alone. Her parents and grandparents always try to attend her functions, but when they are not available she misses them. She loves travelling with her family but they cannot go for a trip because of her parents' busy schedule. But whenever they go, she enjoys that time. She is little introvert who prefers to spend time alone by reading books.

Case Study- V: Ayantika Debnath

She is 14 years old girl. She studies in class IX. Her mother is a professor by profession. She spends more time with her grandparents because her mother is too busy. Yet she tries her utmost to give her time. Grand*ma* gives food to Ayantika in time and she sleeps with her at night. Grand*pa* helps in her studies and if she wants anything, she comes to grandparents. She wants to be a doctor. Since her childhood, everybody in her family supports her. Her mother only goes to school to bring mark sheets. Most of the time she is busy with her computer. She does not share anything with her mother because her mother feels tension for this. So Ayantika shares everything with her father who is very helpful. Every member of the family loves her and cooperates with her in taking decisions. Aside from study and computer learning she goes to class for learning dance and her grandfather takes her to the training class. She is very loveable and everyone loves her very much.

Case Study- VI: Debashree Mukherjee

Debashree is a 17 years old girl. Her mother is a teacher. After the marital separation between her parents, she started staying with her father, but he died when she was very young. She lives with her grand mother, who runs the family by her income from the widow-pension, after the death of her grand father. Debashree's granny spends money for her education. Her mother got married to another man. At present she does not have any relationship with the previous family and her own daughter. Debashree loves to talk and has many friends.

Grand*ma* usually takes care of her and prepares tiffin for her school also. She mostly spends her time with grand*ma* and rest of the time with her friends. She also likes to read books. But during the time of any school event, she misses her parents very much. Despite being close to the grandmother, she cannot share her mind totally with her. So, she has to be more depended on her friends.

She was previously a good student but afterwards she has taken some wrong decisions regarding her early marriage. Finally she has to leave her husband's house and come back to her granny's place. Now she is regretting for her past activities.

Conclusion

The above discussions show that the teenagers who feel neglected and ignored often are afraid of speaking their mind out. Most of them are comfortable in virtual world rather than being in the real world. Probably this sense of solitude has grown because of the nuclear family structure. Those who have a healthy atmosphere at their house are better behaved, composed and lively, than the others who have an atmosphere full of bitterness. The influence of the elders on the children leads their life towards betterment but when the children themselves try to make their own decisions things get adverse because of their lack of experience. In the case of a child the role of grandparents is also important.

Parents and grandparents both are needed to build a child. Particularly in joint families, the impact of grandparents in child's life is immense. Previous generations may teach the next generation about the past as well as they can help the child in shaping their future. Now-a-days, the kids spend time in virtual world, but if they get the scope to stay with their close family members, they can get a better life. Grandparents' care is seen as a relief for children in many cases. But at the end of the day how we see each other is important and every relationship should be cherished.

References

Dewey, J. 1916. *Democracy and education*. New York: Macmillan.

Gordon, R. A., Chase-Lansdale, P. L. & Brooks-Gunn, J. 2004. 'Extended Households and the Life Course of Young Mothers: Understanding the Associations Using a Sample of Mothers with Premature, Low Birth Weight Babies', *Child Development*, 75 (4): 1013-38.

Gray, A. 2005. 'The changing availability of grandparents as carers and its implications for childcare policy in the UK', *Journal of Social Policy*, Volume 34 (4):557-577.

Tan, J.P., Buchanan, A., Flouri, A., Attar-Schwartz, S. & Griggs, J. 2010. 'Filling the parenting gap? Grandparent involvement with U.K. Adolescents', *Journal of Family Issues*, 31(7): 992-1015.

Vandell, D. L., McCartney, K., Owen, M. T., Booth, C. and Clarke-Stewart, A. 2003. 'Variations in child care by grandparents during the first three years', *Journal of Marriage and the Family*, Volume 65 (2): 375-381.

Whitley, D. M., Fuller-Tomson, E. & Sarah, B. 2015. 'Health Characteristics of Solo Grandparent Caregivers and Single Parents: A Comparative Profile Using the Behavior Risk Factor Surveillance Survey', *Current Gerontology and Geriatrics Research*, Volume 2015 (1): 1-10.

Chapter - 16

Motherhood: Beyond Gender- A Study among the Birhor, Souria Paharia and Mal Paharia of Jharkhand

Rimi Sarkar, Samita Manna

Motherhood is a particular state or condition after becoming a mother. So, the position of mother should be prestigious and important in any society. A mother sacrifices a lot for bringing the child into this world. Irrespective of society mothers are worshipped, praised and welcomed by the other members of the family as birth of a child is really a mysterious one and mother performs this job. This is the most wonderful wonder of the world. This miracle is done by the mother. According to Kumari (1997:46), 'It is through the mother that a new life is shaped and released into the world...when mothers become shy of their motherhood and lose their motherliness Matridevo Bhavo losts its meaning too.'

Men and women are different from biological and psychological points of view. Historically, patriarchy has dominated the whole system and subjugated women almost in every aspect of life. In Indian society, husband was treated as '*Pati Param Guru*' (husband is almighty). In patriarchal system of India there is a tendency to control and suppress what is unacceptable to the male dominated society. Success and failure of women are associated with the motherhood or womanhood predominantly in tradition bound societies across the world.

According to Buongpui (2013), the status that men women enjoy in the society is culturally and socially determined. The reasons of discrimination against women are social, cultural and economic. Religious and cultural beliefs consider that women are subordinate to men and this consciously and subconsciously percolates to children in the family through the process of socialisation. Society accepts it as normal to keep them as inferior to men and this becomes the starting point of the discrimination and consequest marginalisation.

It is normal practice to consider an elderly male member of the family as the household head. As compared to such male members elderly female members like wives or mothers are considered a liability and therefore inferior or subordinate to their counterpart in a family. In countries like India such practice has much to do with strong patriarchal values that assign the role of managing the family to the male members. Motherhood is a common but life changing phase in the life of a woman. A woman because of her physiological possibilities is capable of bearing children. Through the act of carrying a child in her womb and giving birth to a child a woman attains her motherhood (Krishnaraj, 2010). Schaffer (1977) states that motherhood is a complex pattern involving both interactive qualities with one another and assigning tasks associated with the role. The role of the mothers and the meaning of motherhood are not same in all socio-cultural contexts. In India, there is a religious and historical tradition of equating women with mother. Motherhood in this country has always been glorified from the ancient times (Dutta, 2014).

Motherhood is a social construction. It varies according to the need of the society. But the role of mother and mothering are exceptional. Patriarchy, which otherwise enslaves the women often is forced to welcome motherhood. Motherhood and pregnancy are the special domains of femininity. Leskosek (2011) has rightly said that 'throughout the history motherhood was described as the women's basic mission, profession, and an inseparable part of her nature. Women are supposedly drawn into motherhood by their instincts which at the same time guarantee their children's healthy growth and development'.

Motherhood is a social institution. From the very beginning the girl child develops within herself a desire to be a mother. Scholars like Nancy Chodorow thinks that this kind of feeling comes from her close association with her mother. Learning sex role becomes evident from the fact that most of the girls take the role of their mothers when they play with their dolls. Society for its own interest creates different sets of norms and sanctions for the boys and girls which are indoctrinated through the process of socialisation.

Feminist anthropologists have demonstrated that gender identity is socially constructed and culture or values play a major role in the day to day practices related to women's work. Patriarchy treats work as paid work done outside home. Motherhood is a state or condition of a woman after becoming a mother. So it is a generic term. But when the sociologists or social scientists focus on motherhood for the subjective understanding and scientific interpretation, motherhood stands as a social fact. Each woman has to obey the societal rules and regulations to become a perfect mother. Institutionalisation of motherhood is also essential to reproduce patriarchy which depends on mothers who teach the patriarchal values to conform to the particular patriarchal system within which they live. As an institution motherhood has been designed by patriarchy to consolidate and extend males' control over women. Childbearing and childrearing under patriarchy, in other words, the experiences of mothering, lie at the heart of women's oppression (Firestone, 1970). The consideration of women bodies as an instrument of reproduction and rearing of children, a function of institutionalised motherhood, is also reflected in the popular discourses. The mothers who conform to the standards set by the ideal motherhood norms are treated to be good mothers and they receive necessary social approval as mothers against those who do not. Hence, patriarchal motherhood appears to be discriminatory since it is based on the ideology of demarcation between the mothers.

Discussions on motherhood in particular within the feminist thought have largely remained marginalised. Despite the fact that mothers' struggles, needs and experiences are crucial to feminist thought, they have seen as corresponding to traditional family values. According to Kawash, the deconstruction of woman and the post-structuralist analysis of gender and power left motherhood to the side, an embarrassing theoretical relic of earlier view of essential woman and her shadow, the essential mother (Kawash, 2011).

The attributes of womanhood are linked to the attributes of motherhood like fertility, maternal love, nurturance etc. The ideology of motherhood differs according to the socio-cultural context, ethnicity and class. For instance, in India where the mother goddesses, as mothers, are highly sacred, mother does have respect, but this is to a very limited extent and that respect is usually for mothers of sons. Chodorow believes that the 'mothering role' has a psychological influence on girls and boys. According to her, 'women's capacities for mothering and abilities to get gratification from it are strongly internalised and psychologically enforced and are built developmentally into the feminine psychic structure' (Chodorow, 1978:76).

II

Motherhood as a gender identity reveals a more complex phenomenon to understand its fluid nature. Society changes with its new set of rules and laws. Today's society is facing various challenges from the developmental points of view. Women are no longer confined to the four walls and this is especially true in case of the educated and professional women. Consequently, various changes are also taken place in the domain of motherhood.

Motherhood denotes an institutionalised term which has been historically constructed in the system dominated by patriarchy (O'Reilly, 2006). In tribal societies, however, this might not be the case. Motherhood is a very enjoyable occasion for the tribal family. Food and comfort are equally extended for both boys and girls. Motherhood is a normal experience of their livelihood. The tribal community possesses a unique identity and cultural heritage of its own. The children learn their community norms, values, mores etc. from their mothers and the society where they live in. Tribal women enjoy more freedom and liberty than the other non-tribal groups. In tribal society the birth of a child is not an uncommon matter. No special attention is given to the woman if she gives birth to a boy.

Girl children are not neglected there, so the child sex ratio in their society is not alarming. There is no specific motive or intention to kill the female foetus for disfavouring women. There is no discrimination between girl and boy. Unlike other social groups, tribal women occupy an important place in their society. The birth of a child brings joy to the parents and equally to close relatives. They were unaware of the family planning programme to some extent. But a few of them have done ligation but they are in general against this process. Because they believe that after operation, they may become physically weak and may not be able to do any hard work. Besides they think motherhood is the greatest gift of god.

III

For this study, Jharkhand state has been purposively selected. Different blocks and villages have been selected from various districts like Hazaribag for Birhor tribe, Godda district for Souria Paharia and Dumka district for Mal Paharia tribe. Five blocks are selected for the study of the Birhors. From these blocks, seven villages have been chosen. Besides, three Souria Paharia-dominated villages have been selected. In similar ways from two blocks, Dumka and Shikaripara, five Mal Paharia-dominated villages have been chosen. 150 families of each tribe have been selected from the respective villages. All data have been collected through direct interview method with the help of a structured scheduled consisting of a number of open-end and closed-end questions, along with non-participant observation.

This paper tries to explore the motherhood of the Birhor, Souria Paharia and Mal Paharia tribe known as PTGs of Jharkhand. They accept motherhood as natural and normal phenomenon in their life where mothers are not blamed for the birth of a girl child. The women enjoy motherhood after giving birth to a boy or a girl.

Birhors' Motherhood

The Birhors, one of the most primitive tribes of Hazaribag district of Jharkhand, are nomadic hunters, food gatherers and rope makers. Birhors are generally found in different places like Palamu, Garhwa, Daybed, Singhbhum, Giridih, Lohardaga, Ranchi, Hazaribagh. They are also famous for hunting and rope making from indigenous fibers of trees and creepers known as *chop*. In their society motherhood is a natural and pleasurable event. Birhors believe that the universe has been created and presided over by Sing Bonga (Sun God) and his wife Chandu Bonga. Beside that they believe in Hapram (ancestral spirits).

Basically, in Birhor society, child marriage is practised where the age of the bride varies from 11-14 years and that of the bridegroom from 15-18 years. But sometimes adult marriage is also practised. A few marriages occur within 15 years of age when girls attain puberty which is known *Bekar*.

The birth of a child is an enjoyable occasion for the couple as well as for the family members and the community. The marriage is considered as successful when the couple is blessed with a child. It is a joyous occasion for the family. The food, care and other facilities and love are equally extended for all children.

Sahu in his book *Birhor Tribe- Dimentions of Development* (1995) mentions that *Chatti* and *Manhjutthi* are two rituals in their society. *Chatti* is purification ritual. After birth of a child, on the sixth day, the mother and child are allowed for purificatory bath. He has also stated that *Chatti* is the final purification of Birhor. In their society pregnant woman gets a special care and position. There are various traditional beliefs and practices existing in relation to pregnancy and childbirth among the Birhors. *Manhtutti* is the ritual which is observed during pregnancy. In this ritual some married women sing a traditional song to make the would-be mother happy and cheerful. All married ladies bless her by putting a *tilok* (a blissful mark) on her forehead.

The Birhors have supernatural beliefs in different types of trees and animals. They believe that there are different types of spirits which have enormous effect in their day to day life. The main sacred head among the Birhor is called *Naya*. In the pregnancy period the woman has to maintain the taboos, some of which are for their health. She would not go to all places. Birhor women believe that problems in pregnancy and childbirth were due the to influence of evil spirits living in forest and rivers. Metallic wear, hooks, chillies and lemons etc., are generally used to prevent evil spirits from the pregnant women.

The birth of a child takes place in the respective house of the child. The most senior and the experienced women of the community attend the birth event. After the child's birth the midwife cuts the umbilical cord by a sharp bamboo. The mother and the child are considered as polluted for at least five days. The period of pollution indirectly helps the mother to take rest after delivery. On the sixth day of the birth of the child the female members of the community are invited to bless the child and the mother.

However, the Birhors have argued that they know the proper application of traditional medicines for birth control. Accordingly, they can stop pregnancy or resume pregnancy of a woman. Almost all the Birhor women are unaware of the sexually-transmitted diseases. The knowledge of HIV/AIDS and the causes for its spread are not known to any Birhor woman at Hazaribag. Among the Birhors the practice of child marriage is prevalent. The majority of girls are married at the age of 11-14 years. As a result, they are married before their puberty. Due to low age at marriage many Birhor women die during the time of child birth. Till now women follow many superstitions during or before pregnancy. They tie *joributi* (one type of sacred thread) on the male and female child. In general *Premjori* is used for male and *Hathjori* for female child. They also use *jotibuti* as a contraceptive measure for effective traditional medicine to stop their pregnancy.

According to the census of 2011, the number of Birhor tribe is 10,726 in which male is 5,472 and female is 5,254 and the sex ratio is 960 and child sex ratio is 968 which is not alarming. But their numbers are gradually being decreased, so the hospital officials do not provide any suggestion for ligation to the mothers. So Birhors are not going through any family planning programme.

Souria Paharias' Motherhood

The Souria Paharia is also one of the primitive tribes of Jharkhand, who live in isolated, hilly, forest areas of Dumka and Sahibganj districts of Jharkhand. The main economy of Souria Paharia tribe is shifting cultivation with occasional supplements from surrounding forest produces. Child marriage is not uncommon. Marriage of the girls aged 12-13 years and boys aged 15-16 years is found. Birth is an important event in

Paharias' life too. In their society there is no family planning programme for controlling the birth of children. The pregnant women enjoy their motherhood. Due to early marriage, a woman sometimes gives births to 5-6 children. No matter whether it is a boy or a girl, they believe that the birth of a child is a reward from god. Paharia women get special prestige during the time of their pregnancy. During the time of pregnancy the women maintain certain rules and regulations. The later part of pregnancy is more vulnerable. The Souria women are found to work in the field even at the advanced phase of pregnancy. As a result, many Paharia women's deliveries occur in the field. There is hardly a case where a trained doctor or midwife has attended a delivery. So delivery of child is a quite natural thing to them.

The new born baby is highly welcomed in the Paharia society. Generally, a midwife with the help of elderly women and relatives attends the pregnant woman's house during the time of delivery. When the child is born, the umbilical cord is cut by the midwife. Birth pollution period continues from seven days to fifteen days. Souria Paharia observes the naming ceremony between the third and fifth day after the child-birth. All members of the community celebrate this occasion with great pleasure and joy. It is observed that the Paharias welcome natural birth of the child; there is no discriminatory process by which male and female child would be separated. So, the trend of child sex ratio is not declining in their society. In Jharkhand, according to the Census of 2011, the population of Souria Paharia is 46,222. In their society sex ratio is 1012 and child sex ratio is 1034. In Paharia society there is division of labour. But it is not under the domination of male persons. So women play a vital role in economic sector. Side by side, parents take a major part in concerning children's rearing and upbringing. As the Paharia people are nature based people they maintain their lifestyle in simple and spontaneous way. This simple and natural ways of life keep them far away from the artificial and mechanical urban life. Modern technological development, gender disparities, killing foetuses for gender discrimination are not their concerns still today.

Mal Paharias' Motherhood

The Mal Paharias, as the name indicates, are a hill tribe settled in the hilly ranges of the Rajmahal Hills and the neighbouring region of the Santhal Parganas. Due to shifting from place to place, their village integrity and solidarity have been violated. Chief economic activities of Mal Paharias are agriculture and collection of forest products. In their society, child marriage is still prevalent and it occurs at the age of 13 to 15 years.

Family is the smallest unit of social organisation in the Mal Paharia society. Family is nuclear with husband, wife and their unmarried children. Pregnant woman is highly welcomed in Mal Paharia community. During this period some restrictions are imposed on her. But they do everyday activities. In their society the husband-wife relationship is very cordial. The couple follows the division of labour. The rearing and caring of the children are the duties of the wife and husband both. They accept motherhood as natural process in their life as the mothers are not blamed for the birth of a girl child. Mothers' opinion is very important for determining the future life of the girl children as they often follow their mothers for bearing the tradition of their culture. The mother has decision-making power in her family, economy, and socio-cultural spheres.

Mal Paharia mothers took the decision concerning children's upbringing and marriage. In their society women do not depend much on men for their sustenance. They have right to take decisions in important matters of the family. In their society girl children are not neglected so the sex ratio and child sex ratio is not distressing. As per the census of 2011, the sex ratio of Mal Paharia is 1003 and child sex ratio is 997. There is no discrimination between girl children and boy children, though in patriarchal society male children are also welcomed by their parents, but girl children also have equal status.

Conclusion

From this study it has been seen that in tribal society, the tribals have expressed their desire to get a boy child after two girl children. In their society the female child is treated almost as an equal to the male child. It is expected that each new female born in tribal society will be a potential mother; they will be honoured like the mother earth; and the female child also gets equal respect from their tribal neighbours. Female children are assets of the tribal households. During the time of marriage, the bride-groom is expected to pay a bride-price to the parents to compensate for their loss. Child marriage is an age-old practice, which has been the regular practice in tribal society. Marriage in tribal society is regarded as pure and sacred and it is considered as a cultural practice in their communities.

Regarding gender-specific education, the tribal communities have shown no preferential attitude towards education. For the case of bride price among the tribal groups, it is found that a majority of tribal groups support bride price.

The historical roles of a woman both as a wife and as a mother have to be contextualised with a cultural dimension. With the advent of modern technological revolution in the 20th century in the Western societies, the women folk came out of the private domestic sphere and took part in public work spheres. Besides, it is assumed that the reality of motherhood to a mother is of paramount reality which comes to her perception and understanding through everyday life experiences of routines, interactions and events relating to her child and mothering process. Bias free motherhood from male-female difference is prevalent in the tribal societies. This picture indicates that there is no discriminating attitude towards girls and boys. To them the journey of motherhood is as natural as their daily life. That is why they enjoy it with their own cultural uniqueness and heritage.

References

Buongpuri, R. L. 2013. 'Gender Relations and the Web of Traditions in northest India', *The NEHU Journal*. Vol. 11. No. 2.

Chodorow, N.1978. *The Reproduction of Mothering*. Berkeley: University of California Press.

Firestone, S.1979. *The Dialects of Sex: The Case of Feminist Revolution*. London: The Women Press.

Kawash, S. 2011. 'New Direction in Motherhood Studies', *Journal of Women in Culture and Soci*ety. Vol. 3. No. 4.

Krishnaraj, M. 2010. *Motherhood in India*. New Delhi: Routledge.

Kumari, L. M. 1997. *The Role of Women in Society: Sita Must Live*. New Delhi: Sterling Publisher Pvt. Ltd.

Leskosek, V. 2011. 'Historical Perspective on the Ideologies of Motherhood and its Impact on Social Work', *Social Work and Society*. Vol. 9. No. 2.

O' Reilly, A. 2010. *Encyclopedia of Motherhood*. New Delhi: Sage.

Sahu, C. 1995. *Birhor Tribe- Dimensions of Development*. New Delhi: Sarup Book Publishers Private Limited.

Schaffer, R. 1997. *Mothering*. Cambridge: Harvard University Press.

Chapter - 17

Homeless and Helpless: A Glimpse on Rohingya Mothers

Suchismita Majumder

Biologically women are attributed with the capacity to become mothers by nature. Motherhood, the most common experience of female life, is the state of having and raising a child. Motherhood is also common among animals but it is the culture and the context that make human motherhood distinct from animals. Recently the Rohingyas, mainly a Muslim ethnic group from Northern Rakhine state of Western Myanmar, have attracted the attention worldwide for their acute discrimination and persecution in the hands of Myanmar military and for their appalling magnitude of displacement. Historically it is evident that Rohingyas have been connected with the land of Rakhine for generations. But they are excluded from the list of 135 national ethnic groups by the Myanmar Citizenship Law of 1982. Continuous flights of them from Myanmar to escape persecutions make Rohingyas a group of footloose people. They are, in fact, homeless. In current years the plight of this community has become too immense to describe. Forced migrants like Rohingyas have to face disparate and complicated life situations because of their incessant movements. The situation is more precarious for mothers.

Focusing on some imprisoned Muslim Rohingya mothers in West Bengal the present study reveals the helplessness of these mothers and their children at various parts of life. These respondents (Rohingya mothers) are incorporated at different points of time from February 2015 to October 2017 and they are divided in five categories mainly on the basis of their children's location. The paper also consults with some secondary sources including previous research papers, reports of organisations and some other documents. The study attempts to show how the unequal standard of privileges and restrictions of human society construct motherhood, the blessing to have a new life, a matter of discomfort for the marginal groups like Rohingyas.

'Motherhood is a particular state or condition after becoming a mother'. Sacrifice of a mother to bring a new life in this world is a reality that can't be overlooked. Generally mothers are respected, admired and greeted in every society (Manna & Patra, 2016:3). Animals are also gifted with motherhood. Becoming mother is a biological fact. But as 'man is a social animal, motherhood is also a social fact along with its biological connotations' (Majumder, 2016:137). Animal mothers are guided by the laws of nature whereas human mothers are the subject to societal rules and regulations that are not equally beneficial for all groups of people and the Rohingyas are one of the best examples of this fact.

For last one and half years the newspapers, TV channels and social media are increasingly becoming overloaded with the Rohingya issue. Though Rohingyas have appeared in the lime light recently their plight is going on for more than 40 years and their controversial background is even older than that. Formally they are identified as 'illegal Bengali migrants from neighbouring Bangladesh' by the Myanmar[1] Government as well as by Myanmar people.On the other hand the community itself along with important international bodies like U.N. recognises themselves as 'Rohingya', mainly a Muslim ethnic group related with Northern Rakhine state of Western Myanmar formerly known as Arakan[2] (Kipgen, 2014).

Historically it is evident that Rohingyas have been living in the land of Arakan for a very long period of time. Arakan is separated from Bangladesh only by the river Naff that flows between Akyab district of Myanmar and Teknaf Upazila of Bangladesh (Ullah, 2011). It is the claim of the Rohingyas that they are connected with Arakan from 10th century. Bhaumik has emphasised (2013) that the existence of the Rohingyas in this land at the time of British arrival can surely be established.

A report by Chris Lewa has stated that ethnically and religiously Rohingya Muslims are related to the Chittagonians of Southern Bangladesh. According to the definition of Andrew Selth, Rohingyas '... are Bengali Muslims who live in Arakan State... most Rohingyas arrived with the British colonialists in the 19th and 20th centuries' (Leider, 2014). The 'Rohingya language' is recognised by some linguist as a version of '*Chittagonian*, a regional dialect of Bengali which is also used extensively throughout south-eastern Bangladesh' (Imran and Mian, 2014:235).

The conflict between Muslims and Buddhists of Arakan began to take place at the end of colonial period (Bhaumik, 2013). The Rohingyas had been regularly and systematically expelled from the process of nation-building in Myanmar since independence of the country in 1948 (Lewa, 2009). In 1982, they were excluded from the list of 135 national ethnic groups by the Myanmar Citizenship Law and thereby became stateless (Cheung, 2011).

According to Article 1 of the 1954 Convention, a 'stateless person' is one 'who is not considered as a national by any State under operation of its law' (UNHCR, 2014).The present number of stateless people in the world ranges from about 11 to 15 million (Goris, *et.al.*, 2009). A stateless person is someone who is not the responsibility of anyone in this world.

Stateless position of Rohingyas justifies all kinds of inequitable actions against them. Though some years like 1978, 1991-92, 2012, 2016 and finally 2017 are marked for severe human rights infringements and huge dislocation of Rohingyas from Myanmar, everyday life of Rohingyas is inflicted with maltreatment from the beginning to the end. Forced unpaid labour, physical torture, murder, rape, sexual exploitation, restriction on every fundamental aspects of life (like family, marriage, education, occupation, movement) are the most common forms of persecution applied extensively against Rohingyas since 1978 and particularly from 1990s. To avoid oppression in the hands of military along with local Buddhist Moughs and to save life the Rohingyas are running away from their home and from their ancestral land on each and every day. In the last few decades they have scattered in different regions of South and Southeast Asia and even beyond that (Lewa, 2009; Imran and Mian, 2014).

Arakan becomes absolutely hostile from June 2012 for the Rohingyas (Keane, 2012) after riot breaks out between the two communities, Buddhists and Muslims centering a rape and murder of a young Rakhine woman by three Muslim youths. The violence of June and October 2012 in Arakan 'caused some of the 140,000 internally displaced to attempt to flee across the border' (Goodman, 2014). Since then the rate of exodus from Burma keeps on increasing consistently.

After the mass flight of Rohingyas (approximate 250,000) in 1991-92 at the time of Operation Pyi Thaya Bangladesh has stopped to receive Rohingyas officially (Cheung, 2011). From mid-1992 to before 2017 massacre the reluctant attitude of Bangladesh remains constant. India is the next option after Bangladesh. Many uprooted Rohingyas have moved towards India on and after 2012 following the regular persecution in Burma and the disinclination of Bangladesh towards them.

The emergence of Arakan Rohingya Salvation Army (ARSA)[3] in 2016 amidst the ongoing turmoil since 2012 and the repeated attacks of Rohingya insurgents on military personnel and security officers of Myanmar turned the total situation into a volcanic one in August 2017. Displacement of 87,000 Rohingyas in Bangladesh takes place between October to December 2016 (Human Rights Watch, 2017). The arrival of displaced Rohingyas numbers 620,000 on November 17, 2017 in Bangladesh (UNHCR, 2017).

The repeated migration of the community since 1978 contributes to build their identity as a group of 'Forced Migrants'[4]. In recent years their plight has become too immense to describe. The incessant movement of Rohingyas from one land to other has made their life complicated and extremely unsafe. The situation is graver for mothers as they are not alone. Mothers are always attached with children. Different kinds of state-initiated as well as state-supported harassment in Myanmar and the resulting escape have carried pitiful consequences for Rohingya mothers and children for a quite long period of time.

II

Motherhood is such a fact that cannot be restricted within its own periphery. It is intimately related to the facts like childhood, parenthood and many others. More specifically motherhood and childhood are the two sides of the same coin. Without one, other is incomplete. In the following sections the researcher has tried to convey how Rohingya mothers are powerless other than to give birth to children as a natural process. On the other hand since birth Rohingya children are deprived of all the resources that are required for their upbringing and development. In this way both motherhood and childhood of Rohingyas are getting shattered. The increasing vulnerability of mothers along with their children is highlighted in this paper.

The study is a descriptive type of research. The researcher has conducted interviews with 10 imprisoned Rohingya mothers (respondents) in some Correctional Homes (Prisons) of West Bengal from February 2015 to November 2017 at different points of time. Since 1992, Prisons of West Bengal are known as Correctional Homes according to the West Bengal Correctional Services Act. These Mothers are the primary cases of this study and they are selected purposively considering the uniqueness of their situation. Though the locations of all these respondents are prisons (at the time of data collection) their background and experience reveal diverse aspects of agony of the Rohingyas. These primary cases are divided into five categories following the location and condition of the children of respondents. The secondary sources of information include previous research papers, news media, reports of organisations and some other documents.

Table 1: Location of the Respondents at the Time of Interview

Correctional Homes	*Time of Interview*					*Total*
	February 2015	*April 2015*	*July 2016*	*March 2017*	*October 2017*	
BCCH	0	0	0	1	0	1
DCCH	0	1	0	0	2	3
BDCH	4	0	0	1	0	5
MDCH	0	0	1	0	0	1
Total	4	1	1	2	2	10

[BCCH- Berhampore Central Correctional Home, DCCH- Dumdum Central Correctional Home,[5] BDCH-Balurghat District Correctional Home, MDCH- Malda District Correctional Home]

The respondents under study faced various kinds of harassment in their life in Arakan. Birth place of all these women was Burma. They lived mainly in Akyab[6] and Maungdaw district of Arakan. 8 respondents left Myanmar after the beginning of 2012 chaos and they were affected by the riot either in 2012 or in the following years (before August 2017). No victim of the latest turmoil (August 2017 and later) was available at the time of data collection. The purpose of coming to India for these respondents was to settle here. All of them had family members in this country. They reached India after 2012 and before August 2017.

Secondary data have discussed the situation of August 2017 and after. When the researcher began her work in February 2015 the Rohingya issue was not so well-known like today. But the gravity of the situation was not much less as it is now. In fact the two types of information, primary and secondary, attempt to make it clear that the 2017 massacre is the extreme outcome of those torments that Rohingya community has been bearing for years. As a result the misery of mothers and children is going on in the same way.

III

The interactions with these 10 mothers reveal their underprivileged background and marginal position. 8 mothers among the 10 are illiterate. Other 2 have minimum education. None of them have completed primary level. They never work outside home. Rohingya women keep themselves busy with household chores. Husbands and other male members of their family remained involved in agriculture, fishery and small business in Burma. In foreign land Rohingya men become engaged with different kinds of daily work.

Table 2: Age Distribution of the Respondents

Age (Years)	*Respondents*
21-30	4
31-40	4
41-50	0
51-60	2
61-70	0
Total	10

To highlight the defenceless position of mothers and the rootless existence of Rohingya children some case studies (both primary and secondary) are discussed in the following categories. But these categories are not in water tight compartments.

Category I

Loss of children on the way to escape from Burma is the common experience of Rohingyas. But this kind of disaster also occurs in other situations. Here the unpleasant incidents of 3 Rohingya mothers are discussed.

Anjuma Bibi was an illiterate Rohingya mother of two daughters. She was 30 years old in 2015. Her husband was most probably murdered in Rathidaung area in the riot of 2012. The man went to market and did not return from there. After that along with 2 daughters and other 31 villagers Anjuma escaped in 2013 from home that was set in fire. Walking 13 days through jungles and hills she entered Bangladesh. For 11 days they could only manage banana leaves and amloki for surviving. Her elder daughter was lost in the jungle on the way. The girl was 11 years old at that time. Anjuma did not know from where she was arrested in India. She was in BDCH (Balurghat) along with her youngest daughter for 21 months as U.T.[7] in February 2015. Her brothers were in Jammu and they had refugee cards of India.

Sitara, another respondent left Burma in 2014 and entered India in the same year with her husband and 5 children through Hilly border, South Dinajpur. They lived for two years in Jammu. Sitara along with her family was again going to Bangladesh to meet her brothers. In the border (Hilly) she was arrested and her husband escaped with the 5 children. Sitara had no contact with her family since imprisonment. She was completely shattered when I met her in March 2017 in Balurghat.

Here among 7 children of the respondents 6 are lost. There is hardly any hope to get them back in future. One daughter of Anjuma is with her in captive situation. The experience of children who have lost mothers and parents are more shocking and pathetic. Here the story of a 10 years old Rohingya boy named Abu is mentioned to highlight the hardship of Rohingya children who are living the life of orphans. It is a secondary case[8].

> Abu was the victim of August 2017 massacre. His mother and elder brother were murdered and he failed to find out his father before leaving Burma. Walking 5 days through forest he reached Bangladesh along with his sister Shorifa and other villagers. Abu and 5 years old Shorifa are now living in a 'tarpaulin shelter with a family that once lived in' their village. For crisis of food, frequently they have 'just one small bowl of rice and lentils a day or just boiled rice with salt'. For last 10 months Abu has been wearing the same t-shirt. He cannot speak more because of the mental shock with which he is struggling hard.

Category II

Arrest and imprisonment with children are common picture of Rohingya mothers since the population begins to be visible in prisons of West Bengal. Sometimes both the parents along with their children are found in captive situation but other times it is also noticed that mothers are alone with children and the fathers are kept in some other place.

Margina Begum an illiterate Rohingya mother who migrated to Bangladesh in her childhood at the age of below 5 years with her parents to save life. She was one of the few lucky Rohingyas who got refugee status in Bangladesh. She spent some long years in the Kutupalong refugee camp where she got married. Margina's husband, Md. Harul was also an illiterate Rohingya who migrated to Bangladesh in 2011. They became the parents of three children in four years. All the children were born in the Kutupalong Camp. But they did not have any birth proof. In the mean time Margina's parents and other siblings moved to India. With the target to reach Delhi, Margina crossed West Bengal border with her husband and three children. All of them were arrested from Bongaon station.

In February 2015, a good portion of imprisoned women in Balurghat was found to lose their husbands either in Burma or in the mid-way of migration. Anowara was such an unfortunate woman who became captive with 7 children. Her husband was missing and her brother living in Jammu was unwilling to take her responsibility. Again in 2017 some Rohingya mothers were detected only with their children in prisons by the researcher. One of them was Asma. She was with her 2 children in Berhampore prison. Asma's husband was in Bangladesh.

Loss or permanent separation of husband creates difficulty for women. In such cases they literally become vulnerable to any kind of misfortune. In this category all the 12 children of the respondents are found in prisons with their mothers.

Category III

Parting from families while in prisons and Children's Homes after arrest in West Bengal causes long term detachment of children from their mothers as well as from their parents. It is also a common fact of many Rohingya families. Individuals of 6 years and above and below 18 years are not allowed in prisons and they are sent to Children's Homes. In such situations the case number remains same for children and for their family members detained in prisons. It creates another sad situation.

Kalima, an illiterate woman of 35 years, was an eye witness as well as a victim of 2012 riot. Her brother and father were murdered in Arakan and her sister became the prey of a rape attempt. Being unable to bear the shock her mother lost life. Observing fire in the locality Kalima along with her husband, four children and a sister escaped in 2013. They were among a group of total 40 members. In words of Kalima: 'we could not take a single dress with us.' After crossing West Bengal border unlucky Kalima and her four children were arrested whereas her husband and sister could escape to Jammu. The three children of the detained mother were sent to some Children's Homes and the youngest one was only permitted to live with her in the prison. After losing parents and homeland and parting from husband and children the poor woman was spending approximately 2 years behind the bar in February 2015.

Like Kalima, Samia's children are also divided between prison and Children's Homes. This story is more shocking as Samia does not know in which Homes her 2 children are placed. Moreover they are placed in two different Homes and one of them is a boy and other one is a girl. Samia along with her mother-in-law and other 3 children remain locked up in Dumdum prison in October 2017. She knows nothing about her separated children who cannot be traced for last 7 months after arrest. Samia's husband is in U.S.A. Her sister is in Delhi and her brother-in-law is in Hyderabad. Throughout the day she is weeping badly remembering her two children.

Here out of the 9 children of respondents, 5 are found in Children's Homes and 4 are in prisons with their mothers. Chakraborty (2015) and Maitra (2017) have discussed the problem and the pain of this type of separation in their studies.

Category IV

In case of Sitara (respondent of Category I) it is seen that the mother has no connection with her children as they can escape with their father. But the agony of Beruja surpasses the anguish of many Rohingya mothers and it is really difficult to find a counterpart of her who is bearing the pain of losing all the 4 children in the fire of riot.

Not only her children but also her husband was burnt alive. Beruja however managed to escape from the burning village with her uncle and his family. After crossing border they were arrested from Hilly. She did not know anyone in India. She was left with no option other than to depend completely on her uncle who had some connections in Jammu.

Category V

The pain of older mothers who are in captive situation is focused in this category. Just as young mothers are becoming incarcerated with their little kids the older mothers are also getting imprisoned with their adult and sometimes teenager children.

Amina (respondent) was 60 years old in October 2017. She repeatedly expressed her wish to have a glimpse of her 6 children who were scattered in 4 countries namely, Burma, India, Malaysia and U.S.A. The memory of children made this old and weak woman sad and she could not speak more. She had been suffering from acute skin disease when I met her in Dumdum prison along with her daughter-in-law Samia (another respondent discussed in category III). Amina lost all of her strength to think about the future anymore.

The 12 children of Ayesha, another elderly respondent of 55 years, were scattered in 6 places in 4 countries. Her husband was murdered by the local Buddhists in Burma. She left Rakhine finally in the beginning of 2016. When I found Ayesha in Malda jail she was passing 6 months of imprisonment but her appearance expressed that she was still inside the battlefield. Ayesha was arrested along with her 3 children and some other companions. After arrest her children were sent to two different Children's Homes of West Bengal. Her son was kept in Ananda Ashram and her two daughters were sheltered in Silayan Home. They were teenagers. The other nine children of Ayesha were adult and they were not in confined situation.

It is observed that among the 18 children of these two mothers, 15 are adult and they are in different countries including India. In cases of old mothers some of their children always remain out of prison. At the dusk of their life these mothers are devoid of any shelter and support and their children are floating without any aim and destination.

IV

The persecution against Rohingyas is a regular occurrence of Arakan and it becomes extremely brutal and intensified since 2012. Maximum of these discussed cases give a clear picture of the atrocities that Rohingyas have faced in Burma. The mothers' experiences of murder, death, loss and separations of children are shocking and these are the everyday realities of Rohingya life.

The pain of mothers living with the dreadful memories of slaughter and loss of their kids is beyond any description and analysis. But the matter is more serious for the children who are left alone because they can be exploited by any kind of immoral activity. They are extremely vulnerable. How their life is going on is a very difficult question. Engagement of young Rohingyas with impious deeds is already documented in different reports. News in dhakatribune.com in 2018 has disclosed the abuse of a 12-years old Rohingya boy by the drug peddlers for carrying *yaba* from Teknaf to Dhaka (Rabbi, 2018). Missing children can invite dangerous consequences. They will be careless in the same way as the world is careless about them.

Separation of mothers and children between prisons and Children's Homes generates emotional insecurity and uncertainty because many a time after partition there are very few chances to meet the children. It completely depends on the goodwill of the concerned authority. The mothers and their children have no activity either in prison or in Children's Homes. They are passing their days with the memory of horrible past and with the tension of uncertain future.

In this entire process absence or permanent loss of fathers is also a matter of gloominess for children. Among 10 mothers only Margina is found with her husband and children. 4 mothers are widow. Husbands of Kalima and Samia are in Jammu and U.S.A. respectively. 2 married women lost their husbands either in Burma or in course of migration. Asma is a separated woman.

Her husband is a Bangladeshi and he does not keep any relation with his wife and children.

As per the reliable information sources Asma along with her two children is pushed back to Bangladesh. It is difficult to imagine the situation of a single mother who is thrown to an unknown risky place in border with two little children. There is none to support her. Asma's husband keeps no contact and her natal family is in India. The situation of push back for mothers with children is dangerous. The ultimate condition of other respondents is not known to the researcher. They are either pushed back or released on bail. Some of the respondents are still languishing because of the ongoing Supreme Court case. No decision can be taken regarding Rohingyas until the end of the case.

It is known from the lawyers that Rohingyas are getting bail since 2013 depending on the goodwill of judges. At the same time a section of them are also pushed back to Bangladesh. When the bail prayers of Rohingyas are not granted they have to languish long and then to make an end of this worthless imprisonment many a time they are deported to Bangladesh.

There is no doubt that a chaotic situation is continuing for long and the ongoing Supreme Court cases make the situation a more confused one.

V

As a community Rohingyas are completely unwanted in Burma. The narrations of the respondents and of the other riot victims mentioned in earlier research papers bring forward the nature of torment by military upon pregnant women and little children. Rohingya mothers are at risk since they become pregnant in the land of Myanmar. An attitude to smash the entire community makes pregnant women vulnerable to physical torture, rape and other kinds of sexual abuse. Restless Beings are informed during their visit in the makeshift camps of Bangladesh in 2017 that '20.83% directly saw girls get kidnapped, raped or targeted because they were pregnant' (Restless Being, 2018).

Physical ordeal is not limited to the Rohingya mothers only. The little children even cannot escape the brutality of Burmese authority. Heartless slaughter of Rohingya children is documented by UNICEF in 2018.

'They threw my son in the air and cut him with a machete. Then they threw petrol bombs and burned down our houses'.— Aisha, a Rohingya mother of 19 years and a victim of 2017 massacre said (UNICEF CHILD ALERT, 2018). But this kind of shocking event was also prevalent before 2017. '... In the conflict of 2012 Myanmar military placed many Rohingya children upon iron net and under the net they arranged fire'. Children were literally just roasted like chicken (Majumder, 2018:7).

Discrimination is so deep-rooted that even the medical facilities cannot stay free from practising violence. Fear of murder keeps Rohingya mothers away from institutional delivery. They are unable to avail any kind of maternal health care. In this study except Asma and Margina other respondents have delivered their children in the land of Burma and they have the only option of home delivery.

To register the name of new born babies after birth is another difficult task. No question of birth certificate arises as home delivery is prevalent. 'In 1994, the authorities stopped issuing Rohingya children with birth certificates' (Lewa, 2009:12). Family book that contains the names and pictures of all the family members is the only basic identity of Rohingyas in Arakan (Majumder, 2015). To enlist the name of the new born in the family book, money is demanded from parents. Rohingyas are not provided with any more documentation regarding the childbirth other than to join the name of the neonate in the family book.

Long term deprivation from the basic necessities of life contributes to the poor educational background of Rohingyas. They don't have the culture of schooling. 10 mothers in this study have total 50 children. The learning backdrop of these children is no way better than their mothers. The condition of girls is more marginal because of the conservative attitude of the community. Moreover Rohingyas are not entitled to government job in Myanmar so they are not interested to study more.

In Bangladesh, Rohingya children are nothing but rootless. Getting married and giving birth to children in the land of Bangladesh is a common fact of Rohingyas. Marriage between Bangladeshi and Rohingya is also not uncommon. But still they remain invisible as the country has stopped to provide shelter officially to the Rohingyas for a quite long period of time.

Birth place of Margina (respondent) and her husband is Burma. They get married in Kutupalong refugee camp. Three kids of them have taken their first breath in Bangladesh without any birth proof. Now these children are in a prison of India with their parents. The only identity of all these brood and their parents is 'Rohingya Muslim', a statusless group of people.

On the other hand, Asma (respondent) also got married in Bangladesh only at the age of 13 years. She entered in the country in 2007 with the purpose of getting married. Her husband was a Bangladeshi citizen. Asma was his second wife. The two children of Asma were born in Cox's Bazaar. But after the birth of the two babies Asma's husband did not look after her.

Like Margina's kids the children of Asma also do not have any birth proof as home delivery is the single choice of Rohingya mothers even in Bangladesh. These mothers and their children are generally deprived of pre and post natal care everywhere. Marriage with Bangladeshi does not give any status to Rohingyas rather it creates more confusions regarding the identity of the children. However, the children of only Rohingya parents are no way less complicated in matter of identity. They are just hovering from one place to other as they cannot be identified with any state and they don't have a place to call home.

After August 2017 the situation becomes extremely precarious. While escaping mass execution by military many Rohingya pregnant women give birth to their children in roadside under the open sky devoid of any required facility for child birth. Even the care of family members is not in their fate (Bhuiya, 2017). At the same time following the mass inflow there is an attempt to provide minimum health services to the expectant Rohingya mothers in Bangladesh but for the magnitude of the problem it is really difficult to tackle the situation (UNICEF, 2018). Since 1978, Bangladesh is bearing the pressure of Rohingya population. In this background it is not hard to understand the load of another overflow of 10 lakh more (estimate of January, 2018) Rohingyas along with a lots of pregnant women in the country ('Over 10 lakh Rohingyas registered so far', 2018).

VI

Being the captive of different unfavourable situations, the ultimate destiny of these mothers and their children is a big question mark right now. 'Mothering is normally related to certain activities and practices concerned with looking after helpless and dependent infant, nurturing them, taking care of their physical and emotional needs and socialising them for better future' (Ghosh, 2016:18). Rohingya women become mothers as a result of natural instinct and process but the activities related to mothering are not possible for them to perform. The matter of socialisation in a proper way and other necessities of civil society are beyond question. They are not in a position to make future plans either for themselves or for their children.

Lack of proper policy makes this problem so big and vast that it has become almost impossible to deal with the situation. Because of its multifarious dimensions it is a challenge to put things in order. Primarily it is the responsibility of Myanmar where the existence of Rohingyas is evident since the colonial period or even before that. But neighbouring countries cannot avoid their accountability. Imprisonment and forced eviction are not the solutions. Rather these will bring more risky situations. Tracking of Rohingyas in neighbouring countries is the utmost important task at present. International NGOs can do some needful interference in this respect. In India it is important to point out each and every Rohingya. Particularly the imprisoned section needs to be traced and mothers should be placed together with children to avoid any further separation. High fertility and orthodox attitude of Rohingyas towards birth control need to be addressed. Proper counselling of parents is necessary. Otherwise the pressure of population will be more acute on the host countries. Completely separated women and single mothers with children should be enlisted for special safeguard. A team work is important between NGOs, UNHCR and government officials for connecting the families. Some policies are required to initiate the plans. These are the few measures that can be taken as an attempt to tackle the ongoing turmoil, to lessen the agony of the mothers and to assure the security of their children. In this age of intolerance and turbulence not only Rohingyas but also other forced migrants and refugees[9] are facing the same kind of anguish throughout the world whether from Syria or from Mexico.

Since 2017 there is a tendency to label Rohingyas as 'Terrorist'. In India they are announced as 'illegal' by the government. The attachment of a section of this population with various immoral activities as reported from time to time is as veracious as the suffering of this people for some long years. Moreover it is tough to believe that the entire community is engaged with radical activities particularly the children and women who are in need of care and support. So it is high time to protect the Rohingya mothers and their children from any kind of unfavourable situation and his kind of initiative can save not only Rohingyas but also the entire region of South and South-East Asia from an upcoming disaster.

Notes

1. Myanmar was formerly known as Burma. It was renamed by the then State Law and Order Restoration Council (SLORC) military government in 1989. In this paper both the names are used.
2. In 1989 the SLORC (State Law and Order Restoration Council) military government changed the state name from Arakan to Rakhine. It is situated in Western Myanmar. The researcher has used both the names in this paper.
3. ARSA (Arakan Rohingya Salvation Army) is a Rohingya insurgent group active in Northern Rakhine State, Myanmar. The previous name of ARSA was Harakah al-Yaqin.
4. Forced Migration is defined by the International Organisation of Migration as 'A migratory movement in which an element of coercion exists, including threats to life and livelihood, whether arising from natural or man-made causes.' Rohingyas are the forced migrants as their life is always under threat due to the ongoing conflict in Arakan.
5. From the second half of 2017 Balurghat District Correctional Home has developed into a Central Correctional Home. But as it was a District Correctional Home at the time of collecting data it is mentioned in that previous position.
6. Akyab is the old name of Sittway. Rohingyas pronounce it as I-cap. It is observed that the respondents are always using the old names like Burma, Arakan and I-cap. They are more comfortable with these terms.
7. The inmates of a prison belong to three categories. These are U.T. (Under Trial), Convict and R.P. (Released Prisoners). Under trial are those who are facing trials in the court and their guilt have not been proved yet. Maximum Rohingyas who are arrested for their illegal entrance are found in this category. Convict is one whose fault is proved and who is punished for a certain period of time. Released Prisoners are those who have completed their term of punishment but are not yet released from the prison on certain ground. Some Rohingyas are also found in Convict and R.P. category. As they are foreigners they

cannot be released after punishment period on certain grounds and in such cases they remain as R.P.

8. This story is taken from the facebook wall of The Founder/Co-Director of Restless Beings. https://www.facebook.com/RahimaShroom- is the link for availing the story that was posted on 29 May 2018. Restless Being is a U.K. based international human rights organisation working on three key fronts including Child Rights, Refugee Rights and Women's Rights. The Organisation is concerned with the plight of Rohingyas and working on this population in Bangladesh.
9. A 'Refugee' is a type of forced migrants. Generally the term refers to any person who seeks refuge/shelter in a foreign country being uprooted from his own. But the term has a technical definition offered by 1951 Refugee Convention.

References

Bhaumik, S. 2013, June. 'The East Bengali Muslims in Assam and Rohingyas of Myanmar: Comparative Perspectives of Migration, Exclusion, Statelessness', *Refugee Watch*, 41, 30-46.

Bhuiya, A. H. 2017, September 8. 'Pathe Pathe Rohingya Sishur Janma', *EiSamay*. Retrieved from https://eisamay.indiatimes.com/world/rohingya-women-children-drown-while-fleeing-myanmar-violence/articleshow/60425948.cms

Chakraborty, M. 2015, September. 'Stateless and Suspect: Rohingyas in Myanmar, Bangladesh and India', *Policies and Practices*, 71, 40-51.

Cheung, S. 2011, December 15. 'Migration Control and the Solutions Impasse in South and Southeast Asia: Implications from the Rohingya Experience', *Journal of Refugee Studies*, 25 (1), 50-70.doi: 10.1093/jrs/fer048

Ghosh, B. 2016. 'The Institution of Motherhood: A Critical Understanding', in Manna, S & Patra, S. (Eds.), *Motherhood Demystification and Denouement* (pp. 17-29). Kolkata: Levant Books.

Goodman, J. 2014, January16. 'No Respite for Rohingya in Bangladesh', *Aljazeera*. Retrieved from https://www.aljazeera.com/indepth/features/2014/01/no-respite-rohingya-bangladesh-201411675944519957.html

Goris, I., Harrington, J., & Kohn, S. 2009, April. 'Statelessness: What It Is and Why It Matters', *Forced Migration Review*, 32, 4-6. Retrieved from https://www.fmreview.org/sites/fmr/files/FMRdownloads/en/FMRpdfs/FMR32/FMR32.pdf

Human Rights Watch. 2017, December 19. *Massacre by the River: Burmese Army Crimes against Humanity in Tula Toli.* Retrieved from https://www.hrw.org/report/2017/12/19/massacre-river/burmese-army-crimes-against-humanity-tula-toli

Imran, H.F. A. & Mian, Md N. 2014. 'The Rohingya Refugees in Bangladesh: A Vulnerable Group in Law and Policy', *Journal of Studies in Social Sciences*, 8 (2), 226-253. Retrieved from http://citeseerx.ist.psu.edu/viewdoc/download?doi=10.1.1.1000.1419&rep=rep1&type=pdf

Keane, F. 2012, June 11. 'Old Tensions Bubble in Burma', *BBC News*. Retrieved from https://www.bbc.co.uk/news/world-asia-18402678.

Kipgen, N. 2014, April. 'Addressing the Rohingya Problem', *Journal of Asian and African Studies*, 49 (2), 234-247. doi: 10.1177/0021909613505269.

Leider, J. P. 2013. 'Rohingya: The Name, the Movement and the Quest for Identity', in *Nation Building in Myanmar* (pp. 204-255). Yangon: Myanmar Egres & Myanmar Peace Center. Retrieved from http://www.burmalibrary.org/docs21/Jacques-P-Leider-2014-01-28-Rohingya-The_Name-The_movement-The_quest_for_ identity-en.pdf

Lewa, C. 2009, April. 'North Arakan: An Open Prison for the Rohingya in Burma', *Forced Migration Review*, 32, 11-13. Retrieved from https://www.fmreview.org/sites/fmr/files/FMRdownloads/en/FMRpdfs/FMR32/FMR32.pdf

Maitra, A. 2017, March 14. 'Bari Jabo Kobe? Plight of a Homeless Young Rohingya', *Refugee Watch Online*. Retrieved from https://refugeewatchonline.wordpress.com/2017/03/14/bari-jabo-kobe-plight-of-a-homeless-young-rohingya/

Majumder, S. 2015, September. 'Rohingyas Languishing Behind the Bar', *Policies and Practices*, 71, 1-24.

Majumder, S. 2016. 'Motherhood: A Social Fact-A study on the Mothers of Tea Garden', in Manna, S & Patra, S. (Eds.) *Motherhood Demystification and Denouement (*pp. 137-147). Kolkata: Levant Books.

Majumder, S. 2018, March. 'Unprotected and Uncared: What is next for Rohingya Children?', *Quest Multidisciplinary Journal of Humanities and Social Sciences*, 3(3), 1-Retrieved from http://www.sncwgs.ac.in/wp-content/uploads/2018/12/Unprotected-and-Uncared-What-is-next-for-Rohingya-Children.pdf

Manna, S & Patra, S. (eds.) 2016. *Motherhood: Demystification and Denouement*. Kolkata: Levant Books.

'Over 10 lakh Rohingyas registered so far. 2018', January 25. *The Daily Star.* Retrieved from https://www.thedailystar.net/rohingya-crisis/over-ten-lakh-rohingyas-refugees-registered-so-far-1525021

Rabbi, A. R. 2018, May 28. 'Rohingya Children Used as Yaba Mules', *Dhaka Tribune.* Retrieved from https://www.dhakatribune.com/bangladesh/crime/2018/05/28/rohingya-children-used-as-yaba-mules

Restless Being. 2018, February. *The Genocide of the Ignored Rohingya.* Retrieved from http://www.restlessbeings.org/projects/rohingya/the-genocide-of-the-ignored-rohingya

Ullah, A. AKM. 2011. June 9. 'Rohingya Refugees to Bangladesh: Historical Exclusions and Contemporary Marginalisation', *Journal of Immigrant & Refugee Studies*, 9 (2), 139-161. doi: 10.1080/15562948.2011.567149.

UNHCR. 2014, May. *Convention Relating to the Status of Stateless Persons.* Retrieved from http://www.unhcr.org/ibelong/wp-content/uploads/1954-Convention-relating-to-the-Status-of-Stateless-Persons_ENG.pdf

UNHCR. 2017, December 1. *100 Days of Horror and Hope: A Timeline of the Rohingya Crisis*. Retrieved from https://www.unhcr.org/news/stories/2017/12/5a1c313a4/100-days-horror-hope-timeline-rohingya-crisis.html

UNICEF CHILD ALERT. 2018, February. *Lives in Limbo no End in Sight to the Threats Facing Rohingya Children.* Retrieved from https://www.unicef.org/publications/files/UNICEF_Rohingya_Lives_in_Limbo_Feb_2018.pdf

UNICEF. 2018, May 17. 'More than 60 Rohingya babies born in Bangladesh refugee camps every day', UNICEF. Retrieved from https://www.unicef.org/press-releases/more-60-rohingya-babies-born-bangladesh-refugee-camps-every-day-unicef

Chapter - 18

Motherhood: Challenges Faced by the Sex Workers

Atulita Banerjee

Motherhood is the experience of having or bringing up a child. But it is not a natural phenomenon. A mother's behaviour is socially and culturally constructed. Each and every culture has some specific rules to govern the role of the mothers. Motherhood has become institutionalised and it is considered as a very important phase in a woman's life. Most of the people equate 'motherhood' with the experience of having or bringing up a child. However, most of the people possess a gender biased point of view when they talk about motherhood. They generally describe motherhood as an inevitable part of a woman's life constituting the most important event that can never be replaced or altered.

Understanding motherhood

Society has assigned, rather imposed motherhood as a universal role of women. '...perhaps mothers of high culture and low culture maintain some similarities... they perform their roles as caregivers... They are mentally stable and do not permit any interference of abuse for children. In that sense, the term 'mother' and 'motherhood' are eternally ascribed with the dignity of divinity or supremacy' (Ghosh and Chattopadhyay, 2018:50).The gender socialisation has given birth to a world of fantasy among most of the women of mainstream society of a divine feeling related to motherhood. The patriarchal society has unnecessarily glorified motherhood and all the activities related to it have deliberately been internalised the wish of 'being a mother' as a pleasure package in most of the girls' mind.

But the glorification of motherhood is not applicable for each and every segment or group of women. There is a marginalised segment of women, viz., the sex workers, who do not get the scope of fantasising motherhood because of the harsh reality of their livelihood. The ghoulish atmosphere of the brothels disturbs the socialisation process of the children and as a result the ideal mother-child relationship fails to develop in such cases.

Prostitution and taboo

Prostitution provides sexual services in exchange of money, food, clothing or any other thing. It is an ancient practice in which feminine dignity is degraded because of the social stigma related to this. Even in contemporary society sex workers are labeled as 'dangerous outcast'.

Objectives of the study

- To explore the views of sex workers as mothers;
- To find the relation between sex workers and their children;
- To examine the challenges related to motherhood faced by them for their stigmatised position;
- To compare the approaches of the permanent brothel based sex workers and the seasonal or part time sex workers towards their children's future.

The present study has been conducted in an urban brothel of North 24 Parganas district in West Bengal. It is located under Naihati Municipality. The study has been conducted with the help of a NGO named 'Naihati Prolife'.

Motherhood is a matter of perception related to anybody's feeling of security, liberty, care etc. Therefore, mainly the qualitative method has been applied to analyse such a delicate issue. Case studies have been applied to explore the challenges faced by them, through in-depth interview. Unstructured questionnaire has been used. A mixed method or a method of triangulation has been used to explore the reality.

A few case studies have been mentioned in the following:

(i) Usharani Jha (name changed) is a permanent Commercial Sex Worker (CSW). At present she is around 50 years old. She previously worked in a brothel near Bangaon of North 24 Parganas. She has one daughter who is persuing her masters in English. She dreams of a safe and secure future for her daughter. Usharani herself was a victim of trafficking at her teens.

(ii) Parvati Shaw is another middle aged CSW who was brought into the brothel by a pimp after her husband's death with her children (a boy and a girl child) in search of a job. When she joined the profession of CSW the girl was of 6 years of age and the boy was a new born baby. Her husband died in an accident. She was driven out of her in-laws house. Now the girl has completed her midwifery course and doing job in a private nursing home. The boy on the other hand is a school dropout at secondary level. Presently he is living his livelihood doing some odd jobs.

(iii) Laxmi Rani Das is an ex-sex worker of this brothel, aged around 60 years and presently a 'madam' of this brothel. She has two sons. Both of them are school drop-outs. One of them is presently working as a pimp in this brothel and the other has no fixed job and thus performs different odd jobs at times. Laxmi Rani prevents the under aged and unwilling girls to join in the profession.

(iv) Dulari Ram (name changed, aged around 30 years) is the wife of an industrial labour who works in this brothel as a seasonal worker mainly for the wellbeing of her children. She has two children and the job of her husband is not secured. Dulari visits the brothel especially during the festive seasons (such as Kali puja) and stays here for nearly a fortnight. Her family is not aware of her job type.

(v) Razia Bibi was brought to this place when she was only 17 years old. She is a victim of human trafficking. Now she is around 25 years and has a son of 5 years. Razia wants her son to get educated properly and join a mainstream profession in future. Her son is a student of class one. She desperately dreams of a better tomorrow for her son.

(vi) Keya (title not mentioned) is a unique example of a CSW who works in this brothel with the consent of her husband. Her husband, a former industrial worker, has become paralysed after an accident in his workplace a few years back. Keya works for two square meals of her family. She has two children who are studying in a SSK. Keya is looking for a better and secured future for her children.

(vii) Ritu Thapa (name changed) is a 28 years young HIV positive mother who has lost her child (who was also HIV positive) but still has a daughter aged around 10 years. Ritu has been working in this brothel as CSW for last 8 years after being driven out from her family after her husband's second marriage and now also working as a peer educator. She mainly works to generate awareness among those who are new in this brothel.

Ritu is under ART (Anti Retroviral Therapy) for last 6 years or so.

(viii) Radha Paswan's story is no exception than other CSW stories of this brothel. The only exception is that she was trafficked in this brothel after her husband's death when she was three month's pregnant. Here she gave birth to her girl child and started working as a CSW. Radha is presently in her forties and her only daughter is a student of class X in a local school. Radha looks after her daughter seriously especially monitors her education and her strongest desire is the settlement of her daughter in any mainstream job after the completion of her education.

(ix) Debika (title not mentioned) is a 50 years old CSW of this brothel. She has a son who is a school dropout in class eight and presently runs a small tea stall, and a daughter who is presently married. As she has basic education, she takes care of the studies of some of the children of this area.

(x) Mita Debnath is a middle aged irregular CSW of this brothel who has no biological child of her own but having a strong feeling of motherhood she takes care of two girl child, one left by her biological mother in train and the other rescued from the dustbin. She herself is illiterate but almost ready to face all challenges for the proper upbringing of her two foster daughters. She wants to keep both of them from this 'life of disrespect' (as per her version) and provide them proper education so that they can get a normal life. She said that they were not her biological children but they were her life and so she wanted to ensure prospecrity in their future life by providing them proper education and a smooth mainstream life.

Findings

In case of permanent CSWs:

- Constant exposure to derogatory labels would lead to a negative self-image, and even worse, self-hatred.
- This is a special type of single motherhood. As the proper identity of the childrens' father is unknown in brothel, so they get identified with their mother's identity only. This is to some extent similar in nature of the previous societies with sexual unions, where the children were identified by their mother's identity. Engles (1884:60) says, 'Unrestricted sexual union between males and females was widely prevalent in human society. Any women and men could choose one or more sexual partners. For this reason, there could be no certainty about fatherhood of the children born out of these sexual unions'.
- A different kind of gender consciousness is noticed.
- Aspiration to educate daughter is high among them for ensuring a secure future of the girl child.
- Boys, rather than the girls of the area, are more prone to dropout and hence are less educated. Probably due to lack of control over the male children, mothers become unable to take care of their day to day routine. It is obvious that the parental observation is one of the most important thing in preventing them from being dropouts. But due to either shortage of time and ignorance, or both, they are unable to pay full attentions to their childrens' study. (Ghosh, 2018).

In case of seasonal CSWs:

- Engaged in this profession for the betterment of their children's livelihood especially their education and healthcare facility.
- Motherly feelings compel them to join this profession.

- Even sometimes their husbands force them to work as temporary sex workers for ensuring their children's as well as family's financial security.

A special case

On 13th Nov, 2015, spine chilling news was published in *Dailymail*, where one 71 years old lady was found guilty. She was a prostitute mother who allowed her clients to sexually abuse her own daughters (source: www.dailymail.co.uk). One of them tried to end her life at the age of 7 years. But an absolutely opposite scenario is observed in this study where

- One aged ex-sex worker has played a vital role to save the under aged trafficked girls from getting into this vicious cycle.
- Motherly feelings encourage her to save the girls and to protect them.

Perspectives

In Sociology of Crime, there is a theory developed by Becker, called as labelling theory, which has been used to differentiate an accused person from the rest of the society by attaching a label of 'criminal' with his/her name. In fact, the children of brothel also get conscious about their existence with a label of stigma. The questions that come in mind at what age does a child realise that he or she is unclean? When does a young boy understand his place of birth has robbed him of any right to an education or healthcare or a girl that she exists for only one awful thing? (Jackman, 2013). In the case of CSWs, though they do not commit any punishable crime and get into this occupation for some odd circumstances, but still they get labelled by the society as social offenders and get a stigmatised position in society. They face all the odds and challenges, but for the sake of their children's life they go as far as they can.

Conclusion

- Mothers are being glorified in mainstream Indian society. Being a sex worker one has to face so many challenges, one of those is motherhood. The mother as a sex worker has to perform various roles for her offspring. They play both the roles of a mother and a father. Sometimes she is passionate, otherwise, she turns into masculinity, which mainly happens in cases of 'single' or 'solo' mother (Klett-Davies, 2007).
- Even in the mainstream society single mothers often face obstacles in course of bringing up their child; so it is obvious that as a single mother permanent CSWs face much more difficulties in bringing up their children.

Questions that hammer:

- Isn't their motherhood more challenging than the motherhood of the women of the mainstream?
- How should these mothers be described? Is their motherhood, in any respect, less glorified than the motherhood of the mainstream mothers?

References

Engels, F. 1884. *The origin of the family, private property and state.* Chicago: Charles. H Kerr & Co.

Ghosh, B. and Chattopadhyay, K. 2018. 'Mother and Motherhood: A sociological construct', in Manna, S., Patra, S. and Roy, S. (eds.): *Sociology of Motherhood and Beyond, Roots and Rejuvenation.* Kolkata: Levant Books.

Ghosh, S. 2016. 'Mother's socio-economic status and issues of child rights: A study in North 24 Pgs, West Bengal' in Manna, S and Patra, S. (eds.): *Motherhood: Demystification and Denouement.* Kolkata: Levant Books.

Jackman, C. 2013. (Oct 26). 'Daughters of Brothel', *The Sydney Morning Herald* (https://www.smh.com.au/world/daughters-of-the-brothel-20131021-2vvll.html) accessed on 18th October, 2019.

Klett-Davies, M. 2007. 'Going it Alone? Lone Motherhood'. *Late Modernity*. Hampshire: Ashgate Publishing Ltd.

www.dailymail.co.uk/news/article-3317270/Prostitute-mother-allowed-clients-sexually-abuse-daughters-drove-one-attempt-suicide-aged-SEVEN.html accessed on 18th October, 2019.

Chapter - 19

I am a Mother too: Motherhood among the Prostitutes of Kalighat

Sajal Sammadder

An unsolved story

The term motherhood invites glorification but mothers are also women. 'Women', are considered to be the commodities of men from time immemorial. This can be due to the fact that the lives of women who practise prostitution are often defined by their work, which makes it difficult to portray them in other roles (Sleighhtholme and Sinha, 1997, as cited in Kelbisow, 2009: 10).

In Indian mythology, there are several references to *Apsaras,* which are demigods, performing as prostitutes like Urvashi, Menaka, Thilothamma, and Rambha. Even some of the earliest scholarly works like *Arthasasthra* written by Kautilya, *Kama Sutra* of Vatsyayan, *Mrichchha Katika* of Dandin and even *Meghadhoot* written by Kalidas, discussed about prostitutes. Religious practices regularly promoted prostitution during these eras. The 'nagarvadhu' since that times came to be associated with the word 'prostitute', a most degrading profession in India, one who sales her body against money.

But the harsh reality is that this oldest and undesirable occupation is spreading its roots. Approximately there are 15 million prostitutes in India. West Bengal alone accounts for

26 percent of the total number of prostitutes in the entire nation. According to a survey, approximately 1500 women sell their selves for sex in Kalighat, an area for lower-class and middle-class people situated along the banks of the Ganges, nearly 500 meters from the famous Shakti Pith Kali Temple in Southern part of Kolkata, West Bengal. Most of these prostitutes are mothers, willingly or unwillingly.

The three narrow lanes, with sprint waste-water, namely, Nepali Goli (Lane), Boro Goli and Post-Office Goli, occupied mostly by the men playing cards and gambling, scattered all over buckets and utensils, barely leaving place for a person to walk, but a paradise of illegal acts and other criminal activities, are the oldest brothel of Kolkata. Here in Kalighat most of the prostitutes live within a space of 6 feet by 6 feet area of rented home.

Tremendous aggravation and vulnerability drive hundreds of women to these redlight areas which constitute of Bengalees, Nepalees and Biharis. They are Hindus, Muslims, Christians and from other religions. According to local information, around 200 prostitutes are HIV positive. Along with these women their children also suffer as they grow in the same environment.

Most of the kids of the prostitutes do not recognise their biological fathers. Some of these children do not recognise their mother's status as a prostitute, while some of them do not disclose what their mothers do. With the absence of conventional family organisation these mother-child relationships have always been an unsolved-story.

The hidden truth

In India alone, there are approximately 5.4 million children of the sex-workers, according to the National Human Rights Commission (NHRC). A major portion of them breathe with their mothers in grimy air of redlight areas (NHRC, 2008).

But the present legislation in India does not deal with the basic requirements of the prostitutes and their offsprings such as education, healthcare, job training, housing, nutrition and so on.

During the first decade of the twenty-first century, the argument against decriminalisation gained support as prostitution became linked with the growing awareness of global sex trafficking (Davies, 2009). Lack of identification and appreciation of prostitutes as 'mothers', lead to neglegence or victimisation of their children. Children face regular discrimination and harassment due to their mother's profession. The objective of this paper is to understand the challenges and experiences of the prostitutes as mothers.

Even though prostitution is illegal in India, the country still has Asia's largest redlight district (Karandikar, 2008; Menen, 2007). Most children of the prostitute are in criminally controlled sex trade as a universal practice and are ready to perform different odd jobs connected with the sex trade. These studies examine the needs of the children and of their mothers to be successful in rendering the responsibilities of motherhood. A number of children share exceptionally insecure bonds with their mothers.

Objectives

The importance of this study is dual. First, the literature reveals a scarcity of empirical study or documentation in audio-visual medium on the needs of prostitutes and their children. Second, the experiences of these women and their children show that support programmes and laws can be modified to empower them and reduce their societal exclusion. Additionally, there is a lack of research on the views of NGOs about the needs of prostitutes and their children and the challenges that Non-government Organisations (NGOs) are facing in providing services to this group. As per the Immoral Traffic (Prevention)

Act- ITPA of 1986, pimps and *babus* or live-in lovers who live off prostitute's earnings are guilty in the eyes of law. Any adult male living with a prostitute is assumed to be guilty (imprisonment of up to 2 years with fine) unless he can prove otherwise. But the reality is that no NGO or other functioning agency has taken any action to amend this law. Existence for them is tough. The sex workers face constant aggravation and cruelty not just from their clients but also from the brothel managers and pimps. There are lot of such violence that keep going on in the life of these prostitutes where no actions are taken in favours of the prostitutes either by the government or by the NGOs. The objective of this paper is to understand these hidden truths.

Methodology

The study was conducted in Kalighat redlight area under Kolkata (South) of West Bengal, namely, Nepali Goli (Lane), Boro Goli and Post-Office Goli, where I visited brothels, local temples, clubs inside the congested locality and informed local youth, women, children, shopkeepers about the study. I briefed them about the scope and goal of the approach with my associate and a key informant. I use qualitative study and deductive analysis to examine the lives of their children from the perspective of socialising agents, e.g., family, peers, school and colleges. Lastly, they have agreed to reply to the important questions: How are the children of sex-workers socialised? What are their challenges? What are their experiences? What do they need to develop them or to sustain in mainstream society?

In addition, I have observed and tried to understand the lives of the prostitutes and the needs of their children through the lens of social exclusion problem. I have examined how prostitutes and their children have been methodically excluded from the mainstream society. I have realised that prostitutes faced so many challenges such as hesitation to use surnames for their children. They are also worried about the health and education of their children. I have tried to understand the reality from the interactions between the participants and me.

It has been found that in Kalighat there are approximately 100 flying sex workers who come from outside to these brothels. Presently there are around 25 prostitutes who have been detected as HIV positive. Around 15 sex workers are already under medication for primary detection of HIV. There are around 70 sex workers died in AIDS (who were tested as HIV positive) in the last 30 years.

Discussion

I am a mother too...

'I am a son of a prostitute. You can mention my real name ....' Vinod, an artist and an art teacher of age of about 38 years, a resident of Kalighat Brothel, boldly declared. He stayed with his wife Putul who was also the daughter of a prostitute. But it is not common that a son or a daughter of a prostitute live without denial of their mother's status. Most of them feel ashamed to disclose what their mothers do as sex worker. In India, prostitution is part of a larger network of criminal activity that involves multi-million dollar business (Karandikar, 2008; Menen, 2007).

According to the Department of International Development, the discrimination against the prostitutes can occur within public institutions, such as the legal system, or in organisations that manage education and health services, as well as in households and the community. These types of institutionalised exclusion can in turn lead to denial of income, assets and services.

Vinod also has stated that although he and his wife are the children of prostitute mothers, but they do not want their children to have the same destiny which they have suffered. Studies by Datta (2000, 2001, 2004 and 2006) revealed that out of 105 children whose mothers were in prostitution, less than

20 remained in the care of their mothers. In a separate study, Weiner (1996) found that only 19% of 1,963 prostitutes have retained the custody of their children. In the case of Vinod and Putul, they were kept in the custody of their mother's landlady, the brothel keeper.

It was because of unremitting anxiety among mothers that their children either will be forced into the sex trade or become the victims of sexual exploitation. These areas, which are full of criminal activities such as drug trafficking, gambling, and gang violence, create an unsafe environment for women and children. Sloss and Harper (2004) have agreed that prostitute mothers have acknowledged the risks to which their children have been exposed under their care, and they have felt grateful when the children have been taken out of the family as this measure would have spared them of abuse or neglect.

The Kalighat brothel being narrow habitat trapped from all side and jam-packed of flesh trade is not hygienic place to live for women and children, who reside in these areas with risk of infectious diseases, such as typhoid, malaria, hepatitis, and sexually transmitted diseases, such as HIV/AIDS, gonorrhea, and syphilis. Vinod's mother Mira Debi died in HIV. Many prostitutes in Kalighat are tested HIV positive (as per local report). These infections have put a prostitute's ability to care for her children in serious jeopardy.

Conclusion

Vinod never like to mention his title or last name. As a child of a sex worker Vinod faced difficulties in getting admissions in schools when the school authorities came to know mother's profession. After 17 years of age he came to know who was his father. Most commonly children do not know their biological fathers here. They consider fathers as the dominant 'male' in their mothers' life. These people never take any liability of the children or their mothers.

These women also face cruelty from the customers, pimps, brothel keepers and local criminals, and do not have any say on the price, kind of service, or health precaution. In some cases, the brothel keepers provide facilities for baby sitters so that the mothers can give time to the customers.

Amidst these hard realities the big question arises: what is the nature of the mother-child relationship? It has been found that some mother-child relationships are cordial, while others share a love-hate relationship with their mothers. But the reality is, even when the mother is hated both by the child and the society, her arms wrap strongly around the child, hugging her to her chest. Because mother is someone who loves her child before she meets up. Nearly all of the mothers in flesh trade have resigned to their destiny. The only hope in their lives is their children, whom they want to protect from all these challenges and raise them as respected citizens. Vinod's mother, Mira Debi, did not disclose that she was his mother till her death in HIV. A social-activist Vinod now realizes that 'she is a mother too....'

References

Datta, R. 2000. 'Exposing the Prety Woman Myth: A qualitative examination of the lives of female street walking prostitutes', *Journal of Sex Research*, 37(4): 344-353.

Datta, R. 2001. 'Et tu, Brute? A qualitative analysis of street walking prostitutes' interpersonal support networks', *Journal of family issues*, 22(8): 1066-1085.

Datta, R. 2004. 'I fell off (the mothering) track': Barriers to 'effective mothering among prostituted women'. *Family Relations*, 53(2): 190-200.

Datta, R. 2006. *Exposing the 'pretty woman' myth: A qualitative investigation of street level prostituted women*. USA: Lixington Books.

Davies, N. 2009. 'Prostitution and Trafficking- The Anatomy of a Moral Panic', *The Guardian* (London), Oct 20, 2009.

Karandikar, S. A. 2008. *Gender-based violence among female sex workers of Kamathipura, Mumbai, India: A contextual analysis*. (Unpublished Doctoral dissertation, The University of Utah). Retrieved from http:/

/search.proquest.com/docview/304430358?accountid=14677. (304430358) dated 10/11/2020.

Kelbosow, S.A. 2009. *I am also a mother: Examinig the child care challenges of sex workers in Addis Ababa, Ethiopia*. Netherlands: Unpublished dissertation.

Menen, R. 2007. *Karma Sutra- Essays from the Margin*. New Delhi: Saga Books.

Slieghtholme, C. and Sinha, I. 1997. *Guilty without trial: women in the sex trade in Calcutta*. New Jessey: Rutgers University Press.

Sloss, C.M. and Harper, G.W.2004. 'When street sex workers are mothers', *Archieves of sexual behavior*. 33: 329-341.

Weiner, A. 1996. 'Understanding the social needs of street walking prostitutes', *Social Work*, 41(1): 97-105.

Index

B

C

D

H

I

N

S